T0305395

The Evaluation and Optimization of Trading Strategies

Founded in 1807, John Wiley & Sons is the oldest independent publishing company in the United States. With offices in North America, Europe, Australia and Asia, Wiley is globally committed to developing and marketing print and electronic products and services for our customers' professional and personal knowledge and understanding.

The Wiley Trading series features books by traders who have survived the market's ever-changing temperament and have prospered—some by reinventing systems, others by getting back to basics. Whether a novice trader, professional or somewhere in between, these books will provide the advice and strategies needed to prosper today and well into the future.

For a list of available titles, please visit our Web site at www. WileyFinance.com.

The Evaluation and Optimization of Trading Strategies

Second Edition

ROBERT PARDO

WILEY

John Wiley & Sons, Inc.

Published by John Wiley & Sons, Inc., Hoboken, New Jersey.
Published simultaneously in Canada.

For general information on our other products and services or for technical support, please
contact our Customer Care Department within the United States at (800) 762-2974, outside the
United States at (317) 572-3993 or fax (317) 572-4002.

Wiley also publishes its books in a variety of electronic formats. Some content that appears in
print may not be available in electronic books. For more information about Wiley products,
visit our Web site at www.wiley.com.

Library of Congress Cataloging-in-Publication Data:

Pardo, Robert, 1951–
    The evaluation and optimization of trading strategies / Robert Pardo. – 2nd ed.
      p.   cm. – (Wiley trading series)
    Rev. ed. of : Design, testing, and optimization of trading systems. c1992.
    Includes index.
    ISBN 978-0-470-12801-5 (cloth)
    1. Investments–Data processing.   2. Futures–Data processing.   3. Options (Finance)–Data
processing.   I. Pardo, Robert, 1951– Design, testing, and optimization of trading systems.
II. Title.
    HG4515.5.P37   2008
    332.64′5–dc22

                                                                      2007038106

Printed in the United States of America.

10   9   8   7   6   5   4   3   2   1

Contents

Foreword

M y relationship with Bob Pardo goes back to 1996 when he approached my firm, DUNN Capital Management, in search of trading capital for his XT99 system. After some extensive system evaluations, we entered into an agreement to help research, develop, and trade Bob's XT99 for Bob, DUNN, and our clients. I am pleased to report that this arrangement has proved beneficial to all parties and that it is still going great guns. When Bob recently asked if I would write the foreword for this second edition I assured him that I would be more than delighted to do so.

Because of my scientific background and training we have always viewed system design and development as a diligent application of statistical analysis of the performance of trading models and of their test results. Accordingly, we were very pleased to find that many of these features were used in developing the XT99 model platform and that it was so amenable to further testing and fine-tuning.

When my colleagues and I had the opportunity to read the first edition of this work, we were particularly interested in Bob's presentation of the virtues and benefits of using the walk-forward method to guide system development.

I am aware that many consider the first edition of this book to be a classic. Generally speaking, it is pretty difficult to improve upon a classic, but in this case it was necessary. As Bob outlines in his preface, to say that our world of computing, trading, and money management has changed since 1991 when the first edition of this book was published, would be a *dramatic* understatement. Given the vast changes that have occurred since the first edition, a new edition of Bob's book addressing these matters is entirely in line. The good news here is that not only did Bob update the original material; he also reorganized it, explained the material with even greater clarity and insight and added some new insights that he has learned in the intervening years. Did he improve on a classic? You'll have to be the judge of that yourself.

I have always been impressed with Bob's technical toolbox and his innovative ideas. Bob's focus, dedication, and originality as a researcher and trader are very apparent in this second edition. I think that serious system developers will find this second edition a very interesting and profitable read.

Enjoy it.

William A. Dunn, PhD
Chairman
DUNN Capital Management
Stuart, Florida
May 2007

Preface

THERE AND BACK AGAIN

The first edition of *Design, Testing, and Optimization of Trading Systems* (DTOTS, as I always think of it) was published in 1991. It would be an understatement to say that the world has changed dramatically in the 17 years between the 1991 edition and this one. Some would say the markets have changed also. I disagree.

The markets do what they always do: incorporate all of the changes in communication, technology, wealth, and trading styles into the instantaneous calculation of their fair value.

I have always considered the defining characteristic of markets to be their ability to adapt and alter themselves accordingly to the changing style of market participants.

In this introduction, we review the principal changes that have occurred during this time and their impact on the markets and trading. Many will seem obvious. Please bear with me in this walk down memory lane, however, for the sum total of these changes has altered the nature of trading and our industry in ways that directly reflect upon the current art of the design and evaluation of trading strategies.

"How?" you might ask, and that would be a very good question. Let me start by offering my reflections on that subject because it is highly relevant to the topic at hand.

The Trading System: From Rock Bottom to Rock Star

The first, and perhaps foremost, difference was that in the early 1990s, the argument that raged was about whether trading systems actually worked. For those who are relatively new to the industry, this might come as a bit of a shock. There is now such a widespread, and somewhat unquestioned, belief in the many virtues of algorithmic trading (AT) that it almost borders on religious belief.

As one who was rather instrumental in the acceptance of the benefits of algorithmic trading, I find *both* of these polar opposite beliefs somewhat troubling. I was trained in and always have been a fierce advocate of the scientific method and the empirical approach. I have always believed in the critical method.

In our business, the trader who does not apply these methods consistently, rigorously, and religiously along with a healthy dose of skepticism is a trader doomed to failure.

I believed then, and even more so now, that algorithmic trading, when performed correctly and based upon exhaustive research, is the most effective method for large-scale trading. Those of you who go on to read this book will find out in detail why I believe this to be so.

In short, the benefits of AT are many. Central, however, are the elimination of highly fallible human judgment, the precise quantification of risk and return and their application in risk and asset allocation, and the ability to trade a relatively unlimited number of markets. Add to this the current technological ability to enter algorithmically calculated trades electronically and without human intervention and we now have the best of all possible worlds: mathematically sound and objective trading signals entered at the speed of light without the (easy) possibility of human interference. Of course, there will be more on this later.

If one examines the current climate of the professional commodity trading advisory and money management industry, one will find that algorithmic, or systematic, commodity trading advisers (CTAs) outnumber the discretionary trader 3.5 to 1.[1] This would suggest that the majority of CTAs have adopted the algorithmic trading philosophy. Since it is fair to assume that professional money managers are knowledgeable and sophisticated, pervasive AT adoption would also suggest that it is the choice of the expert.

It is somewhat troubling then, that the trading public, including those who aspire to professional trading, with all of their varying degrees of sophistication, have almost assumed an unquestioning, naïve, and somewhat gullible blind faith in trading systems. It is shocking to me that the relative sophistication of the typical consumer of commercial trading strategies is not that much different today from what it was around 1990.

So, we have witnessed a most dramatic shift in philosophy since the publication of DTOTS, from an ignorant and oftentimes hostile disbelief in the efficacy of the trading system to a dogmatic and somewhat mindless faith in the trading system, and worse, nearly any trading system that seems to make a good case for itself.

Why is this important? It demonstrates two major factors. The first is that the overall depth of education of the trading public has not significantly improved in the last 15 years, whereas there are certainly far more books, software, and instruction available today than circa 1990. I would call much, but not all, of this information, however, to be of a lateral sort of knowledge, as in a variety of kind, in contrast to in-depth, as in a penetrating knowledge of cause and principle.

The second—and this relates to the first—is that solid knowledge of the principles of trading strategy design and evaluation has not become the common knowledge that one would have thought. This is particularly noticeable to me since I wrote the first edition of this book to remedy what I felt was a dramatic deficiency in the trading literature. Also, because before the publication of DTOTS, I, and the employees of my various businesses, spent a lot of time and money educating our clients in these principles. Perhaps I can make more of an impact with this edition.

COMPUTING

Perhaps the most amazing transformation in the last 15 years has been the exponential expansion of computing and communications capacity. Let us consider the facts. In 1991, the fastest computer chip available was the Intel 80386 at 25 Megahertz. Today the fastest chip is the Intel Core 2 at 3700 Megahertz. This is a 14,800 percent increase. The number of operations of an Intel 80386 at 25 MHz was approximately 8,500,000 per second. The number of operations of an Intel Core 2 at 3, 333 MHz is 57,000,000,000 operations per second. This is an increase of more than 670,000 percent!

The amount of RAM (computer memory) typical of an Intel 80386 was 1,000,000 bytes or 1 *megabyte* (as in 1 million) of RAM. The typical computer today is equipped with 1,000,000,000 bytes or 1 *gigabyte* (as in 1 *billion*) of RAM. This is a 1,000-fold increase. The current trading applications can use this massive amount of RAM to hold data, multiple time markets, and multiple markets in multiple time frames. However, whereas the computers can now hold massive amounts of data, the dual bottlenecks of the grossly inefficient Windows XP operating system prevalent on most computers, together with effectively obsolete (but, of course, the leading vendors will vehemently deny this) trading strategy development applications makes processing massive amounts of price data, multiple markets, and multiple time frames highly impractical, if not essentially impossible. This matter has only been made worse by the even poorer performance of Windows VISTA. The processing time involved is typically so massive with these commercial applications as to make it highly undesirable, if not practically impossible.

In contrast, Pardo Capital Limited uses in-house proprietary applications for most of the heavy-duty computing that we professional trading firms must do when developing trading platforms.

The typical amount of hard drive storage space on an Intel 80386 was 40 megabytes. The typical amount of hard drive storage space on current computers is 250 gigabytes. This is a 5,000 percent increase. Back in the 1990s, storage space and RAM were at a premium; now they are so cheap and massive that for the purposes of the trading strategist they are as if infinite. With this massive storage capacity, it should now be possible for the strategist to store his research in a comprehensive, searchable, and hence statistically analyzable database. However, what is lacking is the trading software that places the strategist's research in sophisticated databases. Also, save for those who create their own software applications, the ability to analyze such a research database in a sophisticated manner is unavailable.

Why is this important? If processing power has increased by 14,800 percent, RAM by 1,000 percent and storage capacity by 5,000 percent, it would not be terribly unreasonable for the strategist to expect that trading applications that perform testing and simulations and that update real-time market analysis should have enjoyed a performance boost at least somewhat similar in proportion. However, they have not. They have not even come close. This is highly relevant.

As both a software developer and a trading strategy developer back in the 1990s, I would have been put into a frenzy by the prospects that such increased computer capacity would have offered to the design and optimization of trading systems.

The truth is that, because of the bottlenecks presented by inefficient operating systems, database management tools, and trading applications, the average trader has not been able to harness the possibilities that lurk in his PC. They are now only available to those who have the resources to assemble teams of application designers and developers with the knowledge and sophistication to design and create such complex applications and harness the full capacity of the hardware available and to come.

The evening of the trading strategy playing field that was emerging in the early 1990s has long vanished. Once again, the large trading entities have a massive advantage. And believe me, they use it to the fullest extent possible.

Need we look much further than a $9.54 billion profit for 2006 for Goldman Sachs or the huge assets ($26.3 billion) under management and outstanding returns (annual returns exceeding 20 percent) of D.E. Shaw for proof of the benefits of the skillful application of such strategic and technological excellence?

THE INVESTMENT INDUSTRY

In 1990, the investment and asset management industries looked antiquated compared to today. Total assets under management by commodity trading advisers were $10.5 billion. As of March 2007, total assets were $172 billion and growing at an unprecedented rate. This represents a growth of more than 1,600 percent in the last 17 years. In 1990, the CTA industry was primarily an American industry. While it is still domestically dominated, there is an appreciable number of European CTAs that are active today. This globalization of the CTA is very likely to accelerate.

The number of hedge funds and assets under management have both enjoyed an ever-greater explosion. Hedge funds numbered 610 in 1990. As of 2005, they numbered 8,661. Total assets under management by hedge funds in 1990 were $40 billion. Now it is in excess of $1 trillion. That is more than a 25-fold increase.

There has been a similar growth in mutual funds. In 1990, there were approximately 3,100. Today there are over 8,600. Assets under management then were slightly in excess of $1 trillion. Today, it is in excess of $10.4 trillion.

During this time of staggering increase in professional money management, the number of individual traders and investors has remained largely the same.

Another development is that of the proprietary trading shop. Whereas the larger trading firms such as Salomon Brothers. (Remember them? They are now part of Citigroup.) Goldman Sachs and Morgan Stanley have always made proprietary trading a significant part of their operations. "Prop trading" (as it is now affectionately called) has become a considerably more significant part of trading. Even relatively insignificant brokerages have prop desks. There are also a significant number of firms, small, medium, and large, dedicated solely to prop trading. With the trading floor becoming a thing of the past, and electronic trading and traders filling this gap, the prop trading firm has taken on a new meaning.

What does this all mean? It means many things, but perhaps the two most significant observations are that the bulk of trading capital is firmly in the hands of a professional class of trader and the efficiency of the markets has never been higher and this efficiency will only continue to improve.

Another very significant development in the world of trading is that trading, now more so than ever before, is perceived as the fastest way to achieve great wealth. For the last two years running, the top earning CTA/hedge fund managers have earned in excess of $500 million in a year.

What does that mean? As never before, trading attracts the very best and the very brightest. One needs to question the societal impact of a significant proportion of a generation's intellectual elite being drained by an essentially nonproductive activity. This is especially significant in light of the large and increasing number of world-threatening crises facing the world today.

It also means that the resources that have been and will continue to be dedicated to the pursuit of trading advantage and profit will become increasingly vast. And when we consider the billions upon billions of dollars currently dedicated to this pursuit, this is a somewhat daunting concept. That the brightest minds are employing vast resources to exploit trading profits means that trading has become and will continue to become increasingly difficult. The markets will continue to become more and more efficient and perhaps exhibit some new behaviors as a result. And as a result of this, new trading opportunities will develop, and the game goes on.

TRADING STRATEGY DEVELOPMENT TOOLS

To say there has been a significant proliferation of tools available to the trading strategist today compared to the early 1990s would be a dramatic understatement. In 1990, there were three major technical analysis and trading strategy development software applications: *Advanced Trader*, *Metastock* (and very limited in those days), and *SystemWriter* (which evolved into *TradeStation*).

To get an idea of where we at are today, we need only to review the Traders' Tips monthly feature in *Technical Analysis*. There we find scripting code from nine different applications. And this is just the tip of the iceberg. There are any number of higher-end applications geared toward the professional trader. Of course, there are also the general-purpose applications such as Excel, Mathematica, and Matlab (the latter two widely used by professional trading houses). There is even a programming language called *R*, which has been constructed for those focused on mathematically oriented applications. There is also the ever-present Visual Basic in its various flavors, which is also widely used in professional houses because of its ability to create applications relatively quickly and without a tremendous need for sophisticated programming abilities.

Without belaboring this point, clearly there are many more choices available to the trading strategist these days. Yet this very proliferation presents the strategist with both an obstacle and an opportunity. More on this in Chapter 4: The Strategy Development Platform.

This, of course, says nothing about the vast plethora of add-in products and other more specialized tools that exist now and did not circa 1990.

There are hundreds of add-ins for Metastock, TradeStation, and Trader-sStudio.

These add-ins range in functionality from trading strategies and indicators to those that extend the capabilities of the host product such as those that do a rudimentary form of portfolio analysis.

This also says nothing of the more specialized tools that provide the strategist the ability to create neural net trading applications, perform genetic algorithms to trading strategies, do fractal analysis of the markets, and apply sophisticated data-mining capabilities to trading strategy issues.

Yet this vast proliferation of trading strategy development applications, add-ins, and advanced technological trading applications is a bit of an illusion. Yes, one can purchase and use all of these different products if one is so inclined. But try to tie it all together into a seamless and functional trading application and one sees wherein the problem lies. It is nearly impossible to do so.

Where is the application that lets the strategist design, create, and apply her own custom genetic search algorithm to a Walk-Forward Analysis of a trading strategy that employs an autoregressive integrated moving average (ARIMA) forecasting model of volatility, a neural net that predicts the magnitude and direction of tomorrow's close change, which auto-adapts to market conditions and has a genetic algorithm that balances one's portfolio automatically, strangling models trading stagnant markets with a strategy that is losing in the last year and feeds the strategies that are profiting unusually well and markets that are really moving?

Why is this important? Yes, such a trading platform would be quite sophisticated. These technologies all exist now, however, and did so in the 1990s, too. The computer hardware is now up to the task. There are strategists who can design and create applications like these and even more sophisticated ones, at that. Yet, the trading strategy development application that would make such a thing possible does not yet exist (at least to my knowledge and I am always looking). One might ask, so what? That, however, would be a rather uninformed question. For the existence of such a trading strategy development application with the ability to integrate and apply such technologies at a usable speed would really be a development that would be at least somewhat in proportion to the vast explosion of computer hardware that we have seen over the last 15 years.

You can count on the fact that if one of the large prop trading firms desires to apply a trading approach as complex—or vastly more so—as what has been mentioned, they have the resources to pull it all together to create and trade such a trading model.

The point is that this capability should be available to the average trader and investor too. The capability is there. The leading trading strategy development software application vendors have been complacent—

perhaps they just lack imagination—in the extreme. Part of the problem here as always been that most of the developers of the trading strategy development applications do not have a trading background; as such, they are not as driven by trading profit as traders are to continuously seek out cutting edge technology that can provide the trader with an edge. And the trading community at large, primarily the individual trader and investor, has been willing to accept this sorry state of affairs. Perhaps they too lack imagination...?

THE RISE OF ADVANCED MATHEMATICAL CONCEPTS IN TRADING

In the last 15 years, traders have been exposed to a broad horizon of advanced mathematical concepts. For the individual trader, this has been more in the form of hearsay and less in the form of concrete application. Again, it is a case of the haves versus the have nots.

Morgan Stanley had the resources to hire the head of the mathematics department of Columbia University, David Shaw, and appoint him head of quantitative trading and provide him with the staff, computers, programmers, and other resources to apply his advanced mathematical concepts to trading.

D.E. Shaw & Company
He is among the best. He went on to form his own top trading firm and now hedge fund D.E. Shaw. His firm, although far from a household word and not a name even known to many traders, routinely do 10 percent of the volume on the New York Stock Exchange in search of small profits on huge transactions exploiting very hard-to-detect (for the average trader) miss-pricings (as they are now affectionately called by the new generation of "quant traders") of various sorts.

Renaissance Technologies Corporation
Chances are you haven't heard of Jim Simons or of his operation Renaissance Technologies Corporation. Since its inception in March 1988, Simons' flagship $3.3 billion Medallion fund has amassed annual returns of 35.6 percent, compared with annual returns of 17.9 percent for the Standard & Poor's 500 index. Gross or net, Simons may very well be the best money manager on earth.

"Jim Simons is without question one of the really brilliant people working in this business," says quantitative trading star David Shaw, chairman of D.E. Shaw, which boasts returns above 50 percent this year. He is a first-rate scholar, with a genuinely scientific approach to trading. There are very few people like him. Simons surrounds himself with like minds. The headquarters of Renaissance, in the quaint town of East Setauket on New York's Long Island, resembles nothing so much as a high-powered think tank or graduate school in math and science. Operating out of a one-story wood-and-glass compound near SUNY at Stony Brook, Renaissance, founded in 1982, has 140 employees, one third of whom hold PhDs in hard sciences. Many have studied or taught in Stony Brook's math department, which Simons chaired from 1968 to 1976.

Prediction Company

"Founded in 1991 by Doyne Farmer, Norman Packard, and Jim McGill, Prediction Company quickly set out to take the financial world by storm. Based on their earlier work in chaos theory and complex systems, Drs. Packard and Farmer felt the financial markets were an example of a highly complex system that would be amenable to predictive technology. They assembled a team of world-class scientists and engineers to attack the problem.

In 1992, Prediction Company signed an exclusive five-year deal to provide predictive signals and automated trading systems to O'Connor and Associates, a highly successful Chicago-based derivatives trading firm. In 1994, O'Connor was purchased by Swiss Bank, one of the world's largest banks. Swiss Bank extended the exclusive relationship with Prediction Company for another two years. In 1998, Swiss bank and UBS merged to create the world's third-largest financial institution."[2] Prediction Company continues its ground-breaking work with UBS AG.

Why is all of this important? There are any number of reasons. Perhaps first and foremost is proof of the concept that advanced mathematical concepts correctly applied to trading can produce tremendous profit and risk-adjusted returns. Second, and perhaps equally important, is proof of concept of the tremendous effectiveness of advanced knowledge and technology when coupled with resources sufficient to harness this technology to trading.

The dance continues.

TRADING MEETS HIGHER EDUCATION

In 1990, I still considered myself fortunate to find a good book on trading. Do a job search today for trading openings and you will find hundreds of job listings for people trained in financial engineering. The circa-1990 trader asks, "What is that?"

No coincidence is the existence of graduate level training in stochastic calculus and financial engineering and the amazing success of super-quants like David Shaw, Jim Simons, and Doyne Farmer.

If one looks at the history of these developments, one can easily trace its beginnings to an extremely important discovery by the creator of fractal geometry, the mathematical genius Benoit Mandelbrot. He discovered that the distribution of price changes in financial markets follows a fractal distribution, not the standard Gaussian distribution assumed by all financial mathematicians and which is embedded in things like the Black-Sholes options pricing model. This is an earthquake. To a certain extent, I am really not too sure that this is understood or applied by all financial engineers even today.

The tides of change were further fueled by the discoveries of things like genetic algorithms, chaos math, fuzzy logic, complexity theory, and concepts like artificial life, which describes the way complex structures form from simple processes, discovered by another mathematical genius, Stephen Wolfram (also the creator of Mathematica).

Greater computing power made things like neural nets, data mining, and machine intelligence available.

It is my opinion that we have only begun to scratch the surface of all of this amazing information and technology. The amazing success of the super-quants lights the path for us lesser mortals.

This is a gigantic, fascinating, and obviously very fruitful field of inquiry. An exploration of the application of this technology to trading would certainly occupy a volume unto itself.

I simply touch upon this information to point out yet another and highly significant way that trading has and will continue to develop since 1990. I point it out also as a challenge to the trading strategy development application vendors. The world of trading is moving fast and furious, as always. Wake up and smell the coffee.

The Unlevel Playing Field

Back in 1990, in the first edition of DTOTS, I suggested with optimism that the playing field between the individual trader and the professional trader had become relatively level or even. It is now clear that this playing field has perhaps never been as unequal as it is today.

The trading game never changes in two significant areas. The markets are always the markets. They continuously adjust and adapt to the demands placed upon it by traders and investors to continue to function as efficient pricing mechanisms. It is their nature to remain the same through continuous adaptation and change.

Trading is always about making a profit and remaining the last person standing, which means that you leave trading on your terms, ahead of the game and because you no longer wish to trade.

To do that, one needs to find what the old-time floor traders called an *edge*. I personally believe that anyone who succeeds at trading does so because he has discovered an edge. I also believe that there are probably as many different edges as there are traders.

The trading game has never been as profitable as it is today. Nor have the markets ever been more efficient than they are today. Yet, traders the world over continue to make profits. Why? They have found an edge. And, and this is a very big *and*, they stick to the rules of their edge; they follow their well-tested trading strategy religiously.

Let us explore together how these edges are found, polished, optimized, and then employed to produce vast wealth.

Acknowledgments

To say that the first edition of this book both occurred at a pivotal point in my life and career and played a seminal role in its further evolution would be an understatement. Be that as it may, I am eternally grateful, however, to all of those who have supported me and from whom I have learned, and leaned on over the years. I am humbled by their generosity.

I must first thank Pamela van Giessen and her very patient and ever-helpful assistants Jennifer MacDonald and Kate Wood, and apologize for all of the vexation through which I put them through the many lengthy delays in the delivery of this manuscript. It was a much bigger project than originally anticipated.

I would also like to thank my colleague, Perry Kaufman, who, unbeknownst to him, played a large role in getting me started in technical trading, and who has supported me in ways both small and large over the years.

A warm, and deeply heartfelt, thanks to Bo Thunman, who was there at the beginning and for many stimulating conversations over the years.

A word of thanks in honor and memory of Andrew Dziedzic, a brilliant mind taken from the trading community far too soon. Also to Steve Hendel who made that fascinating and unique project possible. They both exemplified that which has made Goldman Sachs the great firm that it is today.

Special thanks to the friends and colleagues who collectively formed what I affectionately referred to as the Brain Trust. Their endless supply of comments, edits, suggestions, and so forth have made this a better work. Thanks to (in alphabetical order) Art Collins, Michael Covel, Bruce DeVault, J.T. McPherson, Kate Pardo, Emil Pesiri, Murray Ruggiero, Ginger Szala, Rich Sternal, and Alfred Tagher. I will be forever grateful for the tremendous time and effort that you have all very selflessly invested in this book.

Thanks to Bill Dunn and Pierre Tullier, who gave me a chance when I really needed one, and who have been steadfast ever after.

Last, but far from least, I would like to thank my family—my lovely wife Nora, my daughter Kate (who is becoming a better writer than her dad!), and my son Chris (who is on the verge of becoming an excellent trader himself.) Nora, Kate, and Chris: Thank you for your love, support, and unfailing confidence in me, even in the darkest hours.

The life of a trader's wife is not always an easy one. My loving thanks to you, Nora. I am glad that we have been able to enjoy the uptrends together and proud that you soldiered through the downtrends. I couldn't have done it without you.

Why a Second Edition?

When Perry Kaufman first asked me to write this book in 1991, the business of trading, the technology of computing, and the climate for trading systems, also known as mechanical trading, and as it is now often called, algorithmic trading, could not have been more different from what it is today. Nevertheless, the first edition has been extremely well received over the years. Consequently, the idea of writing this second edition of DTOTS—as I always think of it—has been daunting for a number of reasons, not the least of which is the risky business of messing with success. You know, "If it ain't broke, . . ."

For now, suffice it to say, that I have been asked often and again, "When are you going to update DTOTS?" Well, we both now know the answer to *that* question. And, I have often been asked, "When are you going to come out with another book?" Stay tuned for the answer to *that* one.

I would like to make one thing perfectly clear from the outset—and also forewarn anyone who did not like the first edition from buying this edition—I still believe that the method that I created, pioneered, and still use to this day, Walk-Forward Analysis (WFA) to be the only 99 percent foolproof method of optimizing a trading strategy. The only model that I trust that does not use WFA is the model that requires *no* optimization. And even that is still not a guarantee of future performance because there can be curve-fitting in a nonoptimized trading strategy.

For the typical trading strategy developer, however, therein lies the rub. Until recently, it has been either extremely tedious or impossible to use WFA. Those who do use it have developed proprietary software, to various degrees of sophistication, to do so.

Furthermore, I still agree with everything that I stated in DTOTS. I still think that I went overboard in sharing some highly valuable proprietary ideas. Given that, it remains a mystery to me that, as extremely well received as DTOTS has been and continues to be, so little of the more subtle and powerful technology which I still apply with very positive results has still not worked its way into the mainstream, as so much of the more accessible material has.

That being said, I have reorganized the material and have made additions, deletions, and changes all through the original. Of course, the intention is toward improvement. There is also a lot of new material, which has allowed me to explore different areas.

I discuss at some length the impact of the radical technological changes that have had an enormous impact on trading of all sorts. I also discuss, with evident and deserved disappointment, how the mainstream trading strategy development tools have sadly lagged this technological whirlwind, much to the detriment of the individual trader and to the benefit of the large, professional trader. I do offer some hope there. For, as I said in DTOTS and I reiterate ever more forcibly in this edition, that successful trading merely requires the trader to find his own unique trading edge and to then consistently apply that edge from his trading comfort zone.

There are also a number of new challenges that face the trading strategist. There is now a bewildering array of software applications from which to choose. There are those applications dedicated to the strategy development process such as TradeStation, Metastock, and TradersStudio, and more general applications that have been used for this purpose such as Excel, Mathematica, and Matlab, as well as mathematically focused programming languages such as R. To make matters more confusing, there are some very high-end products ($25,000 to $100,000 and perhaps more; I have lost track) that profess to provide a more sophisticated solution for the professional trader. From what I have seen, this seems more a marketing exaggeration than a reality, but I haven't really taken all of these products for a spin, so I cannot speak definitively about them as of yet.

To make matters more challenging, most of the real-time quote vendors now offer varying degrees of custom strategy programming and strategy testing, including CQG, which I use as well as eSignal, CyberTrader, and Fidelity's Wealth-Lab.

And here the plot thickens. Along with this tremendous fragmentation of the trading strategy development niche, there is another rather pernicious trend. The real-time quote software vendors typically restrict the use of their software to their data. Worse, they restrict the use of their data to their software. Omega Research has become a brokerage firm and requires a monthly fee or minimum brokerage for the use of their software, and they also make every effort to have their users use their price data.

There are now also options on futures and options and futures on individual stocks. There are stock index futures (S&P, NASDAQ, and Dow futures), there are options on the S&P 100, and there are options on S&P futures. The big institutional trading firms are now very big on detecting and exploiting *miss-pricings* (when I was at Salomon—yes, they are gone, too—we used to call it *arbitrage* and the floor traders used to call it *spreading*).

Why is this type of development a problem for the individual trading strategist? For two reasons: such strategies all require the development of trading strategies with multiple price histories and expirations, and they all require the acquisition, accumulation, and maintenance of expensive, and sometimes practically impossible-to-acquire historical price data.

There is another level of trading strategy complexity that also must be considered. As you might imagine, I speak with a wide variety of professional traders. Some have espoused the view that some of the rather simple trading strategies that have produced hundreds of millions of dollars in trading profits in years past no longer work, or at least, are not as effective, anymore. The reason cited, of course, is the same old reason, "The markets have changed." I do not precisely agree with this, but I do agree that trading has become ever more sophisticated and competitive. I have more to say on this in later chapters.

In support of this contention, it is worth mentioning that my friend Art Collins has quoted Richard Dennis to me (he conducted a series of exploratory interviews with him) as saying that "the Turtle Trading Strategy doesn't work anymore." This may be sobering for the many that have made untold millions from variants of this trading strategy.

Nevertheless, irrespective of whether a simple strategy is effective, there are also equally good reasons to develop more complex trading strategies. Once again, herein lies the rub with the bulk of the consumer-level trading strategy development applications. For a variety of reasons, they are not, for the most part, complex strategy-friendly. The vendors of these applications will vehemently deny this, but for the power user, they are too slow and cumbersome for large-scale development even with simple strategies on a portfolio of markets. They become painfully slow as the complexity—as in multistrategy, multitime frame, and multimarket—of the strategy rises.

What is the trading strategist to do? Let us explore the options.

CHAPTER 1

On Trading Strategies

T rading strategies have been around for as long as people have traded organized markets. Whereas some might quarrel with me in this usage I will state unequivocally that by the terms *automated trading strategy* and its short form *automated strategy*, I mean all of the following terms: *trading systems, mechanical trading systems, trading model*, and *algorithmic trading*.

In the final analysis, I believe that any successful trader, discretionary or automated, does trade with a systematic trading strategy. In the end, as I think you will see if you work through this book, it is difficult to generate long-term and above-average trading or investment returns without a systematic approach.

Interest in technical methods and trading strategies tends to wax and wane with interest in the markets themselves. Interest in the markets tends to wax and wane with the dynamism of the markets and with the attendant opportunity, or lack thereof, for trading profits.

In the 10 years before the first edition of this book, *The Design, Testing, and Optimization of Trading Systems* (DTOTS) published by John Wiley & Sons in 1991, interest in trading systems enjoyed tremendous growth. This was due to two main developments.

The first development was the growth in the markets themselves. Not only did a major bull market develop in equities, but the 1980s led to the introduction and development of a number of new futures markets too numerous to mention. The bulk of this new growth was in financial futures, which have completely eclipsed the commodities markets of the 1970s and the 1980s. More money chased more markets. And the money was smarter too, much of which came from institutional, *professional* traders.

The second development was the explosive growth of inexpensive computing power, which, in turn, brought about growth in the power and availability of sophisticated trading as well as trading strategy development and testing software.

The collaboration of these two primary developments and others produced the beginnings of a renaissance in technical trading methods and trading strategies. One might consider the early 1990s as the birth of algorithmic trading, that is, mechanical and without human judgment.

Since then, as I detailed in the Preface, these trends have accelerated at a pace that makes the early 1990s seem sleepy in comparison. Computing power has reached levels that would have been considered nearly impossible in 1990. The proliferation of markets and trading volume has been almost as explosive. Global trading volume has grown over 1,470 percent. In 1990, global volume of all futures contracts traded was 802,158,782. At the end of 2006, that figure stood at 11,859,266,610. The increase in non-U.S. trading volume has grown over 2,890 percent (7,286,007,180 in 2006 versus 251,771,924 in 1990). The increase in U.S. trading volume was a mere 831 percent (4,573,259,430 in 2006 versus 550,386,858 in 1990). This clearly shows the increasing globalization of futures trading.

This produced, circa 1990, a type of parity with the individual investor and the professional trader, but it has been short-lived. It has been difficult for the individual investor to keep pace with professional traders during the trading renaissance. This combination, however, of inexpensive computing power, sophisticated software, and a growing body of trading methods continues to make it possible for the knowledgeable investor to design and to test trading strategies with, as the pros like to call it, *a positive expectancy*, or as we call it, the potential for trading profit.

These strategies can be on a par with, worse than, or better than those of many professional investment firms. There is nothing to prevent the individual trader working on his own from creating very sophisticated and successful trading strategies. The technology, price history, and the software are all available. In fact, the capabilities of the contemporary investor equipped with testing software and a powerful computer (circa 2007) far exceeds that of the professional strategist working in 1990. In addition to those increased capacities, the availability, range, and sophistication of current technical analytical methods are also many times greater.

A thorough and comprehensive working knowledge of how to properly design and test strategies, however, has never been more important than it is in today's extremely competitive markets. I am also sorry to say that the strategy development software arena available to the individual trader has, for the most part, not kept pace with this growth in computing power, software, and technical methods. The life cycle of a successful trading strategy begins as a "twinkle in the strategist's eye" and ends in cash trading profits. This book presents the techniques required to successfully test, optimize, and trade mechanical strategies.

The benefit of a successfully tested mechanical strategy is obvious—financial gain. The drawbacks of an improperly tested strategy, however, are many. The primary one is financial loss, sometimes as extreme as financial ruin. To add insult to financial injury, these trading losses are often preceded by hundreds of hours of labor and the attendant frustration and disappointment that naturally follow from such a failure.

The trader who diligently applies the procedures provided herein to the development and evaluation of his trading strategy will be able to avoid these costly pitfalls.

WHY THIS BOOK WAS WRITTEN

This book was written to provide a clear-cut and specific road map for the trader who wants to transform a trading idea into a tested, verified, properly capitalized, and profitable automated trading strategy.

The use of technical analysis and trading strategies has become so widespread in the futures trading space that it is now the dominant form of trading by most professionals, and the sophistication and the range of methods just continues to grow. The penetration of many of the types of trading strategies that are pervasive in the futures space, however, is far more limited in the equities and hedge fund spaces.

As the remarkable returns of the rocket-scientists-turned-top-algorithmic traders such as Jim Simons (Renaissance Technologies), David Shaw (D.E. Shaw & Company), and Doyne Farmer (The Prediction Company) have shown, those in these spaces have certainly developed their own original, sophisticated, and extremely effective approach to trading strategies. Interest in the approaches of the futures trading space is also growing in the equities space.

By their very nature, numeric, systematic, and automatic approaches to trading lend themselves to computerized testing. If done correctly, testing can add tremendous value to a trading strategy. In fact, I, and the trading programs at Pardo Capital Limited, would never trade with a strategy that did not prove itself through some form of comprehensive, systematic testing.

Strategy development and testing done incorrectly will lead to real-time trading losses. Make no mistake about this consequence. As the famous computer saying goes, "Garbage in, garbage out." Consequently, because of the inevitable results that follow error, poor procedure, and shoddy craftsmanship, computer testing is best done properly or not done at all.

Because of ignorance of proper testing procedures, some traders have become disillusioned with the very idea of computer testing. Poor craftsmanship in trading strategy development has even led some traders to believe that trading strategies don't work.

Because of ignorance and the difficulties of performing optimization and back-testing correctly, some still believe that testing and optimization are little more than an exercise in curve-fitting. For those of you who are unfamiliar with these terms, don't worry, they are all formally defined in the appropriate chapters.

The procedures and methods presented in this book prove that the benefits of correct testing and optimization vastly outweigh the effort required to learn and to master their proper application. The procedures mapped out in this book set forth in detail the correct way to formulate, test, and optimize a trading strategy.

To set the record straight, this book makes a clear and unambiguous distinction between the terms *optimization* and *overfitting*. Optimization refers to the process whereby a trading strategy is tested and refined so as to produce the best possible real-time trading profits. Optimization then is testing done *correctly*. Overfitting, which no sane strategist ever does intentionally, is optimization that has gone bad. Overfitting, then, is *incorrect* testing.

WHO WILL BENEFIT FROM THIS BOOK?

I hope that this book will provide value for anyone planning to employ mechanical strategies in her trading. It presents, from start to finish, the methods that must be employed to obtain and enjoy the fruits of a profitable trading strategy.

A thorough review of strategy testing highlights one of its greatest benefits: the precise measurement of reward and risk. The value of a trading strategy must be evaluated in two interrelated dimensions: profit and risk. One cannot judge these two components of trading performance in isolation. Trading always involves risk. Trading profit can be correctly evaluated only with respect to its risk, which is its major cost.

A trading strategy, therefore, can be evaluated properly only when profit and risk have been measured precisely and accurately, which can best be done through computerized testing. This absolute necessity of the accurate measurement and correct evaluation of risk and reward alone would be sufficient unto itself to justify the computer testing of a trading strategy.

Perhaps the other, and perhaps the greatest benefit, of trading with an objective, consistent, reproducible, and thoroughly understood automated strategy is the subsequent elimination of human emotion and fallible human judgment from the trading equation.

Whether or not you consider yourself a systematic trader, if you succeed at trading and have done so for some years, the odds are that you trade systematically with a perhaps very complex trading strategy formulated over years of trading.

If you have not already done so, I would urge you to make every effort to extract your trading strategy from the confines of your brain cells and reproduce it in a form that is amenable to some form of testing.

I believe, therefore, that this book holds value for any trader, mechanized, computerized, or not. It comprehensively presents the case for the benefits and necessity of the proper testing of a clearly specified trading strategy. A careful study and application of the methods presented herein will hopefully further refine and enhance the reader's computerized trading skills. Perhaps the noncomputerized trader will acquire an appreciation for the many benefits of this approach to trading and strategy development. Moreover, the noncomputerized trader may finally recognize the benefits of a thoroughly researched analysis of her strategy and make a start with the application of these methods to her advantage.

If you are a trader who is using computerized trading strategies but are not trading profitably, you should definitely read this book. You will most likely find out where you have gone wrong. At that point, you can determine whether you can repair your strategy or not.

More important, if you want to begin strategy development, this book is an excellent place to start. A study of the guidelines presented herein will help identify and eliminate the causes of failure, such as a poor strategy, improper testing methodology, or incorrect real-time interpretation.

I also, and this may surprise some, recommend this book for those traders who wish to pursue the path of discretionary, as in nonsystematic, trading. After studying this material, you will at least be advised of some things to look for in your trading so you can make every effort to both balance risk and reward and be properly capitalized.

Again, at the risk of sounding presumptuous, I also hope that this book will help those computerized trading strategists out there who have been enjoying trading profit as a result of their work. I present a number of testing guidelines here for the first time. The systematic and comprehensive procedures mapped out here are very efficient and effective. I also know that this overall approach is not too widely practiced by many strategists.

I also hope that the detailed presentation of Walk-Forward Analysis, fully detailed in Chapter 11: Walk-Forward Analysis, will bring this powerful methodology and its benefits before the eyes of those who will use it to further enhance their trading profit.

THE GOALS OF THIS BOOK

This book will present, explain, clarify, and illustrate:

- The many advantages that follow from the use of a properly developed automated trading strategy
- How to formulate, test, and evaluate a trading strategy
- How to properly optimize a trading strategy
- The symptoms of overfitting and guidelines to avoid it
- How to incorporate out-of-sample data in the testing of a strategy
- The benefits of and how to do a Walk-Forward Analysis
- How to develop a trading strategy profile
- How to judge real-time trading performance with respect to the trading strategy profile developed through historical testing

I have practiced these principles of trading strategy development presented in this book for years. As such, it is fair to say that they have passed my tests of time and of success in real-time trading.

Of course, there are some refinements and trade secrets that I do not disclose. I can say, however, that if a trading idea has initial merit, then a diligent application of the principles disclosed in this book will produce tradable strategies performing at optimal levels.

If you are new to trading strategy development, I would encourage you to master these principles and put them to the test. In all likelihood, you will save yourself a lot of wasted time, a great deal of grief and frustration, and probably a good deal of money.

You can certainly learn something from this book unless you already know how to effectively apply some form of Walk-Forward Analysis (WFA). It has been my experience that WFA is the only nearly fool-proof method (nothing in trading is 100 percent) of trading strategy optimization. Although some might disagree, I suggest that you put it to the test before forming an opinion about it.

THE LAY OF THE LAND

Everything created under the sun began as an idea. Most ideas are a bit vague when first conceived. As the idea is further explored, however, it gradually gains a more precise form. Once fully formulated and visualized, it takes on a definite and specific form and when formulated in such a way, an idea is capable of becoming a concrete, manifest reality. The same holds true for a trading strategy.

Chapter 2: *The Systematic Trading Edge* presents the benefits, along with some drawbacks, of trading with a computer-tested automatic trading strategy. This unfolds in three parts, detailing the benefits, respectively, of a trading strategy, the historical simulation, and strategy optimization.

A mechanical trading strategy, called simply a *trading strategy*, or *strategy*, is a set of objective and formalized rules external to and independent of the mind and emotions of the trader. The majority of successful traders employ a consistent set of rules, whether or not they are overtly formulated and tested as a formal trading strategy. The use of a consistent set of trading rules is essential to the management of risk and to the creation of trading profit.

After a reading of this chapter, those who still decline to use automated trading strategies will at least know what they are missing. Those who embrace automated trading will rest assured of the merit of the approach. I hope it will provoke those who are still undecided to explore the potential of the automated and tested trading strategy.

Chapter 3: *The Trading Strategy Development Process* maps out the steps through which a trading strategy must evolve, beginning with formulation and precise specification, testing, optimization by way of Walk-Forward Analysis, and culminating in real-time trading. The chapter structure of this book follows this process in its natural order. Essential background material is introduced and interspersed within this overall process, however, as and when it is needed.

Chapter 4: *The Strategy Development Platform* is a brief overview of what the capabilities of a trading strategy development and testing application must include to effectively complete the entire testing cycle from idea to portfolio. A full survey of the plethora of trading development platforms is beyond the scope of this book. It therefore focuses on the various aspects that constitute the full evaluation and development style and what is therefore the minimum feature set needed to complete the process. This chapter also outlines the various processes that need to be completed to take a trading strategy from an idea to an automated, multimarket, multiple time frame trading platform.

Chapter 5: *The Elements of Strategy Design* is an overview of the principles of trading strategy design. Since a full exposition of the principles of strategy design is beyond the scope of this book, the chapter focuses on the essentials of design and the impact that different types of strategies can have on the testing process. It provides the reader with a broad overview of a trading strategy's various components and their purposes.

It also provides a platform and basic foundation for those wishing to enhance their knowledge of this subject.

The prudent, experienced, and well-informed trader is well aware that it is a great deal cheaper and much easier on the nerves, emotions, and confidence to evaluate the performance and value of a trading system using a historical computer simulation. The alternative, of course, is to just start trading with capital and see how things turn out, but that is likely to prove costly.

Chapter 6: *The Historical Simulation* describes what a historical simulation is and what it looks like. The chapter details the various issues that one must address to achieve the most accurate, authentic, and realistic simulation possible of trading with a strategy based on historical data. This approach to the evaluation of a trading strategy is so commonly practiced and widely accepted that I can hardly imagine how anyone ever traded without this process.

Chapter 7: *Formulation and Specification* goes into sufficient detail to clarify the central importance of this first stage in the strategy development process. It provides an illustration of the process of transforming a vague trading concept into computer-testable code.

Chapter 8: *Preliminary Testing* outlines the procedures to be employed in the first round, or preliminary stage, of trading strategy testing. The first step, of course, is to determine whether the strategy has been correctly specified. The next step is to simulate the strategy over a number of small, representative baskets of markets and a diverse set of discrete time periods.

Chapter 9: *Search and Judgment* explores the practical impacts strengths and weaknesses of different types of search and evaluation methods have upon the outcome and quality of the historical simulation and on the optimization processes.

The type of search method employed will determine the amount of processor time necessary to complete the required research. The type of objective function used during the optimization will have a large-to-dominant impact upon the quality of the resulting models. This chapter demonstrates the paramount importance of the objective function. The correct objective function is also one of the keys to the identification of robust trading models and is central to the effective application of Walk-Forward Analysis.

The model parameters selected during the optimization of a trading strategy are based on an objective function also known as *optimization function* and *search parameter*. There's a wise saying that goes "Be careful of what you wish for because you just might get it." This is never truer than in optimization. Optimization and simulation work by their nature are computationally intensive. Extensive literature has been devoted to the multitude of methods available to search through a large number of simulations to identify the optimal and robust parameter values. The goal of these various objective functions or search methods is to identify the most robust model parameters while still keeping the required processing time to a minimum. This chapter also demonstrates the central importance of the objective function to optimization and also to Walk-Forward Analysis.

Many trading strategies have rules and formulas that can accept different numerical values. These parameter values may vary with different types of markets and conditions. Such a trading strategy may often benefit from optimization. If the trading strategy is found to be satisfactory at the end of this first stage of testing, it is time to move on to the second round of testing, which is optimization.

Chapter 10: *Optimization* presents the proper methods to optimize a trading system. Optimization proceeds through two levels. The first is an optimization of the trading strategy over a variety of different markets and time periods. The main purpose of this stage is to determine to what degree the trading strategy is enhanced by optimization. If the strategy demonstrates better performance under optimization, then it is taken to the final round of optimization and testing: the Walk-Forward Analysis.

Chapter 11: *Walk-Forward Analysis* presents this advanced method of strategy optimization, testing, and validation alongside the three major objectives achieved by Walk-Forward Analysis (WFA). The optimization of the trading strategy under an exhaustive WFA measures the trading performance exclusively on the basis of out-of-sample trading, that is, on data other than those used to optimize the strategy.

The first, and far and away the most important, objective of the WFA is to determine whether the trading strategy remains effective on unseen or out-of-sample price history. This, of course, is one of the most reliable and major predictors of real-time trading success. If it *walks forward* well, as we call it, then it is highly likely that it will continue to perform profitably in real-time trading.

The second and next most important objective of the WFA analysis is to determine the optimal parameter values to be used with real-time trading. The third objective is to determine the sizes of the optimization window and the periodic rate at which the strategy is to be reoptimized.

I first introduced Walk-Forward Analysis to the trading public in the first edition of *The Design, Testing, and Optimization of Trading Systems* in 1991. Experience has only continued to prove its merit in the trading arena as the most cost-effective way of producing robust trading strategies that behave in real-time trading in a manner consistent with their historical simulations. Given its efficiency and practicality, it continues to be a surprise to me that it has not attained widespread acceptance and application.

After a trading strategy has been tested, optimized, and walked forward, it must be evaluated, or judged. It must be judged on its merits as an investment competing for capital with the entire universe of investments. It also must be evaluated in comparison to other available trading strategies on the basis of a statistical analysis and review of its own simulation profile and performance structure.

Chapter 12: *The Evaluation of Performance* presents these two essential, typically underappreciated, and often misunderstood procedures.

The simple truth is that with contemporary trading strategy development software and the modern computer, it has never been easier to perform an optimization of a trading strategy. The *proper* ways, however, to test, optimize, and evaluate a trading strategy are not necessarily well known by all of those in the trading community who use these applications.

It is precisely because it is so easy to perform an optimization but so difficult to evaluate it correctly and then successfully trade it in real time, however, that the reputation of optimization has been unfairly tainted by those ignorant of its correct procedure and evaluation.

In fact, it is because of this widespread misuse of optimization that some still falsely equate the term *optimization* with the term *overfitting*. As we see in Chapter 13, *overfitting* or *curve-fitting* is really optimization done incorrectly, carelessly, or gone wrong in some other way.

Chapter 13: *The Many Faces of Overfitting* puts forth the proposition that the *overfitting* of a trading strategy to historical data occurs when testing and optimization are done *incorrectly*. The proper evaluation of an optimization can be a very difficult matter. I personally believe that the most effective way to avoid overfitting during the optimization process is to perform optimization through a Walk-Forward Analysis.[1]

Not all strategists however, have the software necessary to do WFA. The effects of the overfitting or curve-fitting of a trading strategy to its historical data are devastating, and an overoptimized trading strategy often leads to significant and immediate real-time trading losses. To help the strategist avoid overfitting, I dedicate an entire chapter to identifying the symptoms that result from the accidental abuse of proper testing and optimization methods.

This chapter also includes an extensive discussion of a variety of methods designed to detect and avoid curve-fitting, including the most effective way to do this, which is to include out-of-sample testing in your optimization process.

The goal of any trading strategy is to enjoy long-lasting, real-time trading profit. Once the full cycle of trading strategy development has been successfully completed—namely, strategy formulation, testing, optimization, walk-forward analysis, and evaluation—then, and only then, can real-time trading safely begin.

Chapter 14: *Trading the Strategy* presents the guidelines one must follow to assess real-time trading performance in the context of the knowledge of profit and risk arrived at by computer testing and formulated in the statistical strategy profile.

The improper evaluation of real-time performance will cause problems for the trading strategist. It is essential to know, within reason, that the carefully and painstakingly developed trading strategy is performing in real-time trading within the bounds of the trading strategy profile. Without this essential knowledge, the strategist is like the captain of a ship at sea without any sort of navigational apparatus.

CHAPTER 2

The Systematic
Trading *Edge*

T he *New Oxford American Dictionary* defines *edge* as "A quality or factor which gives superiority over close rivals" and *strategy* as "A plan of action or policy designed to achieve a major or overall aim," and finally *trade* as "The action of buying or selling goods or services."

In our definition of the word *trade*, let us replace "goods or services" with the purchase (going *long*) or sale (going *short*) of positions on financial markets operated under the auspices of an organized exchange such as the Chicago Mercantile Exchange (CME), EUREX, or the New York Stock Exchange.

Of course, it goes without saying that the goal or aim of trading is to cause our trading account to grow or to produce a profit.

Let us now combine and extend these definitions to define a *trading strategy* as "A plan of action designed to achieve a profitable return by going long or short in markets on organized financial exchanges."

Continuing, our *New Oxford American Dictionary* defines *systematic* as "Done or acting according to a fixed plan or system; methodical."

Let us combine these definitions to arrive at a definition of a *systematic trading strategy* as:

Acting methodically according to a fixed plan that is designed to achieve a profitable return by going long or short in markets on organized financial exchanges.

Let us recall from Chapter 1 that I take the terms *systematic trading strategy* and its short form, *systematic trading*, to mean, as in synonymous with, the following terms: *trading systems, mechanical trading systems, trading model,* and *algorithmic trading.*

Of course, the overall aim of any trading strategy is the creation of wealth through trading excellence. Trading excellence means the creation of the greatest rate of return possible with the least risk. Furthermore, trading excellence also means the reliable production of excellent returns with the greatest possible consistency from year to year and for the full duration of the trading life of the strategy.

As stated earlier, the only purpose of trading is to produce profits. The main reasons that a properly tested and validated systematic trading strategy helps in the pursuit of trading profit are its:

- Verifiability
- Quantifiability
- Consistency
- Objectivity
- Extensibility

We explore in detail how to do all of these things in the chapters to follow. But, before we do that, let us explore the major advantages or benefits of the systematic trading strategy. This chapter presents the philosophical and practical reasons why someone would choose to trade with a systematic strategy. It is the *why* of systematic trading.

That being said, trading is a human activity, and we humans have a nearly inexhaustible number of reasons to remap and distort our *intended* goals, but that is a topic for a different book. This very tendency toward fallibility, however, is the other highly significant reason that having a systematic trading strategy helps produce profit.

The systematic strategy—unless overridden by well-intentioned but often misguided human judgment—does so without the emotion, fallibility, and error-prone guidance of the all-too-human trader. The properly designed and verified systematic trading strategy pursues trading profit with the relentless consistency and objectivity of computer logic.

DISCRETIONARY TRADING

Let us take a look, and thereby gain some valuable perspective, at some of the advantages and disadvantages of what is known as *discretionary trading.*

The *New Oxford American Dictionary* defines *discretion* as "The freedom to decide what should be done in a particular situation."

That sums up the concept of discretionary trading rather well. The discretionary trader decides what to do each time he makes a trade. It is all put upon the shoulders, as it should be, of the trader. It is up to the skill, knowledge, experience, control, emotional balance, and discipline of the trader.

Let it be known, even though I am known as a leading advocate of systematic trading, that I hold the successful discretionary trader in the highest regard. Discretionary trading demands the mastery of a number of demanding skills.

Aside from all of the technical skills that the discretionary trader must master, first and foremost, the successful ones of long-standing tenure are *masters of themselves*. Remember that the inability to follow a proven strategy is high on the list of reasons for failure of the systematic trader. How much more difficult must it be for the discretionary trader who needs to be *on* and in control of himself day in and day out?

Let us extend this idea a bit further. Consider how difficult it is for the systematic trader when undergoing a drawdown—even when it is in keeping with the risk profile of the strategy—to stay with the strategy and make the next trade, how much more so it must be for the discretionary trader to pull the trigger when faced with loss after loss. Certainly such a condition will have a very corrosive influence on his self-confidence.

As we explore the advantages of the systematic strategy in more detail later in this section, the differences that emerge will be highlighted.

Let us consider the plus side of the discretionary trader. It is quite simple. The biggest plus is that, to date, I do not believe that a systematic strategy has yet been created that equals, let alone exceeds, the performance of the greatest discretionary traders.

Proof of this concept is available by the mere consideration of a short list of some of the household names of the greatest discretionary traders. This short list of the greatest would include the likes of legendary billionaires such as Warren Buffett (I know he is not a trader per se, but he is the second richest man in the world and he got there solely through investing), George Soros, Paul Tudor Jones, Bruce Kovner, and T. Boone Pickens.

The list of the who's who of trading and their multibillionaire status should be sufficient proof positive that discretionary trading and investing can and does work.

RAISING THE BAR

Just because there has not been a systematic trader of record the equal of these great traders, however, does not mean that it is not yet to come.

As I detailed in the preface to this book, systematic trading has not kept pace with the technological advances that have occurred to date. A greater indictment—and there is a causal relationship here to a certain extent—is that commercially available trading strategy development software has woefully lagged behind on all fronts.

The most significant difference between the performance of the highly skilled discretionary trader and that of the systematic trading strategy is merely one of degree and not one of kind.

The discretionary trader has a vast knowledge base of different trading methods and strategies. This knowledge base also holds a store of knowledge about, for example, the strengths and weaknesses of these different strategies as well as their interactions with one another and under different market conditions. Such traders also have the benefit of finely honed reflexes and observational skills that can, sometimes nearly instantaneously, detect a complex pattern in one flash of insight that tells him that the market just made a top. If he is heavily long, he then gets out of all positions as quickly as possible.

Of course, this is highly simplified, but the significant point is that the successful and experienced discretionary trader brings a vast knowledge of different methods of analysis, trading strategies, market knowledge, and pattern recognition to what he does. All this knowledge is then sifted, filtered, and parsed by the human brain through a process of synthesis and experience to arrive at a proper and timely buy-or-sell decision.

In contrast, consider a relatively simple but widely used systematic trading strategy made famous by Richard Dennis and the group of trading students, the famous Turtles, whom he trained in its use. Let us consider a highly simplified version of this strategy. The Turtle Trading Strategy (TTS) is a range breakout method originally derived from a strategy developed by Richard Donchian, an early pioneer of systematic trading.

TTS goes long when an x-day high has been penetrated and goes short when an x-day low has been broken. It exits positions on opposite signals from a shorter y-day high or low. There are other variations, but in the end, it really doesn't add that much complexity, so these wrinkles will be ignored for the sake of this illustration.

This information is all that the TTS trading strategy "knows." Go long at new x-day highs and go short at new x-day lows. Exit long and short positions on opposite signals at y-day highs or lows. In its original form, it factored in no other knowledge or information. Anyone with any imagination can certainly think of a long list of other indications that might be added to this strategy for its enhancement. The point to be noted here, however, is not the relative simplicity of the strategy, although that too is significant, but rather the absence of any other information factored into this decision to go long or short.

This is why I say that the difference, at least at this point in the game, between the skilled discretionary trader and a systematic strategy is one of degree. There is no reason to believe that a systematic trading strategy cannot be made that rivals the knowledge base of the discretionary trader. Just because it has not been done yet, at least to my knowledge, does not mean that it cannot or will not be done.

When computer scientists first began the development of computer programs to play chess, it was said that a computer would never beat a chess master. That barrier was broken in 1997 when IBM's Deep Blue beat Garry Kasparov.

Evidence is mounting that the front-runners in systematic trading are finding ways to develop, test, and trade increasingly sophisticated and highly profitable systematic trading strategies. Recall from the preface the spectacular performance of the trading world's rocket scientists who are making fortunes trading like D.E. Shaw & Company, Renaissance Technologies, and the Prediction Company. I personally believe that we, as the saying goes, "ain't seen nothin' yet."

In support of this seemingly bold statement, consider the implications of the concept of Perfect Profit. I created this concept for use as an important measure of performance for our implementation of Walk-Forward Analysis. I presented this in the first edition of this book on page 125 under a discussion of Model Efficiency. An expanded version of this discussion can be found in Chapter 12 of this book: The Evaluation of Performance.

The definition of "perfect profit" found in Chapter 12 is *"Perfect Profit is the sum total of all of the potential profit that could be realized by buying every bottom and selling every top."*

Of course, this is an idealized and unobtainable goal. Consider, however, the potential (Perfect Profit) profit obtainable for five markets in five years on daily bars. Table 2.1 lists these values for five markets.

TABLE 2.1 Perfect Profit for Five Markets for Five Years of Daily Data

	Perfect Profit Daily Data	
	January 2002 to December 2006	Average Year
Crude Oil	$887,440	$177,488
Eurodollars	$56,887	$11,377
Yen	$601,000	$120,200
Soybeans	$783,450	$156,690
S&P	$2,368,000	$473,600
Total	**$4,696,777**	**$939,355**

Consider that a sustained annualized rate of return of 25 percent or more places a hedge fund or a commodity trading adviser (CTA) in the upper stratosphere of performance. According to the Barclay Trading Group, as of June 2007, only 16 CTAs (out of a universe of 375) produced a five-year annualized compound rate of return of 25 percent or better.

Now consider that the potential profit for one average year ($473,600 = $2,368,000/5) in the S&P futures market measured trading, one contract in a $100,000 account in the daily degree is 474 percent. The total for one average year of Perfect Profit for the five markets in our table is $939,355. That is a return on our account of 939 percent!

Now let us consider that there are more than 11,000 listed stocks, 7,000 listed mutual funds, and over 200 different futures markets, and the potential becomes absolutely staggering. When we factor in the profit potential that is available on crude oil futures on 5-, 30-, and 60-minute bars and we realize that all markets can be traded in a wide variety of time degrees, and whereas potential profit is not infinite, it is vast in the extreme.

It certainly raises the bar on what the aggressive trader might target for his next trading portfolio of strategies. When we consider the extensibility to all markets and time frames that systematic trading makes possible, the enterprising and imaginative strategist might begin to see how it might be possible to begin striving for returns that would have been unimaginable 10 years ago.

Now that we have had a look at what the return potential of future systematic trading platforms may aspire to, let us take a look at the concrete benefits of the systematic approach to trading.

VERIFICATION

The *New Oxford American Dictionary* defines *verification* as "The process of establishing the truth, accuracy or validity of something."

The main reason that we test a trading strategy is to see whether it works, that is, produces a profit. Indeed, perhaps the first and foremost advantage of a thoroughly tested systematic trading strategy is the determination that it, in fact, has a profit potential. Another way of looking at this is that a successful and fully tested systematic trading strategy is in itself a proof of the trading concept.

Without a reasonable estimate of the potential risk-adjusted reward of a trading strategy, it is impossible to know if it is worth trading. Without a reasonable estimate of potential risk, it is impossible to know the true cost of trading with the strategy.

How is it that we determine that a trading strategy has a positive profit expectancy? This is done through the construction and evaluation of a historical simulation. This term will be formally defined and detailed in Chapter 6: The Historical Simulation.

Why is it that the strategist goes through all of the work to painstakingly construct and evaluate a historical trading simulation just to verify the validity of a trading system? The answer to that question is quite simple and most basic. We want to see whether it works, that is, that it produces a trading profit on past historical market data. We also want to develop an opinion of the likelihood that the trading strategy will produce real-time profits in a proportion similar to that of its historical profile. That, however, is an exploration for Chapters 11 and 12.

We are also very interested to see what the profit and risk of the trading strategy is over both ever-changing market conditions and different markets. If we find that the trading strategy produces profit over a range of conditions (necessary) and a variety of markets (desirable, but not necessary), we have further validation of the trading concept. We also know that we have a more valuable trading strategy.

An objectively formulated set of trading rules can be translated into a format that can be understood by a computer. The programmed trading system can then be tested over years of price history and many different types of markets: stocks, bonds, futures, and options. When the trading strategy has undergone a full and exhaustive round of development and testing and the results are positive, we know that we have a profitable trading strategy. We can capitalize a trading account and begin trading with a higher degree of confidence in a positive and lasting outcome.

In contrast, let us consider what is likely to follow if we begin our trading adventure with a bunch of vague, inconsistent, and *unverified* ideas. First, such a configuration cannot be computer tested. We have only our *faith* in the merits of the trading ideas. We have no solid *knowledge* of their past effectiveness or of their risk and rate of return.

Such vague and unverified ideas, of course, can be traded. All that is needed is some trading capital, a clearinghouse, and an account. The results of such an approach, however, are well-documented and predictable. The likely outcome is an assured entry into that very nonexclusive "90 percent-of-all traders-who-trade-lose" club.

As I have previously suggested, even the discretionary trader trades with a plan and systematically determines entries, exits, trade size, and so forth. Trading without a well-defined plan has the same likely outcome as doing anything without a plan—failure. Would you start a business without a plan? Build a house without architectural and engineering drawings? Begin a journey of 5,000 miles without a road map? Why then would anyone begin trading without a trading plan?

It reminds me a of a W.D. Gann quote (paraphrased): "A doctor goes to medical school for four years before practicing medicine; a lawyer goes to law school for three years before beginning the practice of law; why then does a sufficient amount of money with which to trade qualify an unschooled individual to be a trader?"

The Trading Advantage of Verification. When a trading strategy has successfully undergone the full testing cycle from start to finish, it has been verified to have a positive expectancy. It has also been verified that the trading strategy has a reasonably high likelihood of producing real-time trading returns relatively consistent with its historical simulation. Armed with this knowledge, the trader has a sound and rational basis for confidence in the trading strategy sufficient to trade with it and to follow it faithfully.

QUANTIFICATION

The *New Oxford American Dictionary* defines *quantification* as "Express or measure the quantity of."

Another tremendous advantage of a properly developed and evaluated trading strategy is the highly detailed quantitative measures that are the result of this process. An accurate measure of profit and the risk required to obtain it are needed for two main reasons. The first is to determine whether the risk-adjusted reward is equal to, inferior to, or superior to other competing trading and investment vehicles. The second is to determine the optimal account capitalization required to obtain the maximum rate of sustainable return.

Another tremendous advantage of the quantification or statistical evaluation of a trading strategy is that it makes it possible to accurately compare different trading strategies to one another. Because of the varying profit and risk profiles of different trading systems and the profit potential of different markets, the only thing that can be meaningfully compared from one system to another is the rate of its risk-adjusted rate of return.

RISK AND REWARD

A computer-tested trading strategy measures profit and risk. It also provides a large number of other very useful statistics, such as the number of trades, the value of the average trade, statistics about winning and losing runs, and trading performance on a year-by-year basis. These statistics collectively compose the performance profile. Table 2.2 is an example of such a profile.

Perhaps one of the most important benefits of the historical trading profile is the proper evaluation of returns. Profit cannot be evaluated without a measurement of the risk that earning it entails.

TABLE 2.2   Example of a Performance Summary

Summary Report for Session
R1_Test_SP SP-9967.TXT 1/1/1999 to 12/31/2000. System is XTct (38, 38, 3)

Performance Summary: All Trades

Total net profit	$185,450.00	Open position P/L	$2,350.00
Gross profit	$415,325.00	Gross loss	($229,875.00)
Total number of trades	113	Percent profitable	60.18%
Number winning trades	68	Number losing trades	45
Largest winning trade	$31,875.00	Largest losing trade	($22,650.00)
Average winning trade	$6,107.72	Average losing trade	($5,108.33)
Ratio average win/average loss	1.20	Average trade (win and loss)	$1,641.15
Maximum consecutive winners	4	Maximum consecutive losers	3
Average number of bars in winners	5	Average number of bars in losers	5
Maximum intraday drawdown	($34,875.00)	Maximum number of contracts held	1
Profit factor	1.81	Yearly return on account	267.90%
Account size required	$34,875.00		

Performance Summary: Long Trades

Total net profit	$82,350.00	Open position P/L	$0.00
Gross profit	$220,975.00	Gross loss	($138,625.00)
Total number of trades	57	Percent profitable	57.89%
Number winning trades	33	Number losing trades	24
Largest winning trade	$22,475.00	Largest losing trade	($22,650.00)
Average winning trade	$6,696.21	Average losing trade	($5,776.04)
Ratio average win/average loss	1.16	Average trade (win and loss)	$1,444.74
Maximum consecutive winners	4	Maximum consecutive losers	3
Average number of bars in winners	5	Average number of bars in losers	5
Maximum intraday drawdown	($22,650.00)	Maximum number of contracts held	1
Profit Factor	1.59	Yearly return on account	183.17%
Account size required	$22,650.00		

Performance Summary: Short Trades

Total net profit	$103,100.00	Open position P/L	$2,350.00
Gross profit	$194,350.00	Gross loss	($91,250.00)
Total number of trades	56	Percent profitable	62.50%

(Continues)

TABLE 2.2 (Continued)

Number winning trades	35	Number losing trades	21
Largest winning trade	$31,875.00	Largest losing trade	($19,350.00)
Average winning trade	$5,552.86	Average losing trade	($4,345.24)
Ratio average win/average loss	1.28	Average trade (win and loss)	$1,841.07
Maximum consecutive winners	4	Maximum consecutive losers	3
Average number of bars in winners	5	Average number of bars in losers	5
Maximum intraday drawdown	($19,350.00)	Maximum number contracts held	1
Profit Factor	2.13	Yearly return on account	268.43%
Account size required	$19,350.00		

To illustrate this principle, consider two different trading strategies and their risk and reward. Strategy One earns an annual profit of $2,500 with a risk of $500. This is not a terribly profitable system. Yet, neither is it a very risky one. Furthermore, it offers a reward-to-risk ratio of 5 to 1 ($2,500/$500 = 5). This makes the system very appealing on a *risk-adjusted return basis*. Let us calculate required capital at three times risk plus margin of $5,000. Strategy One produces a risk-adjusted return of 38.5 percent ($2,500/((3 × $500) + $5,000).

Strategy Two earns an annual profit of $50,000 with a risk of $50,000. Based solely on its profit, this looks like a very profitable system. However, it just turns out that it is an equally risky one. Its reward-to-risk ratio of 1 to 1 is very unappealing. Strategy Two produces a risk-adjusted return of 32.3 percent ($50,000/((3 × $50,000) + $5,000).

Which strategy is better? If we were to judge by profit alone, Strategy Two would be the hands-down winner ($50,000 versus $2,500.) If we are to judge correctly by the respective risk-adjusted return, however, or what it costs to earn a dollar of profit, Strategy One produces a return that is more than 6 percent better.

Profit and risk are inextricably interrelated. The trader or investor cannot have one without the other.

THE PERFORMANCE PROFILE

The performance profile is a collection of trading performance statistics. It is analogous to an X-ray or an MRI scan of a person. This look under the hood of the strategy provides insight into the internal operation of the trading system. More important, it provides both a road map and a benchmark providing what should—and, more important, what should *not*—be expected from its real-time trading performance. It provides us with a mechanism to check the health of our trading strategy's real-time performance. This is discussed in detail in Chapter 14: Trading the Strategy.

Suffice it to say that this *performance profile* is essential to the proper management of trading a systematic strategy. Without a precise, statistically reliable measurement of risk-adjusted returns, it is impossible to assess whether future profits and losses are in line with the strategy's historical performance.

More important, without a statistically reliable measure of risk, it is impossible to *manage* future trading risk. Of course, this makes rational trading impossible. Risk is the primary dictator of the cost of trading a strategy. Furthermore, without the proper measurement of risk, portfolio management is also impossible.

This profile provides further insight into what type of performance to anticipate during differing market conditions, such as an uptrend or a downtrend, or during conditions of high and low market volume and volatility.

The quantification of the trading strategy also needs to be extended over different markets. The reward-and risk-measurements of individual markets are essential to the design and creation of a basket of markets or a trading portfolio. Without these individual market-risk-adjusted returns, it is impossible to determine appropriate market allocations and to balance a portfolio to achieve maximum risk-adjusted returns.

The Trading Advantage of Quantification. The quantification of the risk and reward of the trading strategy provides the mathematical basis for the correct capitalization for real-time trading of the strategy. The statistical performance profile that is also a result of this quantification provides a set of milestones by which real-time trading performance can be evaluated. Aside from the value inherent in these features, this knowledge should further enhance the trader's confidence in the trading strategy and the assurance of a positive outcome.

OBJECTIVITY

The *New Oxford American Dictionary* defines *objectivity* as "Not influenced by personal feelings or opinions in considering and representing facts. Not dependent on the mind for existence."

In other words, an *objective trading rule* is uninfluenced by those ever-willing assassins of trading profit: unsubstantiated opinion and uncontrolled emotion. Furthermore, the objective, systematic trading strategy is external to the mind of the trader. In other words, it has no reliance on the mind, and its highly varied states, of the trader for correct execution. Once specified and verified, the objective systematic trading strategy has a life of its own, like any other human creation, independent from its creator.

There is nothing wrong with emotions—after all, constructive emotions are the drivers and wellsprings of life. Undisciplined and poorly understood emotions as trading inputs, however, are typically quite unreliable. All the more so because the typical emotions that play heavily, usually wreaking havoc on trading, are fear and greed. Lack of confidence, or self-doubt, is another emotion highly antithetical to trading profit.[1]

What is the typical effect of fear on the trader? As we all know, the emotion of fear triggers the fight-or-flight response in our biological system. If we choose to fight, we dig in. What does a trader do when he digs in? He stays with a trade, for better or for worse.

If we choose flight, we run away from the threat. What is the flight response in a trader? We exit the trade (typically when it is going against us), regardless of whether it is the right thing to do.

What is the typical effect of greed on the trader? Typically, greed motivates a premature trading exit: "I better grab this profit while the getting is good." The trader grabs the profit only to see the trade soar on a profit three times the size of his grab.

The other typical, although opposite, response is to hold on to the trade too long. The thinking runs something along these lines: "I already have $5,000 per contract on this trade; that's good, but I bet if I hold on, I can get another $2,500 per contract." The trader holds on only to find his profit cut in half, or perhaps, turned into a loss on an adverse open the next trading day.

There is an old trading proverb that sums this up rather well: "Bulls make money, bears make money, and hogs get slaughtered."

What is the typical effect of self-doubt on the trader? The typical effect is chronic second-guessing and self-questioning to the point that a trade might not be taken or the position size reduced in a manner inconsistent with his trading rules. What is the typical result of such omissions? Often, the trade not taken is a winner and the downsized trade is a big winner.

The destabilizing effect of undisciplined emotion is the introduction of tremendous inconsistency. Furthermore, fear, greed, and self-doubt can have a tremendously negative impact on trading. These effects can be compounded by the likelihood that such emotions will be affected by whether the trader is healthy or sick, well-rested or exhausted, hungry or satisfied, happy or sad, tense or calm, and so on.

Undisciplined and turbulent emotions—especially fear, greed, and self-doubt—are the enemy of trading consistency. Conversely, objectivity, with its independence from the mind, emotions, and opinions of the trader is the ally of consistency.

The Trading Advantage of Objectivity. The objective systematic trading strategy is external to and independent from the mind, mood, and emotions of the trader. Once formulated and thoroughly researched, the systematic trading strategy has a life and independence of its own. Furthermore, the trading strategy is independent from the whimsy of and buffeting by the often-turbulent emotions of the trader. This objectivity and freedom from the inconsistent whimsy of the trader promotes consistency in trading. The systematic trading strategy, if followed without exception, provides its own form of trading discipline.

CONSISTENCY

The *New Oxford American Dictionary* defines *consistent* as "Conformity in the application of something, typically that which is necessary for the sake of logic, accuracy, or fairness."

Why is consistency so important to trading profit? Consistency, in fact, is arguably one of the major influences contributing to profitable trading. Why? Consistency in trading means the application of the same trading rules—entries, exits, trading size, risk management, and so forth—for each and every trade produced by the trading strategy. The execution of a trading strategy automatically in real-time trading will produce profits and losses that are relatively consistent with the results of its profitable, verified, and robust historical simulation. The alteration of the rules in the execution of a systematic trading strategy will not.

The optimization of the trading strategy produces a robust set of model parameters, which hold reward and risk in a delicate balance. It is certainly true that the more robust and excellent the trading strategy, the less delicate this balance is. But even the most robust trading strategy can and will be eventually ruined by the acceptance or rejection of trading signals that can and will result from human interference.

Only after the risk of a trading strategy has been properly identified and measured can it then be successfully monitored and managed in real-time trading. It is impossible to manage risk successfully when it is undefined or constantly changing. As it is said, "It is hard to hit a moving target." This is never truer than when attempting to manage undefined risk.

What does it mean to "unfaithfully follow" a systematic trading strategy? It means, in general terms, any human—and untested—override, interference, or alteration of the rule of the strategy. One way of looking at these human overrides, or as we'll call it going forward, *trader interference* of a strategy, both in theory and in practice, introduces a new and untested variable(s) or rule(s) to the strategy.

A typical form of trader interference is to not take a trading signal. Of course, the prudent reader might ask, "Why would a trader not take a signal from a proven and tested trading strategy?" This is a very good question indeed and has everything to do with trader psychology, which, of course, is not the topic of this book. In brief, this usually has to do with fear or a lack of self-confidence. The net effect, however, of *not* taking every trade produced by a strategy has the effect of transforming the precisely measured risk, which is balanced with reward in that delicate equation arrived at in the development process, into an unknown and *moving target.*

To illustrate the effect of risk as a moving target in a more concrete manner, let us consider hypothetical System X. X has an average winning trade of $1,000, an average losing trade of $500 and a 45 percent rate of accuracy. Given these statistics, we can reasonably assume that after 100 trades (with every trade taken without trader interference) there will be approximately $45,000 in profits (.45 × 100 × $1000 = $45,000) and approximately $27,500 in losses (.55 × 100 × $500 = $27,500.) This leaves System X with a net profit of $17,500 ($45,000 − $27,500 = $17,500).

Now let us consider System Y. Y is a variant—perhaps an aberration—of X. It has a 45 percent accuracy rate, an average win of $1,000, and an *unknown* (Hmm, can we detect a possible case of trader interference going on here?) loss size. After 100 trades, it can be reasonably predicted that 45 trades will be wins, producing a profit in the vicinity of $45,000, and 55 trades that will be losers. However, the dollar value of these 55 losses is *unknown* due to Y's lack of statistics and rules about risk. The net loss may be $11,000 (assuming an average loss of $200) yielding a net profit of $34,000. This would be great. Or, they may yield a net loss of $82,500 (assuming an average loss of $1,500) producing a *net loss* of $37,500. It could also be worse.

As this simple example illustrates, ignorance of the risk of a trading strategy makes it impossible to properly assess the return of the strategy. Even worse, such ignorance of risk makes it impossible to properly capitalize the trading strategy.

Obviously, no one ever really knows whether the next trade is going to be a winner or a loser. The only good reason, however, why a trader would choose to take or not to take the next signal would be foreknowledge of its outcome. That, however, is impossible. The *real* effect of such picking and choosing of signals is to destabilize the delicate balance between profit and loss uncovered during the strategy development process.

I have always considered it one of the great ironies of trading that, at least from what I have seen, it is the trade *not* taken that is so often a winner, and often enough to matter, a *big* winner. Conversely, the ones taken are typically losers. It doesn't take a rocket scientist to see where that course of action is headed.

Let us get back to our metaphor of risk as a moving target. Extending the logic developed in the previous paragraph, missing winners and picking the trades that lose will wind up affecting the balance of profit and loss by decreasing profit and increasing loss.

Another typical form of trader interference with the systematic trading strategy can extend to trade sizing, and this can, and quite rapidly, lead to potentially devastating results. Consider the following example.

The trading strategy is on a hot streak and it has produced seven wins in a row and decent size ones, too, trading a unit size of two contracts per trade. Feeling flush from the extended winning streak and the big equity increase, the trader feels like the strategy can do no wrong and increases the unit size to ten contracts per trade. Well, anyone who has traded for any length of time knows that all winning streaks come to an end. So does that of our hot-handed trading strategy and its does so with three typically sized losers in a row *at the larger trade size of ten contracts.* Of course, a trade size five times larger than that which produced the winning streak will lose money at a rate five times greater. As a result, the trader winds up giving back all of the profits from the last winning run and much more as well.

Without consistency of entry, exit, risk, and trade size on each and every trade, it is impossible to estimate the probability of success. It is essential to understand that without a thorough knowledge of strategy-specific risk, it is impossible to intelligently trade with any strategy, whether automatic or discretionary.

Consistency also means knowing in advance how to act in any circumstance, based on preestablished and verified rules. Contrast this to the inconsistency and unpredictability of trading responses based on emotions such as fear and greed. Consider the tremendous advantage this confers during those infrequent but oftentimes very dramatic, fast, and either hugely rewarding or painfully costly price moves that occur from time to time driven by sudden, large, and unexpected political or economic events.

The Trading Advantage of Consistency. A sound systematic trading strategy is that it consistently—with the uncluttered logic of mathematics and the relentlessness of computers—applies the same entry and exit rules without exception or deviation. As a result of this, and assuming a relative consistency in market activity from period to period, which is not always the case, the size and frequency of profits and losses will remain reasonably in line with that of its performance profile.

EXTENSIBILITY

The *New Oxford American Dictionary* defines *extensibility* as "An application of an existing system or activity to a new area."

Replace the word *area* with *market* and we now have a clear conception of the first step of extensibility. If we replace *market* with *markets and time frames*, we have yet another important application of this concept. If we further add *systematic trading strategies*, then one can really begin to see the considerable advantage conferred by the extensibility of trading strategies through total automation.

One of the most valuable but often overlooked advantages of the systematic trading strategy is that, given sufficient trading capital and computing capacity, it can be applied to as many different markets and time frames in which it has proven itself to be effective. Taking this logic one very important step further, and given the same provisos, a group of different systematic trading strategies can be traded over a portfolio of different markets and different time frames.

To a large extent, given the mental capacities of the human trader, I don't think there are many people who would even for a moment pretend to be able to trade such a basket of strategies, markets, and time frames. Given the rise of global markets, trading is now possible almost 24 hours a day and 7 days a week. It is true that it would be possible to staff a group of professional traders 24/7 to trade such a complex vehicle. It is also true that any large trading entity these days has a fully manned 24/7 trading desk. This is, of course, very expensive.

But consider how much more cost-effective, quick, and reliable a computerized installation of such a vehicle would be. Such a computerized trading desk would only be limited by its hardware and communication capabilities. It should also be noted that such highly computerized trading desks already exist.

Now consider the recent and rapid rise and availability of electronic trading in the vast majority of markets (and which many experts believe will soon include all markets). Combine this with the rapid rise of automatic order entry and we are looking at the perfect climate for the systematic trading of a basket of systematic trading strategies, over a basket of markets and time frames. And, once again, rest assured that such highly systematic trading is also taking place. By no means, however, is it all-pervasive—at least as of yet.

The Trading Advantage of Extensibility. A profitable and sound systematic trading strategy run by computer makes it possible to trade virtually as many markets for which the trader has capital. This ability to trade a systematic trading strategy by computer makes it possible to cost effectively and efficiently extend trading over a multimarket, multiple time frame, and multistrategy basket blended with an asset management and portfolio overlay. The availability and effectiveness of automatic order entry makes this an increasingly realistic proposition. It is now technically possible to trade a highly complex systematic trading strategy through a computer and with no human involvement other than that of its creation, testing, and implementation.

THE BENEFITS OF THE HISTORICAL SIMULATION

The *New Oxford American Dictionary* defines *simulation* as "Produce a computer model of." It defines *model* as "A description, esp[ecially] a mathematical one, of a system or process, to assist calculations and predictions."

A historical simulation of a trading strategy is a model or representation of the trading performance—a historical profit and loss statement—produced by the rules of the trading model under evaluation.

How is a trading simulation produced? Two things are needed: trading simulation software and a historical database of market prices. The first step, then, is to create a precise formulation of all of the rules of the trading strategy in a computer-testable language. Next, this strategy formulation is then processed by a computer application—a trading simulator—that has the ability to trade, or to apply, this strategy on historical data. The trading simulation software then collects all of the trades—buys, sells, and individual profit and loss—produced by the strategy during this historical period and a number of different statistical performance reports are created from them.

The level of detail and the different types of information contained in a historical trading performance varies from application to application. There are a number of common statistics, however, that are included in all such reports, including, for example, net profit, maximum drawdown, number of trades, percentage of winners, and average trade.

Producing a historical simulation with the proper software is a straightforward process. Once the trade simulation software has been mastered and a historical database of prices acquired, producing trading simulations is a relatively simple process. Deducing that the trading strategy has a positive expectancy is also quite simple: Either the historical simulation is profitable or it is not. However, and this is a big however, determining that the historical simulation has produced a result that is reproducible in real-time trading is quite a different matter.

We explore these topics in detail, including examples, in succeeding chapters. Now that we have a basic idea, however, of what a trading simulation is and what information it provides, let us go on to explore the various benefits that accrue from the creation and examination of a trading strategy.

POSITIVE EXPECTANCY

As we determined in the previous section, one of the main reasons that we test a strategy is to see whether it works; in other words, if it has positive profit expectancy. If the results of the simulation are profitable, at least we now know that we have something that traded profitably in the past and something with which we can work to determine whether it will produce such returns in future trading. An accurate historical simulation of the trading strategy is the only way to determine whether the strategy has a positive expectancy. The alternative, of course, is to just start trading with the untested strategy in real time. I would not recommend this latter course of action, though.

The historical simulation and its evaluation can and must answer two very important questions. First, the strategist needs to determine how effective the trading strategy has been historically. This needs to be evaluated as an investment comparing it to a variety of competing alternatives. This is explored in Chapter 11: The Evaluation of Performance.

THE LIKELIHOOD OF FUTURE PROFIT

The second and *far* more important question is to determine the likelihood of the strategy producing returns in real-time trading in a manner consistent with that of its historical simulation. This is a far more difficult determination to make. This is explored in Chapter 13: The Many Faces of Overfitting.

Furthermore, if one uses Walk-Forward Analysis to optimize and validate the strategy, arriving at this determination with a high degree of confidence is far more straightforward and mechanical. This is explored in Chapter 11: Walk-Forward Analysis (WFA). It is one of the central theses of this book that Walk-Forward Analysis is the most effective remedy for, and method of, avoiding overfitting. The historical simulation of course, is the mode of operation of Walk-Forward Analysis. In fact, as we see in Chapter 10, WFA adds another level of simulation to the trading strategy process.

We can see from this that the historical simulation by itself does not answer this very important question. Rather, this determination is arrived at by the evaluation of the

- Historical simulation itself
- Development process
- Optimization process
- Walk-Forward Analysis

It is the proper and stringent application of the procedures presented in these latter chapters that tell us with a high degree of confidence the likelihood of real-time performance in line with the strategy's historical performance. Of course, it all begins with and could not proceed without the historical simulation.

It is a complicated and sometimes difficult process to simulate, optimize, and evaluate a trading strategy from start to finish *correctly*. We have seen how easy it is to create a historical simulation of a trading strategy. The accurate evaluation of the validity of the historical simulation however, is not quite so simple.

Also, to establish with a high degree of confidence that a trading strategy will work in real-time trading is a complex and more difficult process. As we will see, one of the greatest benefits of Walk-Forward Analysis is the bright light that it sheds on this question.

THE PERFORMANCE PROFILE

After it has been determined that the trading strategy has a positive and desirable profit expectancy that is reproducible in real-time trading, it is time to take the trading strategy out of the realm of history and thought and to enter into real-time trading with the strategy.

It is the historical simulation and the various statistical analyses that are produced in this process and the subsequent analysis aimed at the determination of its robustness that are the foundation of the trading strategy's performance profile.

PROPER CAPITALIZATION

There are two main applications of this profile. The first is to use this information to determine the minimum proper capitalization of the trading account. The pursuit of consistent, high, and sometimes outsized trading profits is what drives the trader to trade. It is the size of the risk, however, that tells the trader how much it is going to cost to achieve this profit.

Reward cannot be properly evaluated in the absence of its attendant risk. The only meaningful and practical measure of performance is in the form of the risk-adjusted return. This central statistical measure of performance is defined and detailed in Chapter 12: The Evaluation of Performance.

What concerns us here is that this measure is central to the proper capitalization of a trading account. Proper capitalization means that an account is funded with sufficient capital to absorb the maximum risk, or drawdown, that the trading strategy may endure. More important, not only can it absorb this drawdown, the account must have sufficient capital remaining after drawdown to continue to trade with the strategy. As they say at the gaming tables, "If you can't pay, you can't play." In other words, if your drawdown wipes out your trading account, you will not be able to continue trading, recoup your losses, and move on to a new high from the many wins to come.

A MEASURE OF REAL-TIME TRADING PERFORMANCE

The second and perhaps even more important application of the performance profile is its application to the evaluation of real-time trading performance. With a properly developed systematic trading strategy, real-time trading performance should conform in general to that of the statistical profile of performance. This is unlikely to be an exact correspondence, of course. This is explored in detail in Chapter 14: Trading the Strategy.

If real-time performance is dramatically different from that of its performance profile, however, whether on the side of profit or loss, then we must satisfy ourselves as to the reason for this discrepancy. If a valid reason cannot be found, then it is even more important to be highly vigilant until trading begins to realign itself to the performance profile. Be aware that strategies that have perhaps gone awry do not always return to normalcy.

We are all too quick, of course, to consider abandoning a strategy if losses begin to exceed our expectations. This is not always the correct thing to do, however. Conversely, we are laughing all the way to the bank when our strategy is more profitable than its performance profile. And, of course, there are valid explanations for windfall-size profits. One does need to keep in mind, however, that outsize losses usually follow outsize profits. The sword of volatility cuts both ways.

In summary, the benefits of the historical simulation are a:

- Determination of positive expectancy and a measure thereof
- Method for determining the likelihood of real-time trading profit
- Method of properly capitalizing a trading account
- Yardstick for real-time trading

THE BENEFITS OF OPTIMIZATION

The *New Oxford American Dictionary* defines *optimize* as "Make the best or most effective use of a situation, opportunity or resource."

To optimize a trading strategy then is to make the *best* or *most effective* use of it. One of the main reasons that we optimize a trading strategy then, is to obtain its peak trading performance. As we see in the next section, Walk-Forward Analysis takes this one step further.

Most trading strategies have rules that accept various different values. For example, a two moving average crossover system will have a value for the length of each of the averages. Whether the analyst chooses to optimize these values, any strategy that can accept different values for its rules is optimizable, if so desired.

The first function of optimization then, is to determine the *appropriate values* for the most robust implementation of the trading strategy. Just as the creation of a historical simulation with trading simulation software is trivial, so is optimization. Doing it correctly, however, and determining the most robust parameter set is nontrivial.

The second, and more important and more difficult, function of optimization is to arrive at an estimation of the *robustness* of the trading strategy. This is explored in detail in Chapter 12: The Evaluation of Performance. Let us just note here that robustness, or the lack thereof, of a trading strategy can show itself in this stage of strategy development.

Anyone who has been around trading for any length of time knows that market conditions are in a relatively constant state of flux. Trends end and change. Volatility rises and falls, as does trading volume. Political and economic events add small, medium, and sometimes gigantic shocks to the markets.

Change is one of the defining principles of a market. Hence, it must be a fundamental axiom of trading life that markets change, and as traders, we must be flexible and adapt to this change. Changing market conditions will definitely have an effect on the performance of a systematic trading strategy.

Another of the main functions of optimization, and more so of Walk-Forward Analysis, is to arrive at and maintain *peak trading performance* in a systematic trading strategy in the face of this continual change.

It is also a function of optimization and Walk-Forward Analysis to *adapt* a trading strategy to different types of *markets*. All markets have their own unique personalities. A trading strategy may perform well in one market with one set of values and poorly in another with those same values. I do not believe that one set of parameters should necessarily be sufficient for every market in which the strategy is traded. In my experience, such a situation is rare. In fact, I tend to prefer different values for a trading model for different markets, in that it offers an additional dimension of portfolio diversification. Optimization will identify the best set of parameter values for each market.

Finally, different traders have different trading capital, time available, computing resources, profit expectations, tolerance for risk, and temperaments. Another application of optimization then, is to adapt the trading strategy to the individual needs of the trader. The degree to which this is possible will vary with the style of the trading strategy as well as with the market to be traded.

In summary then, the benefits of optimization are the:

- Achievement of peak performance
- Evaluation of one measure of robustness of the strategy
- Maintenance of peak performance
- Adaptation to changing market conditions
- Adaptation to different markets
- Adaptation to different traders

THE BENEFITS OF THE WALK-FORWARD ANALYSIS

Walk-Forward Analysis is formally defined and illustrated in its creation and correct interpretation in Chapter 11: Walk-Forward Analysis. For our purposes here, it is sufficient to note that a Walk-Forward Analysis is a systematic and formalized manner of performing what has been referred to as a *rolling optimization* or a *periodic reoptimization*.

One of the primary benefits of the Walk-Forward Analysis is to determine the robustness of the trading strategy. The central and highest benefit of the Walk-Forward Analysis is to determine the degree of confidence with which the trader may anticipate that the strategy will perform in real-time trading as it has in its historical testing.

Another important advantage of Walk-Forward Analysis is to produce peak trading performance as markets, trends, and volatility change. Since the Walk-Forward Analysis provides a method of periodic reoptimization with current price action, this often means that it can produce trading performance superior to that of traditional optimization. Since this periodic reoptimization is done with a strategy-appropriate amount of current price data, this also provides an efficient way to continuously adapt a trading model to ongoing changes in market conditions.

In summary, the main benefits of Walk-Forward Analysis are the:

- Evaluation of the likelihood of a trading strategy performing well in real-time trading
- Measurement of the robustness of the trading strategy
- Achievement of peak trading performance at a level superior to that of traditional optimization
- Maintenance of superior trading performance through more effective adaptation to changing market conditions

THE ADVANTAGES OF A THOROUGH UNDERSTANDING

Any trading strategy that has been developed and tested by the methods presented in this book will offer the trader five major benefits. These benefits flow directly from the thorough, intimate, and precise understanding of the trading strategy that is a product of this approach to trading.

These five important benefits are:

1. A comprehensive and precise knowledge of the strategy's reward and risk
2. A high degree of confidence that your strategy *will perform in real-time trading* as it has in historical simulation
3. A basis for a rational and reliable evaluation of the trading strategy's real-time performance
4. The confidence to stick with the trading strategy during good times and bad
5. A comprehensive knowledge of the trading strategy and of its real-time trading performance, which makes it easier to successfully improve and further refine the trading strategy over time

The first three benefits of the systematic approach to trading were covered in the preceding sections. We have seen how this approach leads to:

- A precise understanding of the trading logic of the strategy
- A detailed understanding of the behavior of the trading strategy
- An understanding of its behavior in different market conditions and
- A method of rationally evaluating its real-time trading performance in light of its historical performance

Items four and five, however, from the previous list will benefit from further elaboration.

CONFIDENCE

As tremendous as all of the preceding benefits of the systematic approach to trading are, they all lead up to perhaps the most important of all of its benefits: confidence. The most solid confidence is one based upon knowledge and understanding.

W.D. Gann had a saying of which I have always been particularly fond. He said, *"Never trade on hope."*

The systematic approach to trading strategy development leads to knowledge. With knowledge we don't need to hope.

The most important knowledge which this process produces is of:

- The workings of our strategy
- Its performance
- Its risk
- Its robustness
- Its likelihood to produce profit in real-time
- A method to evaluate its real-time performance

Armed with such a comprehensive knowledge of a strategy, the trader needs only hope for favorable market conditions. He does not need to *hope* that his strategy will work because he knows that his thoroughly evaluated strategy offers the best possible prospect for trading success.

The bottom line is that the solid knowledge that results from a thoroughly tested and well-understood trading strategy produces a tremendous and well-founded confidence by the trader in his trading strategy. The main benefit of this well-founded confidence is that it increases the likelihood of the trader being able to follow his strategy absolutely and to the letter of the law. It is the following of the well-tested trading strategy with exactitude, and without exception, that is the greatest assurance of long-term trading success. Conversely, deviation from such a well-tested trading strategy will most often lead to trading loss.

Most important, such knowledge-based confidence makes it much easier for a trader so equipped to stay with the trading strategy during its inevitable lean periods of losing streaks, drawdowns, and low returns. The trader so equipped trades with knowledge, not with false hope.

STRATEGY REFINEMENT

A thorough understanding of the theoretical foundation of the trading strategy makes it much easier for the trader to continuously refine and improve her strategy. Equipped with this knowledge, it is far easier and more productive for the trader as she observes the strategy's behavior in real-time trading to look for its strengths and weaknesses with an eye to improving the former and better limiting the latter in future trials.

For example, consider a trend-following system. Assume that the driver of the strategy is the breakout of a volatility channel around a moving average. As the creator and trader, you have observed a tendency for the signals to have an appreciable lag behind market action. Knowing this, you can search for other patterns or indicators that may be able to reduce this lag.

Consider a countertrend strategy. Assume that the driver is some measure of an extreme reading in an overbought or oversold indicator such as a stochastic oscillator. As the creator and trader of this strategy, you have observed a tendency in real-time trading for the best signals to occur at intermediate-term cycle tops and bottoms. With this information, the developer can research cycle detection software as a potential way to filter the trades taken by the strategy.

CHAPTER 3

The Trading Strategy Development Process

The development of a trading strategy is a complex process consisting of a number of different interrelated and interdependent stages. The entire procedure is quite straightforward if one performs every step carefully and thoroughly with a proper attention to each one's significance.

In short, the development and application of a trading strategy follows eight steps:

1. Formulation
2. Specification in computer-testable form
3. Preliminary testing
4. Optimization
5. Evaluation of performance and robustness
6. Trading of the strategy
7. Monitoring of trading performance
8. Refinement and evolution

Each of these topics will be developed in its own chapter. This chapter comprises two parts. The first is an introduction to the philosophical orientation taken in this book. The second is an overview of the development process so as to provide an overall context within which to place the very detailed material in the subsequent chapters dedicated to these topics.

TWO PHILOSOPHICAL APPROACHES TO STRATEGY DEVELOPMENT

There are two main philosophical approaches to trading strategy development. The first approach applies reason in the original design and conceptualization of the trading strategy. This is followed by the systematic and empirical verification of each component of the trading strategy. Every element of the strategy must make sense before the testing process even begins. I refer to this as the scientific approach to strategy development and it is the approach that I primarily follow in this book and in my trading.

The second approach might best be called the empirical approach. To a large extent, the logic and reason of the strategy developer is eclipsed, and to a varying extent, replaced by computer intelligence.

The empirical approach uses various forms of computer software technology to search a space comprising a vast library of indicators, patterns, and price action to assemble a profitable set of trading rules that become the trading strategy if accepted and put to use. In other words, the computer picks and optimizes a trading strategy developed in this manner.

Though the fields of artificial and machine intelligence have come a long way, I do not feel that there is evidence that they are yet up to a task of this magnitude.

The main drawback to this approach is that it is relatively easy for this to devolve into a morass of sophisticated overfitting. Also, the actual logic of the trading strategies that emerge from this process is often not visible to the trader. The trader is, typically, and with good reason, unwilling to invest millions of dollars traded on a strategy that is essentially unknown to the trader.

The Scientific Approach

It might well be said that applying the scientific approach to trading strategy development follows the scientific method. Namely, one formulates a hypothesis and then tests this theory to verify whether it is true—profitable and robust—or false—unprofitable and untradable.

Whether the original theory has been found to be true or false, a dialectical process of further development and refinement can begin. In this process, new theories (the refinements to the original) are formulated and then accepted or rejected as true or false.

The scientific approach to trading strategy development is the methodology that is detailed in this book.

The trading models that emerge from the scientific approach offer an invaluable benefit because the trader of such a system completely understands how the trading model operates and why it is expected to be successful. This approach provides many benefits, not the least of which is the comfort that comes from appreciating the strategy's ins and outs.

A bird's-eye view of this approach would look something like the following example. A theory of market action is proposed that states that a bigger-than-usual momentum surge predicts the beginning of a new trend in the direction of the surge. Let us call this trading strategy the Momentum Surge Strategy (MSS). The strategist formulates a means of trading and verifying the theory.

The strategy would stipulate: "Enter the market long when the market rallies 55 percent of the 3-day average daily range from the previous day's close. Enter the market short when the market falls 75 percent of the 3-day average daily range from the previous day's close. Exit on opposite signals."

The trader then translates these trading rules into a computer testable language, creates a historical simulation of the trading results, and evaluates it. MSS is thereby found to be modestly profitable over five different markets each over five two-year historical periods. Optimization and Walk-Forward testing of MSS uncover the full scope of its profitability, it is found to be sound, and it is traded in real time. Because of thorough testing, real-time performance follows test performance, so the trading continues. Furthermore, the trader is able to continually refine the system.

In my experience, the vast majority of traders employ the scientific approach. It is also the approach that I have followed with much success and satisfaction over the years. Because of my and others' success with it, I follow the scientific approach methodology in this book.

The Path of Empirical Development

The onset of this second approach to strategy creation largely results from the development and refinement of a large array of computerized tools such as neural nets, data mining, genetic programming, and the other forms of computer artificial intelligence technology that are often referred to as *machine intelligence*.

It is beyond the purview of this book to explore the pros and cons of this method in the detail that it demands. In fact, a thoughtful analysis of that topic could easily result in a lengthy tome of its own.

Therefore, let us consider a much simplified and somewhat crude example of this approach that is inadvertently employed by many uninformed traders attempting to find a tradable strategy.

As an example, imagine that a trader is dabbling with a strategy development program that allows for easy profit and loss results along with a whole array of statistical measures on any trading strategy entered into and tested through a historical simulation. Although he tinkers with this formula found in a book, its workings, benefits, and pitfalls are not fully understood.

One or two of the 30 variations of this formula show marginal profit on one period of history in one market and the trader thinks this looks promising. So this strategy is optimized on one year of current data and found to be even more profitable. Trading with it starts Monday. Unfortunately, real-time trading performance is poor. Trading continues until half of the equity is lost and the trader concludes that the trading strategy fell apart.

The unfortunate, but still optimistic, trader starts perusing his library for another system or formula that might work. Once he finds this prospect, the same uninformed process will be repeated and a similar fate will probably befall the untested system.

Now certainly, the new machine intelligence applications that can be brought to bear upon the development of a strategy are far more sophisticated than those of this unfortunate trader. It is the very sophistication and opaqueness of these machine intelligence software applications however, that can mask, beneath the surface of their operation, an outcome similar to the one described earlier can and often does occur.

The sophistication of the artificial intelligence technology employed by these applications often intimidates the strategist into a quiescent and uncritical acceptance of the results. This is made worse because, often, it is very difficult for the strategist to have any idea how these patterns were found and validated or why they should be believed to work.

That being said, I know there are any number of sophisticated, capable, and sincere strategists using these applications to empirically develop valid strategies. I will add, however, that I think, for reasons that follow that this approach is fraught with difficulties that make it very difficult to arrive at sound trading strategies in this manner.

Note that any strategy developed using this approach, however, needs to follow the same stages of testing and real-time trading monitoring as a strategy developed using the scientific approach. Also, given that the strategist may never really know exactly why a signal has been generated, it may be very difficult to determine whether or not the strategy is performing correctly.

There is a further difficulty inherent in this process. The research process is often hampered by the complexity of the machine intelligence research process, the general inflexibility of the software, and large amounts of processing power required to complete a lengthy optimization and Walk-Forward Analysis.

Because of these issues, it may be either highly labor intensive and time consuming, if not outright impossible, to do a comprehensive Walk-Forward Analysis to validate a trading strategy developed with the empirical approach. It is rather well-known that technologies such as neural nets are often referred to as the ultimate curve-fitting technology. I therefore believe that a rigorous Walk-Forward Analysis is absolutely essential to any strategy's final validation.

In my opinion, consequently, it is critical that an empirically developed strategy be put to a rigorous Walk-Forward Analysis and be monitored and controlled without exception by adhering to its statistical profile.

I believe, to a large extent, that most professional traders are reluctant to, and for the most part do not, use empirically derived trading strategies, largely because the rules and trading logic of such strategies are not transparent or visible. The reluctance of the professional trading community to embrace the empirically derived strategy is also due, in part, to the inherent difficulties and high costs associated with the creation and validation of empirically derived strategies. But for many traders, and I include myself, the inability to perform the necessary due diligence on such black-box trading strategies is their biggest drawback.

There is no reason to believe the issues of transparency and high development costs will not be resolved by future technological advances. But, of course, that is not the case as of the time this book was published, so I will continue to adhere to the scientific approach to the development of trading strategies.

AN OVERVIEW OF THE TRADING STRATEGY DESIGN PROCESS

I have found that every successful trading strategy goes through eight stages of development and usage. Like all things, a trading strategy begins as an idea. If the idea is sound, it eventually becomes a wealth-producing trading strategy after following this eight-step development process, which I have found to be the most efficient path from idea to successful systematic trading.

The eight stages are (see also Figure 3.1):

1. Conceptualize and formulate the trading strategy
2. Specify the trading rules in a definitive, objective, and computer-testable form
3. Do a preliminary form of testing of the trading strategy
4. Optimize the trading strategy, which means arrive at the formulation of the strategy that features the most robust and highest level of risk-adjusted returns

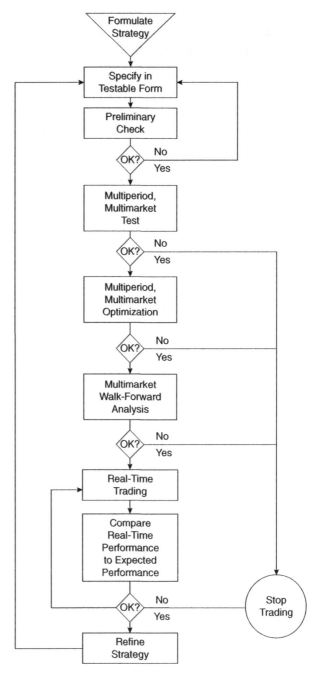

FIGURE 3.1 The Scientific Approach to Trading Strategy Development

5. Evaluate the robustness of the trading strategy and its ability to produce real-time trading profits with the Walk-Forward Analysis method that I recommend

6. Trade the strategy in real time

7. Monitor the trading performance and make sure it agrees with the performance exhibited during historical simulation

8. Improve and refine the trading strategy

Each of these eight stages depends on the success of the preceding step. Continuous feedback, using information from later steps to go back and perhaps improve upon earlier steps, is an essential component of this approach and one of its great strengths. This is most obviously the case in step Seven. With a good system, this approach leads to a continuous evolution, refinement, and improvement of the trading strategy. This approach can also lead to the creation of entirely new strategies, which are derived from observations of the original strategy in operation.

Step 1: Formulate the Trading Strategy

Like anything, a trading strategy begins as an idea. The rules that compose the strategy must be laid out one at a time. The strategy can be simple or as complex as desired but its simplicity or complexity does not matter. What does matter is that you can spell out the strategy completely and consistently.

One of the most dangerous things for a trader to do is to incompletely specify all of the strategy's rules. This is also, unfortunately, one of the most common mistakes that is made in strategy development, especially with traders new to systematic trading.

In its final form, a systematic trading strategy must be reducible to a set of precise rules and formulae. If the trading idea cannot be reduced to such a form, then it is not a systematic trading strategy.

Step 2: Translate the Rules into a Definitive Form

When *all* of the trading rules have been written down and organized into a coherent, logically consistent format, this step is appreciably easier. If the formulation has sufficient precision, is logically inconsistent, lacks key elements, or has errors, this process will be much more difficult.

To be testable, you must first translate the trading strategy into a language format that your selected testing platform can understand.

Metastock, TradeStation, and TradersStudio all have their own scripting languages and their own strengths, weaknesses, and idiosyncrasies.

While some of these vendors will deny this, all of these scripting languages are essentially high level programming languages that are customized to include the features necessary for trading strategy development.

EasyLanguage, TradeStation's development language, evolved from a once very widely used, and now all but defunct, programming language called Pascal. The object-oriented scripting language of TradersStudio will be clearly recognizable to those who are familiar with Visual Basic. Those who are familiar with Excel formulae may well recognize that of Metastock.

No matter which platform is selected, a faithful translation from concept to formulation to exact scripting language is necessary. An inaccurate translation of trading concept to script will, of course, lead to an inaccurate historical simulation. Furthermore, without this scripted version of the trading strategy, the historical simulation and the associated evaluation of performance are impossible.

Step 3: Preliminary Testing

The trading strategy is now in a scripted form that can be tested with two goals in mind. The first objective is to determine whether the trading strategy is doing what it was intended to do. The second goal is to arrive at a preliminary evaluation of trading performance.

In this first stage, you compare the trading strategy as conceived for consistency with its scripted translation. In other words, is the script buying when the short moving average crosses above the long moving average, and selling when the short moving average crosses below the long moving average? In short, have you faithfully and successfully translated the trading idea into a script that you can later use to create a historical simulation and support further testing?

The first goal has been achieved when you have determined that the scripted form of the trading strategy accurately represents the trading strategy as originally conceived. If it does not, the trading strategy script must be corrected and then reevaluated. This process continues until you have achieved the first goal.

The second goal is to get a rough idea of the strategy's profit and risk profile before moving further into the testing cycle. The model should be moderately profitable, or it at least should not lose a great deal over a number of markets and over a number of different time periods. Every test does not have to be a winner; if every test is a loser, however, and particularly if the losses are large, you should probably abandon the strategy. Conversely, if this check produces results that are, or nearly are, tradable, that is good news indeed.

This level of testing is not intended to be exhaustive or definitive but it is intended to teach you two things. First, that the trading strategy has been correctly formulated and is now in a testable form. Second, that its trading performance is anywhere from within acceptable tolerances to good. You know enough now to either reject the trading strategy and move on to the next project or continue with its development.

Step 4: Optimize the Trading Strategy

The definition of the word *optimize* according to the New American Oxford Dictionary is "To make the best or most effective use of."

As this definition suggests then, to *optimize* a trading strategy is to make the most effective use of it. The most effective use of a trading strategy is to earn the highest possible and sustainable risk-adjusted return with it. Achieving this is the true purpose of trading strategy optimization.

Because of a long history of abuse and ignorance of correct procedure, the word *optimization* has unfortunately been falsely confused and has sometimes even been taken as a synonym for the word *curve-fitting.*

Curve-fitting is a statistical term that means to approximate a line or a curve to a body of data. This term is also often misunderstood and is incorrectly taken as a synonym for the term *overfitting.*

Overfitting occurs in the statistical modeling process when excessive attention is paid to creating a curve that matches every twist and turn in the data that are modeled. Overfitting occurs in the trading strategy development process when the trader adds rule after rule and parameter after parameter to the strategy and falsely boosts its trading performance beyond that which is likely to occur in future trading. I explain this in more detail in Chapter 13: The Many Faces of Overfitting.

As the dangers presented by overfitting exemplify, optimization has many pitfalls. If you follow the procedures presented in this book correctly, you can avoid these pitfalls. Knowing how to correctly optimize a trading strategy allows for the best understanding of and profit from your trading strategies. Optimization is simple to understand, and, with current testing software, it is even easier to do. But it is nearly impossible to correctly optimize a trading strategy without a full understanding the principles involved. The ways to avoid these pitfalls are presented in Chapter 13: The Many Faces of Overfitting.

In brief, the process of optimization entails the creation and analysis of a group of historical trading performance simulations using a selected range of different model parameter combinations on the same piece of historical price data. The optimization process selects a small set of top models from this larger group of test results based upon an objective function. Chapter 9: Search and Judgment further describes the tremendous impact of this objective function.

If you pay the proper attention to the appropriate rules during the optimization process, the top models identified thereby will be those that offer the greatest profit potential in actual trading.

A broad improvement of profit performance is expected over that which was found during the first level of testing. For example, a very good test would show anywhere from a 50 to 100 percent overall improvement in performance over that discovered in the first round of testing. This performance improvement will show in many ways, but key here are in the areas of profit increase and drawdown decrease.

It is also important here to examine the robustness of the trading strategy in light of the overall optimization results. This is relatively complicated process and will be explored in detail in Chapter 10: Optimization.

This stage of testing is considered successful if trading performance has increased considerably in all markets on which the strategy has been tested. It is also an important consideration at this stage to begin to notice some of the features that suggest strategy robustness.

Step 5: The Walk-Forward Analysis

This is the most critical stage of the trading strategy development process. In short, this is the go or no-go stage. The trader determines at this stage whether the trading strategy is real. In other words, you determine whether the hypothetical returns that have been produced up to this stage result from overfitting, in spite of your best efforts to the contrary, or result from a robust trading strategy capable of producing real-time trading returns on a par with those uncovered in the earlier stages of the development cycle.

If the strategy's returns are plagued by overfitting and lack robustness in out-of-sample testing, you must return to the drawing board, so to speak, and reevaluate the strategy. Conversely, and happily, if our strategy passes this round of testing, the next step is real-time trading.

How do we evaluate the out-of-sample robustness of our trading strategy? The many approaches to this thorny problem are discussed in Chapter 11: Walk-Forward Analysis. I suggest, however, that the most effective, reliable, and efficient approach to this stage of testing is Walk-Forward Analysis (WFA). Using this approach, in fact, saves a great deal of time and energy by replacing much of the optimization process.

In short, WFA judges the performance of a trading strategy strictly and solely on the basis of postoptimization or out-of-sample trading. It is also the closest simulation possible of the way in which an optimizable trading strategy is most often used by traders. WFA is presented in detail in Chapter 11: Walk-Forward Analysis.

Walk-Forward Analysis's first and most important benefit is the verification of the strategy's real-time trading capability. In other words, does the trading strategy have life after optimization? Will it make money in real time? Of course, the Walk-Forward test is not real-time trading, *but* WFA is a much more realistic simulation of and most closely resembles the way in which many traders do apply optimizable trading strategies in real time.

The second benefit of WFA is a more precise and reliable measure of the rates of postoptimization profit and risk. This is explained in more detail in Chapter 11.

Because WFA produces a statistical profile with multiple optimizations and postoptimization trading periods, it makes a precise comparison and measurement of the rates of out-of-sample returns versus in-sample optimization returns possible.

Finally, WFA provides insight into the impact of changing market conditions on trading performance. Trend changes, which by nature often occur swiftly, and large shifts in volatility and liquidity can have a large and often negative impact on the performance of a systematic trading strategy. A good, robust model will be more capable of responding effectively to such changes.

If a trading strategy passes a rigorous Walk-Forward Analysis, it is ready for real-time trading.

In sum, this stage of testing answers three essential questions that are necessary to trade a system with intelligence and confidence:

1. Will the trading model make money after optimization?
2. At what rate will the trading model make money after optimization?
3. How will changes in overall market conditions such as trend, volatility, and liquidity affect trading performance?

Step 6: Trade the System

After such exhaustive testing and evaluation trading, the system is the easy part, relatively speaking. The signals and stops are generated by computer on a period-by-period basis in accordance with the formulae and rules created in the strategy development process. The only thing that you must do to be assured of the highest likelihood of success is to take all signals from your strategy without exception.

Larry Williams is fond of reminding the systems trader: "Trading strategies work. System traders do not."

Many profitable trading strategies exist. I am relatively confident that strategists will also continue to create new and profitable trading strategies. However, and this is a very big however, successful systematic traders are rare.

Why? Many traders lack sufficient confidence in and understanding of their trading strategies to stick with them when they begin their inevitable periods of drawdown. Many traders also lack the self-discipline required to rigorously stick with a mechanical trading strategy. Experience has certainly proven, however, that systematic trading is an effective way to make money.

A thorough understanding of the performance of the trading strategy, its profit and risk profile, and a system stop-loss will generate the confidence and discipline required to take every signal offered by the system.

The lesson then is quite simple: When a trading strategy has been satisfactorily tested and is performing in real-time trading according to expectation, *trust it*. Stick with it and take every signal.

This is not to say that a trading strategy will not have losing streaks. It will. It is the strategist's job, however, to understand exactly what the typical risk is of the trading strategy. It is also the strategist's responsibility to be adequately capitalized to endure these drawdowns so that the profits to follow can be realized. Last, but not least, it is an important job of the trading strategist to know when to stop trading a systematic strategy. This is discussed in Chapter 14: Trading the Strategy.

Step 7: Evaluate Real-Time Performance

To successfully trade a systematic strategy, the trader must continuously monitor its real-time performance. It is essential to understand that a properly designed and tested systematic trading strategy should continue to behave the same way in real-time trading as it did during the development process. Conditions arise that can alter this equilibrium. It is essential, however, that if they do, the trader understand the causes of this deviation.

Many traders are too quick to abandon a trading strategy when it is losing, even when the frequency and size of losses is in line with the trading strategy's performance profile. The reason is usually ignorance about and lack of confidence in the trading strategy. Poor self-discipline can also have a hand in this premature abandonment.

Conversely, there are few traders who are alarmed when a trading strategy begins to profit at a pace far in excess of its performance expectation. Yet, this too is a serious deviation, albeit a far more pleasant one. The cause of this deviation, however, must also be explained. You may learn something important searching for the cause of this unexplained profit.

Such knowledge may help anticipate future pleasant surprises. It may also point to the probability of larger losses, since larger-than-expected profits are usually a result of growing volatility, and the flip side of rising volatility is often larger losses. This knowledge can also lead to improvements in the trading strategy. Remember, profits beyond expectation can be a warning of a problem to come. Unexpected large profits may be a warning not heeded.

Step 8: Improving the System

Continued observation of the trading strategy's performance on an entry-by-entry, trade-by-trade, and exit-by-exit basis can provide valuable information to the trader. Over time and over many markets, it will certainly reveal the strengths and weaknesses of the trading strategy.

Such intimate knowledge of the workings of the trading strategy combined with observations of its behavior during different market conditions will spark many ideas for improvement of the trading strategy. Of course, as each improvement is made, the entire development and testing process must be carefully reapplied before the new and improved version can be used for real-time trading.

CHAPTER 4

The Strategy Development Platform

A s we outlined in the previous chapter, the strategy development process is a long procedure when done correctly. If one does this with
the exhaustiveness that professional trading demands, it is an even
longer process. The development platforms that are used during this development cycle can, like all tools, either be a great help or perhaps a
great hindrance. Worse, given the utmost necessity of proper optimization, evaluation, and robustness testing, the wrong development application can doom the strategist to failure right from the outset despite her best
efforts.

This chapter is a brief overview of the different attributes that are required of a trading strategy development application to effectively complete the entire testing cycle from idea to portfolio.

A full survey of the many trading development platforms is beyond the
scope of this book. I also do not want to recommend one over another so
as to appear to have compromised my objectivity. The focus then here is
upon the various aspects that compose the analytic capabilities needed to
perform a full evaluation and development of a trading strategy.

First and foremost then is to pick a development tool that has the feature set with which you are most comfortable. All of the various development tools that are commercially available feature the ability to create
custom indicators and trading strategies and to perform what is commonly
referred to as *back-testing*. In other words, these applications all permit
the input of a trading strategy and the creation of historical simulations
of its trading. The majority will also allow the optimization of a trading
strategy.

You might ask at this point if they all can do this, what is the difference? As in so many things, the devil is in the details.

THE SCRIPTING LANGUAGE

As I discuss in Chapter 7: Formulation and Specification, there is quite a variance in both the capabilities and ease of use of the various strategy scripting languages.

Ease of use is a highly personal matter based upon the personality, skill, and experience of the strategist. Generally, familiarity breeds ease of use.

The bottom line is that if you already are familiar with programming in a particular language, the tools that most closely align with this knowledge will be those that will be easiest for you to learn and to use. Conversely, if you are completely unfamiliar with programming, then I would suggest that you look at some scripting samples for the development tool before making a decision.

Also, some of these development products have wizard-like features, or templates, which can reduce some, if not all (so some vendors claim), of the need to be able to program to use these tools.

Most professional strategists would be disinclined to employ a programming wizard because of the likelihood of the wizard's inability to perform the more sophisticated coding that they are most likely to employ.

This too, however, is a case of buyer beware. If you are unable or unwilling to learn to script or program in the language of your selected application, then you need to satisfy yourself that a programming wizard is available and that it is sufficiently powerful to meet your needs. Please be mindful of the fact, though, that in all likelihood, if you are going to pursue systematic trading in a serious and dedicated manner, the use of a scripting wizard is unlikely to provide a long-term solution.

The reality of the situation is such that trading strategy scripting is not really all that difficult to pick up at a basic-to-intermediate level. Of course, that is easy for me to say after 20 years of doing it, but it is still true. Still, there will be some who will pick it up quite easily and some who never really end up getting it.

If you cannot or will not learn to navigate the scripting path, fear not. There are programmers and consultants who can be hired to do it for you. Of course, this adds a new layer of cost, but it is an available option. There are examples of EasyLanguage, Metastock, and TradersStudio scripting languages in Chapter 7 for your review.

DIAGNOSTICS

This is an area that is often neglected by the beginning strategist. As I discuss in Chapter 8: Preliminary Testing, it is necessary to confirm that the script of your trading strategy is actually producing trading signals that behave exactly as you intend.

Many of the strategy development applications have a feature whereby trading signals can be mapped onto a price chart for which the strategy is being tested. Figure 4.1 represents a TradeStation chart with Buy and Sell signals as arrows placed under (buy) and over (sell) the price bars.

A price chart with signals mapped with price information is a very helpful tool during the preliminary diagnostic cycle. It is especially helpful in detecting gross errors in scripting.

There are other graphic features that are very helpful as well. Among these are the ability to color bars that meet certain conditions. Another similar feature is the ability to place some sort of mark on a chart near the price level and bar that triggered the condition. Figure 4.2 is a Trade Station chart with PaintBars with the darker, heavier price bars displaying the desired characteristics. Figure 4.3 is a TradeStation chart with Show Me symbols displayed as large dots under and over the price bar, displaying the desired quality.

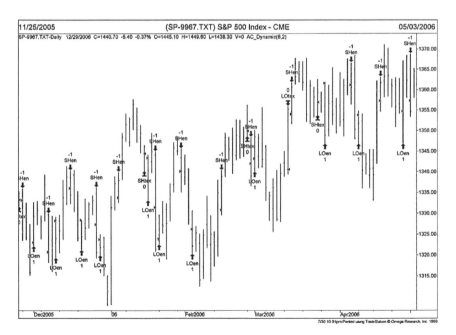

FIGURE 4.1 S&P 500 Index-CME

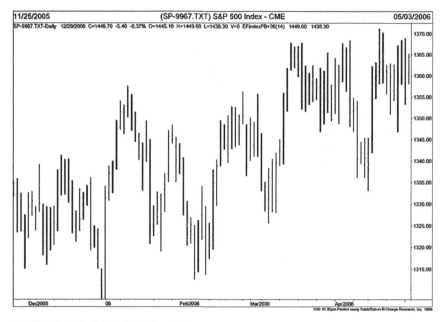

FIGURE 4.2   S&P 500 Index-CME

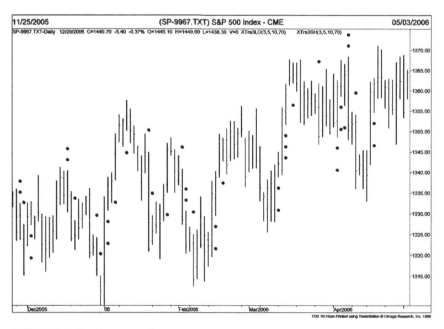

FIGURE 4.3   S&P 500 Index-CME

TABLE 4.1 Diagnosing the Rules of a Trading System

Variables

1020318.00RSIeix:	91.21 Position:	1.00 Position Price:	1200.00
1020318.00RSIeix:	91.21 Position:	1.00 Position Price:	1200.00
1020318.00RSIeix:	91.21 Position:	1.00 Position Price:	1200.00
1020318.00RSIeix:	91.21 Position:	1.00 Position Price:	1200.00
1020319.00RSIeix:	91.00 Position:	1.00 Position Price:	1200.00
1020319.00RSIeix:	91.00 Position:	1.00 Position Price:	1200.00
1020319.00RSIeix:	91.00 Position:	1.00 Position Price:	1200.00
1020319.00RSIeix:	91.00 Position:	1.00 Position Price:	1200.00
1020320.00RSIeix:	84.51 Position:	1.00 Position Price:	1200.00
1020320.00RSIeix:	84.51 Position:	1.00 Position Price:	1200.00
1020320.00RSIeix:	84.51 Position:	1.00 Position Price:	1200.00
1020320.00RSIeix:	84.51 Position:	1.00 Position Price:	1200.00
1020321.00RSIeix:	75.19 Position:	1.00 Position Price:	1200.00
1020321.00RSIeix:	75.19 Position:	1.00 Position Price:	1200.00
1020321.00RSIeix:	75.19 Position:	1.00 Position Price:	1200.00

It often becomes essential, however, when diagnosing more complex strategies and indicators that the strategist be able to see the actual calculations of the formulae in her strategy. This is usually accomplished by placing statements in the script that display information from the strategy. In this way, the strategist can hand-check the calculations of the script to confirm accuracy or to find errors. This information can be printed, posted to a file, or reviewed on the computer screen. Table 4.1 shows variables printed to a file from an EasyLanguage script for the purpose of diagnosis of the rules of a trading system.

It is sometimes helpful on a more detailed level to step through the strategy bar by bar and see how the different variables are functioning. This type of debugging tool is a common feature in the integrated development environments common in the computer programming world. It is not as common, however, among strategy development tools. There are times, though, when this type of feature can be very valuable, especially when debugging more complex trading strategy scripts.

This debugging process can become quite intricate at times. It is important to know what your strategy development tool offers in this regard, particularly if one is inclined to get very serious about this process.

REPORTING

The next feature that is high on the list of priorities is to consider the various types of reports and information that the development tool produces. This has become fairly standardized among the various applications.

Reporting typically includes a performance summary, which provides a variety of statistical measures about the trading performance of the strategy. This will include such essential numbers as net profit, maximum drawdown, number of trades, percentage winning trades, average winning trader, average losing trade, and average trade. These values are also presented broken down by long and short trades. Table 4.2 is a performance summary of a trading strategy on Japanese yen produced by TradersStudio.

A report that details performance on a trade-by-trade basis is also essential. Such a report should include date, price, and signal name for each entry and exit. A trade listing will, of course, also include the profit

TABLE 4.2 Performance Summary

Summary Report for Session
XT99aWK_WF_jy JY-9967.TXT 1/1/1990 to 12/31/2006.
System is XT99AWK()

Performance Summary: All Trades

Total net profit	$85,062.50	Open position P/L	$800.00
Gross profit	$184,987.50	Gross loss	($99,925.00)
Total number of Trades	91	Percent profitable	45.05%
Number winning trades	41	Number losing trades	50
Largest winning trade	$22,425.00	Largest losing trade	($4,912.50)
Average winning trade	$4,511.89	Average losing trade	($1,998.50)
Ratio average win/ average loss	2.26	Average trade (win & loss)	$934.75
Maximum consecutive winners	6	Max consecutive losers	7
Average number bars in winners	51	Average number bars in losers	19
Maximum intraday drawdown	($25,487.50)	Maximum number contracts held	1
Profit factor	1.85	Yearly return on account	19.65%
Account size required	$25,487.50		

Performance Summary: Long Trades

Total net profit	$3,750.00	Open position P/L	$0.00
Gross profit	$71,162.50	Gross loss	($67,412.50)
Total number of trades	47	Percent profitable	34.04%
Number winning trades	16	Number losing trades	31
Largest winning trade	$20,837.50	Largest losing trade	($4,912.50)
Average winning trade	$4,447.66	Average losing trade	($2,174.60)

(Continues)

TABLE 4.2 (*Continued*)

Ratio average win/average loss	2.05	Average trade (win & loss)	$79.79
Maximum consecutive winners	3	Maximum consecutive losers	6
Average number bars in winners	42	Average number bars in losers	17
Maximum intraday drawdown	($19,512.50)	Maximum number contracts held	1
Profit factor	1.06	Yearly return on account	1.13%
Account size required	$19,512.50		

Performance Summary: Short Trades

Total net profit	$81,312.50	Open position P/L	$800.00
Gross profit	$113,825.00	Gross loss	($32,512.50)
Total number of trades	44	Percent profitable	56.82%
Number winning trades	25	Number losing trades	19
Largest winning trade	$22,425.00	Largest losing trade	($3,975.00)
Average winning trade	$4,553.00	Average losing trade	($1,711.18)
Ratio average win/average loss	2.66	Average trade (win & loss)	$1,848.01
Maximum consecutive winners	6	Maximum consecutive losers	7
Average number bars in winners	56	Average number bars in losers	22
Maximum intraday drawdown	($14,775.00)	Maximum number contracts held	1
Profit factor	3.50	Yearly return on account	32.40%
Account size required	$14,775.00		

or loss for each trade and usually a running total. Table 4.3 shows a Trade List of each trade of a trading strategy on Japanese yen produced by TradersStudio.

It is also valuable to be able to review a graphical display of the equity curve produced by the trading strategy in a window below the market on which it was simulated. This is a very quick and easy way to examine the performance of the trading strategy under different market conditions. Figure 4.4 shows a NeoTicker chart with price bars and a corresponding equity curve for a trading system in a window beneath it.

What the strategist should examine here is the performance of the strategy during markets that are trending, cycling sideways, and congested. Conversely, the strategist should also examine trading activity during times of strong profit and drawdown.

TABLE 4.3 Trade List

Trades for Session
XT99aWK.WF_jy JY-9967.TXT 1/3/1990 to 12/31/1999.
System is XT99AWK(10, 10)

Buy/Sell	Entry Name	Market	Entry Date	Size	Entry Price	Exit Date	Exit Name	Size	Exit Price	Trade P/L	Running P/L
BUY	LOen	JY-9967.TXT	8/22/1990	1	114.68	10/30/1990	LOex	1	123.44	$10,750.00	$10,750.00
SELL	SHen	JY-9967.TXT	10/31/1990	1	123.29	1/25/1991	SHex	1	122.10	$1,287.50	$12,037.50
BUY	LOen	JY-9967.TXT	1/28/1991	1	121.86	2/28/1991	LOex	1	121.65	($462.50)	$11,575.00
SELL	SHen	JY-9967.TXT	3/1/1991	1	120.61	4/9/1991	SHex	1	119.69	$950.00	$12,525.00
BUY	LOen	JY-9967.TXT	4/11/1991	1	119.58	5/1/1991	LOex	1	119.57	($212.50)	$12,312.50
SELL	SHen	JY-9967.TXT	5/2/1991	1	118.86	6/25/1991	SHex	1	118.88	($225.00)	$12,087.50
BUY	LOen	JY-9967.TXT	6/26/1991	1	118.99	8/2/1991	LOex	1	119.26	$137.50	$12,225.00
BUY	LOen	JY-9967.TXT	8/13/1991	1	120.14	10/30/1991	LOex	1	123.26	$3,700.00	$15,925.00
BUY	LOen	JY-9967.TXT	11/12/1991	1	124.12	2/10/1992	LOex	1	126.72	$3,050.00	$18,975.00
SELL	SHen	JY-9967.TXT	2/11/1992	1	126.04	5/5/1992	SHex	1	122.60	$4,100.00	$23,075.00
BUY	LOen	JY-9967.TXT	5/6/1992	1	122.80	7/29/1992	LOex	1	125.71	$3,437.50	$26,512.50
SELL	SHen	JY-9967.TXT	8/5/1992	1	125.93	8/20/1992	SHex	1	126.73	($1,200.00)	$25,312.50
BUY	LOen	JY-9967.TXT	8/21/1992	1	126.76	10/13/1992	LOex	1	129.78	$3,575.00	$28,887.50
SELL	SHen	JY-9967.TXT	10/20/1992	1	130.08	12/16/1992	SHex	1	128.41	$1,887.50	$30,775.00
BUY	LOen	JY-9967.TXT	12/17/1992	1	129.17	1/6/1993	LOex	1	127.54	($2,237.50)	$28,537.50
SELL	SHen	JY-9967.TXT	1/7/1993	1	127.35	2/2/1993	SHex	1	127.81	($775.00)	$27,762.50
BUY	LOen	JY-9967.TXT	2/5/1993	1	128.13	7/9/1993	LOex	1	138.91	$13,275.00	$41,037.50
SELL	SHen	JY-9967.TXT	7/12/1993	1	138.71	7/28/1993	SHex	1	142.29	($4,675.00)	$36,362.50
BUY	LOen	JY-9967.TXT	7/29/1993	1	142.09	8/31/1993	LOex	1	143.39	$1,425.00	$37,787.50
SELL	SHen	JY-9967.TXT	9/1/1993	1	142.46	11/16/1993	SHex	1	141.48	$1,025.00	$38,812.50
SELL	SHen	JY-9967.TXT	11/23/1993	1	139.36	1/19/1994	SHex	1	137.80	$1,750.00	$40,562.50
BUY	LOen	JY-9967.TXT	1/21/1994	1	138.21	3/4/1994	LOex	1	142.11	$4,675.00	$45,237.50

SELL	SHen	JY-9967.TXT	3/7/1994	141.73	1	3/30/1994	SHex	1	143.97	($3,000.00)	$42,237.50
BUY	LOen	JY-9967.TXT	3/31/1994	144.04	1	5/19/1994	LOex	1	143.23	($1,212.50)	$41,025.00
SELL	SHen	JY-9967.TXT	5/23/1994	142.70	1	6/14/1994	SHex	1	144.13	($1,987.50)	$39,037.50
BUY	LOen	JY-9967.TXT	6/17/1994	143.88	1	7/27/1994	LOex	1	148.14	$5,125.00	$44,162.50
SELL	SHen	JY-9967.TXT	7/28/1994	147.72	1	9/2/1994	SHex	1	147.02	$675.00	$44,837.50
BUY	LOen	JY-9967.TXT	9/6/1994	147.46	1	10/6/1994	LOex	1	146.28	($1,675.00)	$43,162.50
SELL	SHen	JY-9967.TXT	10/7/1994	145.92	1	10/19/1994	SHex	1	148.74	($3,725.00)	$39,437.50
BUY	LOen	JY-9967.TXT	10/21/1994	149.27	1	11/25/1994	LOex	1	147.12	($2,887.50)	$36,550.00
SELL	SHen	JY-9967.TXT	11/29/1994	146.73	1	1/19/1995	SHex	1	145.72	$1,062.50	$37,612.50
BUY	LOen	JY-9967.TXT	1/27/1995	145.90	1	5/4/1995	LOex	1	163.12	$21,325.00	$58,937.50
SELL	SHen	JY-9967.TXT	5/5/1995	162.68	1	6/2/1995	SHex	1	162.07	$562.50	$59,500.00
BUY	LOen	JY-9967.TXT	6/12/1995	162.65	1	7/6/1995	LOex	1	160.50	($2,887.50)	$56,612.50
SELL	SHen	JY-9967.TXT	7/7/1995	160.03	1	9/27/1995	SHex	1	141.45	$23,025.00	$79,637.50
BUY	LOen	JY-9967.TXT	9/28/1995	141.99	1	10/13/1995	LOex	1	140.75	($1,750.00)	$77,887.50
SELL	SHen	JY-9967.TXT	10/16/1995	140.96	1	11/15/1995	SHex	1	139.85	$1,187.50	$79,075.00
BUY	LOen	JY-9967.TXT	11/20/1995	139.24	1	12/19/1995	LOex	1	138.80	($750.00)	$78,325.00
SELL	SHen	JY-9967.TXT	12/22/1995	137.82	1	4/26/1996	SHex	1	132.77	$6,112.50	$84,437.50
BUY	LOen	JY-9967.TXT	4/29/1996	134.32	1	5/24/1996	LOex	1	131.04	($4,300.00)	$80,137.50
SELL	SHen	JY-9967.TXT	5/28/1996	130.25	1	7/25/1996	SHex	1	130.22	($162.50)	$79,975.00
BUY	LOen	JY-9967.TXT	7/30/1996	130.15	1	8/14/1996	LOex	1	129.95	($450.00)	$79,525.00
SELL	SHen	JY-9967.TXT	8/19/1996	129.82	1	11/13/1996	SHex	1	125.94	$4,650.00	$84,175.00
BUY	LOen	JY-9967.TXT	11/14/1996	125.79	1	12/6/1996	LOex	1	124.42	($1,912.50)	$82,262.50
SELL	SHen	JY-9967.TXT	12/9/1996	123.91	1	3/5/1997	SHex	1	116.93	$8,525.00	$90,787.50
BUY	LOen	JY-9967.TXT	3/10/1997	116.80	1	3/11/1997	LOex	1	116.58	($475.00)	$90,312.50
SELL	SHen	JY-9967.TXT	3/12/1997	116.13	1	5/14/1997	SHex	1	118.79	($3,525.00)	$86,787.50
BUY	LOen	JY-9967.TXT	5/15/1997	120.30	1	7/23/1997	LOex	1	119.35	($1,387.50)	$85,400.00

(Continues)

TABLE 4.3 (Continued)

Trades for Session
XT99aWK.WF_jy JY-9967.TXT 1/3/1990 to 12/31/1999. System is XT99AWK(10, 10)

Buy/Sell	Entry Name	Market	Entry Date	Size	Entry Price	Exit Date	Exit Name	Size	Exit Price	Trade P/L	Running P/L
SELL	SHen	JY-9967.TXT	7/24/1997	1	119.07	8/15/1997	SHex	1	117.74	$1,462.50	$86,862.50
BUY	LOen	JY-9967.TXT	8/21/1997	1	117.83	8/22/1997	LOex	1	117.49	($625.00)	$86,237.50
SELL	SHen	JY-9967.TXT	8/25/1997	1	116.80	1/21/1998	SHex	1	109.10	$9,425.00	$95,662.50
BUY	LOen	JY-9967.TXT	1/23/1998	1	109.96	2/25/1998	LOex	1	108.12	($2,500.00)	$93,162.50
SELL	SHen	JY-9967.TXT	3/4/1998	1	109.35	4/17/1998	SHex	1	106.03	$3,950.00	$97,112.50
BUY	LOen	JY-9967.TXT	4/22/1998	1	106.27	5/6/1998	LOex	1	104.99	($1,800.00)	$95,312.50
SELL	SHen	JY-9967.TXT	5/12/1998	1	104.48	6/30/1998	SHex	1	100.91	$4,262.50	$99,575.00
SELL	SHen	JY-9967.TXT	7/2/1998	1	100.08	8/27/1998	SHex	1	98.51	$1,762.50	$101,337.50
BUY	LOen	JY-9967.TXT	8/31/1998	1	99.03	11/17/1998	LOex	1	110.02	$13,537.50	$114,875.00
SELL	SHen	JY-9967.TXT	11/20/1998	1	110.36	11/24/1998	SHex	1	110.48	($350.00)	$114,525.00
BUY	LOen	JY-9967.TXT	12/8/1998	1	111.11	1/27/1999	LOex	1	114.06	$3,487.50	$118,012.50
SELL	SHen	JY-9967.TXT	1/28/1999	1	112.77	2/12/1999	SHex	1	114.14	($1,912.50)	$116,100.00
SELL	SHen	JY-9967.TXT	2/23/1999	1	108.52	3/24/1999	SHex	1	111.09	($3,412.50)	$112,687.50
SELL	SHen	JY-9967.TXT	3/30/1999	1	109.00	4/26/1999	SHex	1	109.80	($1,200.00)	$111,487.50
BUY	LOen	JY-9967.TXT	4/28/1999	1	109.72	5/11/1999	LOex	1	108.19	($2,112.50)	$109,375.00
SELL	SHen	JY-9967.TXT	5/12/1999	1	108.02	6/7/1999	SHex	1	107.99	($162.50)	$109,212.50
BUY	LOen	JY-9967.TXT	6/8/1999	1	107.66	7/1/1999	LOex	1	107.35	($587.50)	$108,625.00
SELL	SHen	JY-9967.TXT	7/2/1999	1	107.58	7/29/1999	SHex	1	111.43	($5,012.50)	$103,612.50
BUY	LOen	JY-9967.TXT	7/30/1999	1	111.72	10/13/1999	LOex	1	116.51	$5,787.50	$109,400.00
SELL	SHen	JY-9967.TXT	10/14/1999	1	117.27	11/2/1999	SHex	1	119.70	($3,237.50)	$106,162.50
BUY	LOen	JY-9967.TXT	11/4/1999	1	118.98	11/16/1999	LOex	1	117.70	($1,800.00)	$104,362.50
SELL	SHen	JY-9967.TXT	11/17/1999	1	118.11	11/30/1999	SHex	1	121.37	($4,275.00)	$100,087.50
BUY	LOen	JY-9967.TXT	12/7/1999	1	120.85	12/31/1999	Still Open		120.37	($800.00)	$99,287.50

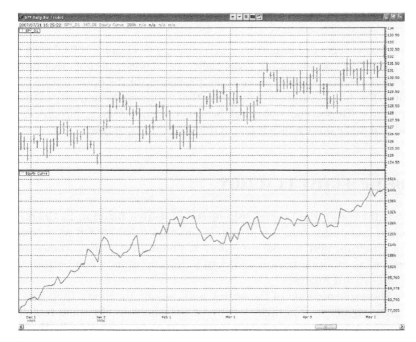

FIGURE 4.4 SPY Daily Bar Trades

It is also an attractive feature to examine trading performance on an interval-by-interval basis, such as yearly, quarterly, even monthly with very active strategies. It is a good indication of robustness if the trading performance of a strategy over time is spread relatively evenly over the entire historical simulation. This is discussed in more detail in Chapter 12: The Evaluation of Performance.

Essential to any strategy development tool, of course, is its ability to produce real-time trading signals. All such worthwhile tools have this ability. As the scale of trading increases, however, the quality of this feature may or may not become an issue. Also, in this era of electronic order entry, the ability to have your strategy development tool route signals to order entry software becomes important. This varies dramatically, of course, from application to application.

A feature that I have always found valuable is the ability to review stops and signals on a historical bar-by-bar basis.

Many software vendors offer additional reports beyond these basic and essential forms of reporting. They are quick, of course, to tout the value of these different reports. It is up to the strategist to determine whether they have merit above and beyond the essentials.

OPTIMIZATION

The next category of importance in a strategy development tool is its ability to perform optimization. Essentially, the majority of tools that provide for back-testing will also make some provision for the optimization of the values for the indicators and formulae that compose the majority of trading strategies. They are all not equal, however. Some of these differences can and will make quite a difference in the life of the strategist.

THE OBJECTIVE FUNCTION

We will explore the crucial role of the objective function in Chapter 9: Search and Judgment. The objective function (also known as *optimization function* and *fitness function*) is preeminent in importance when performing an optimization and even more important when performing a Walk-Forward Analysis.

The sophistication of the search and ranking functions, therefore, are of great significance in the selection of a strategy development tool. This, unfortunately, is a much-neglected aspect of most of these tools. The ranking and sorting functions are pretty typical and not all that useful.

The more sophisticated and experienced strategist has, no doubt, developed various ways to work around this problem. The very best solution would be an application that allows the strategist to implement an objective function customized to his particular needs.

SPEED

This is another often-neglected aspect of the trading strategy development tool. The bottom line is that for the professional and serious amateur trading strategist, processing speed is critical. As I detailed in the preface, most trading strategy development tools are woefully inadequate in this area and have definitely not kept pace with the extraordinary advances in computer technology.

Why is speed important? This should be obvious. To many who are new to this area, however, it is not. Speed is important to the professional strategist because of larger and more complex portfolios that will typically include multiple strategies, multiple time frames, and a large basket of markets. Optimizing a relatively simple, two-parameter strategy on five years of daily data over a small scan range for one market is not all that speed critical.

Consider, however, the optimization of a multiple strategy, multiple time frame, and multiple market trading platform employing complicated models and multiple parameter, intensive scan ranges, and *then* speed becomes absolutely critical. Consider doing this with Walk-Forward Analysis and we really begin to see how critical speed becomes.

Great speed is a window into many possibilities. Slow speed closes trading doors by making these possibilities prohibitively expensive in resources and time.

Unfortunately for those who are restricted to commercial trading strategy development tools, most of them are not particularly quick.

AUTOMATION

The ability to design a research process and then set the application to do this automatically is essential to large-scale trading strategy development. For example, we wish to optimize 3 different trading strategies for 20 different markets. We also wish to have the program save the appropriate reports to a directory and file names of our choosing.

This is impossible to do, unfortunately, for most commercially available programs. For the strategist confined to the use of these commercial applications, it becomes a tedious and laborious process to perform the research process described earlier.

Whereas there are tools that allow for the automation of some Windows processes and applications, experience has demonstrated time and time again that these methods of automating strategy development applications are very limited and often prove to be an unsatisfactory and unreliable process.

In addition to eliminating tedium, resulting in a more efficient allocation of the strategist's time that the automation of the optimization process yields, it also has the decided impact of offsetting to some extent the slowness of processing with which most of these applications are plagued. With automation, research can be planned to run in large batches at times when computers are least used, such as nights and weekends. The strategist is also freed from nursing his research and can spend his time on more productive pursuits.

WALK-FORWARD ANALYSIS

Of course, any development platform that can do optimization can be made to do an out-of-sample test, and this can be extended to a full Walk-Forward

Analysis. Given the number of walk-forward windows one needs to apply to perform a full Walk-Forward Analysis, however, if the research project described earlier is tedious when done without automation, doing a full-blown Walk-Forward Analysis makes it look relatively effortless. It can be done, but it is time-consuming.

In fact, given the level at which computers now function and the degree of software evolution, there is no valid reason for trading strategy development tools not to have built-in Walk-Forward Analysis.

Our new add-in,[1] of course, performs Walk-Forward Analysis as specified herein. There are also a few other TradeStation add-ins that claim to do Walk-Forward Analysis. Based on my review of these, however, none of them do it in the manner specified in this book.

It is one of the central theses of this book that a strategy that has not been validated with out-of-sample testing and, ideally, a full-blown Walk-Forward Analysis should *not* be traded in real time.

Successful strategies, of course, have been traded without the benefit of this form of testing, and I am sure that people will continue to develop some successful strategies without it. It is just my contention that it is a lot of work to do so without it. Also, in the absence of this validation of real-time trading potential, the degree of confidence the strategist is likely to have in his own strategy will be greatly reduced.

PORTFOLIO ANALYSIS

The analysis of the performance of a trading strategy over a portfolio of markets is the last—and some say one of the most important—stages in its development.

The vast majority of professional traders, commodity trading advisers, and hedge fund managers trade a portfolio of markets. Many also trade with multiple strategies (that is, a group of different strategies traded on one market) over their portfolio of markets. Some also trade on multiple time frames with multiple strategies and a basket of different markets. Those who trade equities are likely to trade a large portfolio of hundreds, if not thousands, of different stocks. The vast majority of professional money managers will also employ various forms of asset allocation and position-sizing mechanisms, adding another layer of necessary complexity.

From this, I hope that you are able to see clearly that the issue of evaluating a complex, multilayered portfolio is absolutely essential. All professional traders have some means of performing this essential research.

The strategist would ideally like such a multilayered portfolio-testing capability to be built in to his chosen strategy development application.

This is not, unfortunately, the case with many. Such a capability exists in some of the very high-end applications, but not in the more common ones.

IN CONCLUSION

This chapter was never intended to be an exhaustive feature-and-product survey of trading strategy development tools. Rather, it assumes that most of these products that allow for the scripting of custom indicators and trading strategies and that feature some form of back-testing all share a lot of basic, necessary features in common. The focus in this chapter is on those essential capabilities that are necessary to complete the full cycle of trading strategy development.

The purpose of this focus is intended to serve as an alert to the trading strategist. If a trader has a clear idea of her end destination before she begins her development process, she is more likely have a more productive and successful outcome. This chapter sheds light on each of the various development milestones that must be achieved to transform a trading idea into a profitable multiple strategy, multiple time frame, multiple-market portfolio with sophisticated asset allocation and position sizing mechanisms.

This information should also prove helpful aiding strategists of all levels to avoid some of the potential bumps along the path of this development process. It is best to know the capabilities of your tool at the inception of a project. Know your platform before you begin your development process. Know how it will help you. Also know how it will hinder you.

If used as intended, this chapter will assist you in the design of the strategy development protocols that you will need to successfully develop your trading strategy from start to finish.

CHAPTER 5

The Elements of Strategy Design

A formal definition of the terms *trading strategy* and *systematic trading* was presented in Chapter 2. To recap, the central concept of a trading strategy is the systematic application of formalized trading rules. Foremost among the key benefits of a trading strategy are its objectivity, consistency, and comprehensiveness.

In this chapter I present the basic elements that compose a trading strategy. A trading strategy can range from the very simple to the extremely complex. They come in all forms. Some examples of classic trading systems are: moving average crossovers, volatility breakouts, price channel breakouts, single-bar patterns, multiple-bar patterns, chart patterns, candlestick patterns, swing-based, and indicator-based systems.

This chapter can present only the basic elements of strategy design. This is primarily due to the potential complexities and the huge variation that is possible among trading strategies. The full treatment of the design of trading strategies is too large for one chapter.

The focus of this chapter then will be in two areas. The first is to give concrete form, along with some basic examples, to the idea of a trading strategy. The second is to provide a basic framework of understanding of the different strategy components and what their impact is upon the overall strategy development process.

A simple trading strategy with one optimizable variable will be easy to build, test, optimize, and evaluate. Conversely, an extremely complex strategy will be far more difficult and time-consuming to build, verify, and optimize. Also, the complexity of the trading strategy makes it more difficult to evaluate the results and verify their authenticity. Complexity, if not managed well, can be very deceptive. It can be the ultimate hiding place of overfitting.

THE THREE PRINCIPAL COMPONENTS OF A STRATEGY

All trading strategies have three major components:

1. Entry and exit
2. Risk management
3. Position sizing

These will all be formally defined and illustrated with examples in the sections to follow. This section provides an overview.

Entry and Exit

Entries and exits are the *engine* or *driver* of trading in a strategy. They can be very simple or extremely complex. They can be filtered by one or many different elements. An entry can be at a specific price level or at the market or on the open or close. A trading strategy can employ more than one entry or exit. It can use one method to enter a trade and an entirely unrelated method to exit. The variety of entries and exits is really without bounds.

Risk Management

All trading strategies have different forms of risk. One must accept that all trading strategies are going to have losing trades. They can occur one at a time or in series. The best trading strategies are those that have an overt method of managing these risks. The management of risk does not mean its elimination, although, of course, that would be the ultimate and ideal form of risk management. Rather, it means keeping risk within measured, anticipated, and affordable boundaries. Proper risk management limits risk.

It is also a part of *good* risk management to acknowledge that if risk is becoming unmanageable—as in excessive or beyond the strategy's known boundaries—then trading with the strategy should either be ended or reduced to more tolerable levels.

The cardinal purpose of risk management is to limit losses to trading capital so that it is always possible to continue to trade after extended periods of loss or drawdown.

Let us consider the somewhat ideal alter ego view of risk management that will serve us as an inspiration and a guiding light. This view of risk management is to lose the least amount of money necessary to allow the trading strategy to achieve maximum trading profit.

Position Sizing

A trading strategy can trade either a fixed number of contracts or shares in each position or it can vary the number of contracts or shares in each trade according to some rule(s) or principle(s).

This is an underappreciated and poorly understood principle of trading strategy design. And this is so with good reason. It is easy to arrive at a sizing algorithm. It is, however, a difficult thing to do *well*.

The difficulty of effective position sizing is further compounded (pun intended) by the fact that it becomes a necessity with a profitable trading strategy. If a sound position sizing strategy (or algorithm) is not employed, the effective rate at which trading equity is compounded will remain suboptimal.

It is a point of interest worthy of mention that many professional trading strategists believe that the sizing principle is more important than the trading strategy itself. What does this ultimately mean for the design of a trading strategy? This suggests that perhaps it will be more productive to find the most effective sizing principle than it is to spend a great deal of time attempting to improve the entries and exits of the strategy.

AN OVERVIEW OF A TYPICAL TRADING STRATEGY

There are two minimum requirements for a trading strategy: a rule to enter the market and a rule to exit the market.

A strategy typically consists of buy-and-sell conditions that mirror, or are the opposite of, each other. For example, a buy signal occurs when price rises through a three-day high and a sell signal occurs when price breaks through a three-day low. This is an example of what is called a *symmetrical* trading strategy.

A strategy can also consist of completely different buy-and-sell entry conditions. For example, a buy signal occurs when a five-day high is broken and a sell signal occurs when a five-day moving average falls below a 20-day moving average. This is an example of an *asymmetrical* trading strategy.

A trading strategy may include risk management in the form of a stop-loss order. Risk management is a way to limit the amount of capital at risk during the life of a trade. A typical risk management approach is to set a stop-loss order that is the maximum, yet subject to slippage, loss to be taken on a trade. For example, assume that a long position is initiated at a price of 1,495.00 in S&P futures. The strategy calls for a maximum risk of $1,000 or 4.00 points. Therefore, after the position is entered, a protective sell stop is also entered. If our risk is $1,000, or 4.00 points, then our sell stop will be 1,491.00 (1,495.00 – 4.00).

A trading strategy can also include profit management. This is a method of protecting the open equity profit that must develop during the life of a winning (and sometime losing) trade. A typical profit management approach for a long position is to set a trailing stop at a fixed dollar amount below an equity high, that is, the highest price achieved during the trade. Assume a strategy that calls for a trailing stop of $2,000, or 8.00 S&P points. This point value will trail under progressively higher prices during our long position. Assume that the long position is entered at a price of 1,390.00 and an equity high point of 1,410.00 is reached on the fourth day of the position. A sell stop is entered at 1,402.00 (1,410.00 – 8.00 points). This locks in a $3,000 profit, subject to slippage (1,402.00 – 1,390.00).

Another type of profit management is the target order. This is a more proactive or aggressive way of capturing trading profits. A typical approach to the target order is to place a price order at a price above or below the position price. Assume a strategy that employs a $2,000, or 8.00 points, profit target. A long S&P position is taken at 1,375.00. A price order is then entered to sell at 1,383.00 (1,375.00 + 8.00 points). If the market rallies to this price, our sell order will capture a profit of $2,000.

A TRADE EQUALS AN ENTRY AND AN EXIT

We will start at the very basic level and build from that foundation. Those familiar with trading and trading strategies should feel free to skip anything with which they are already acquainted.

We formally defined the term *trade* in Chapter 2. A trade is composed of at least one buy and one sell. A trade begins by entering, that is, taking a position in, the market either by *going long* (buy) or *going short* (sell) and ends with an equal and opposite offsetting or liquidating trade that *closes the trade out.* For example, a long trade starts when the trader buys ten contracts of S&P index futures and ends when he sells ten contracts of the same future. A short trade takes the opposite course.

A trading strategy with a positive expectancy enters the market on a condition(s) that has proven itself capable of identifying an opportunity to make a trading profit. Such a trading strategy will exit the market when there is nothing left to be gained in the current trade.

In line with this formulation, the *perfect entry* is one that always occurs at the *best price* (the lowest buy and highest sell) and produces a profit. The *perfect exit* extracts the last dollar of profit from a trade.

Of course, any trader knows this is a perfect ideal and impossible to attain in practice. It is valuable, however, to hold this concept in mind as a guiding principle when designing a trading strategy. Let us now get into some details, definitions, and examples.

Definition: An *entry rule* initiates a new long or short position.

An entry can occur only when the system has no current position, or is *flat*. Some examples of buy, or long, entry rules (sell, or short, entry rules are the opposite) are:

- A 5-day moving average crosses from below to above a 20-day moving average
- The Relative Strength Index closes below a reading of 20
- The daily close rises by 1 percent and the weekly close rises by 1 percent
- Today's close is higher than yesterday's close plus 50 percent of the daily range
- Today's close is higher than the previous three closes

Definition: An *exit rule* closes out a current long or short position.

An *exit* can occur only when a strategy has an open long or short position. A symmetrical trading strategy exits its trades on an opposite entry signal. An example of an exit from a symmetrical moving average trading strategy that uses opposite entries is:

Close out, or exit from, a long position when the 5-day moving average crosses from above to below the 20-day moving average. A trading strategy can be reversing or nonreversing.

Definition: A *reversal rule* closes out a position and initiates a new and opposite position.

Of course, a reversal can occur only when there is a position. A reversal is an exit of the current position and the entry into a new and opposite position. The current position is exited and enters a new and opposite position. An example of a reversal rule is to close out the current long position and go short when the 5-day moving average crosses from above to below the 20-day moving average.

A trading strategy that reverses position on every new entry will, of course, always have a position in the market. Of course, a trading strategy can have rules that make it *reverse* only under specific conditions. Under other conditions, it will use the new signal to *exit* the position.

A trading strategy can also be *nonreversing*. In other words, it uses an opposite entry, or some other rule, to exit the position. Such a strategy will then wait for some other rule signal to initiate a new position. A nonreversing rule is simply an entry or some other rule used as an exit rule as defined earlier.

Entry Filters

Entry and exit signals can employ *filters*. In the most general sense, a filter is additional information intended to improve the quality of an entry or exit. The only purpose of a trading filter is as additional confirmation or validation of the entry.

Definition: An *entry filter* rule adds additional information to produce a more accurate and reliable trading strategy entry or exit.

In other words, entry or exit filters add additional indicators, analysis, market facts, or trading rules to the primary entry rules. A filter is really part of a more complex entry or exit rule.

A filter can be very simple, and this single, simple filter can be applied in conjunction with the entry rule. For example, if today's close is higher than yesterday's close, then take the current buy entry signal.

A single, complex filter can be used. For example, if today's close, high, and low are all higher than yesterday's, then take the current buy entry signal.

Multiple simple filters and multiple complex filters can be used. The main purpose of the entry filter is to increase the overall accuracy, reliability, and quality of the trading strategy's buy-and-sell entries.

For the purpose of illustration, let us consider the following short list of filter examples. These are examples of filters on buy signals (sell signal filters are the opposite). The trading strategy will accept a buy entry as confirmed by its respective filter if:

1. The Relative Strength Index is below 30
2. The Relative Strength Index was below 30 on the previous bar and is now above 30 and rising higher
3. Today's high is higher than yesterday's
4. The last buy signal was profitable
5. The close today is higher than the close 20 days ago plus 10.00 points
6. The close yesterday is in the top third of yesterday's daily range

There really is no limit to the level of complexity that can be introduced into a trading strategy with the use of filters. It is important to note that as the number and complexity of the trading filters increases, so can the difficulty of coding and testing a trading strategy. It should also be noted that the likelihood of overfitting also rises with the number of filters. To take this to an absurd extreme, an extremely—and absurd—overfit model would feature a different filter for every bar in the simulation data. Such an overfit model would exhibit exceptional profit in simulation and unprofitable performance in real-time trading.

THE MANAGEMENT OF RISK

The second principal component of a trading strategy is the management of risk. Many isolate and identify many different forms of risk. To some extent, these different categorizations of risk can prove helpful when designing ways to manage them.

The *New Oxford American Dictionary* defines that aspect of risk of interest to us as "The possibility of financial loss." *Trading risk* is defined as "The possibility of financial loss from the activity of trading or investing."

This does sum it up rather well. No matter how many ways one chooses to view, define, and label risk, it is central to the understanding of trading risk to know that it is result of exposure to loss from any open trading position. Put more simply, if you have a position in a market, you are at risk of losing money. Of course, you can make money in trading only by taking positions in the market.

One might say that this is the *central dilemma of trading*. To profit from trading, we must incur risk. As they say, "Nothing ventured, nothing gained." However, and this is the bottom line, without the successful management of risk, there *will* come a day when we will no longer be able to trade because of the cataclysmic trading losses that have come from our *unmanaged* risk.

The essence of good risk management is to risk as little trading capital as necessary so as to maximize profit. This is easy to say. Doing this well, however, is one of the most difficult aspects of trading strategy design.

Risk can be broken down into three broad categories: trade risk, strategy risk, and portfolio risk.

The definition of *trade risk* is: "The possibility of financial loss from an individual market position."

The definition of *strategy risk* is: "The possibility of financial loss from the use of a trading strategy."

The definition of *portfolio risk* is: "The possibility of financial loss at the portfolio level (potentially multistrategy, multiple time frame and multimarket) from the sum total of all trading therein."

Let us examine each of these forms of risk in more detail.

Trade Risk

Definition: A *trade risk rule* seeks to limit the amount of trading capital that can be lost on each individual market position.

The definition says "seeks to limit" risk because there are circumstances that can cause losses to exceed that amount initially set. These are explored in this section.

The primary way that risk is managed at the trade level is through the placement of a stop-loss order—the risk stop—which will automatically liquidate the trading position if exceeded. For this method to be effective, the stop order must be placed when the position is initiated.

Risk at position entry and beyond can be limited to the *approximate* value of a specific dollar amount by using a risk stop set at a price level equal to the desired risk.

Definition: A *risk stop* limits the amount of capital placed at risk at trade inception and through the life of the position. It is a stop order that is entered at inception and is maintained through the life of the position. If the price of the risk stop is touched or exceeded, the position is unconditionally liquidated.

The calculation of the size of the capital to risk can be done in a myriad of ways. Three representative examples are presented. But first, it is essential to understand how and why these risk amounts can be exceeded.

On the whole, risk stops perform their intended function and keep trading losses near their anticipated level. Market conditions can and will occur, however, that will cause actual trading losses from these stop orders to exceed the desired level of risk.

For example, risk can be exceeded because of fast markets and the consequent poor order executions. What is essential to note is that order executions at price levels worse than the price of the risk stop are a fact of trading life. This is the main reason that an accurate measure of slippage must be factored in to trade cost in the historical simulation process. This is addressed in detail in Chapter 6: The Historical Simulation.

The definition of *slippage* is "The transaction expense charged by poor quality executions." It is the difference between the order price and the actual execution or fill price.

The other main reason that levels of risk set by the risk stop are exceeded is *overnight risk*.

Definition: *Overnight risk* is the amount of capital that can be lost by adverse changes in price between today's close and tomorrow's open.

Whereas the gaps between close and the following open are not infinite, they occasionally can be very large. Let us examine the impact that these sometimes large adverse close-to-open gaps can have on a risk stop.

Consider that a risk stop employed to limit position risk must be placed as a Good Till Canceled (GTC) order. To limit risk, a risk stop must be kept in place from the beginning (entry) to the end (exit) of a position. However, this does not limit the trade risk to that set by the stop price. This is because the overnight close-to-open change can and will be larger than that set by the risk stop.

For example, if the market's opening price exceeds the 2.00 point risk stop by 10.00 points, this order becomes a market order on the open and will be filled in the opening range and will incur a loss 8.00 points greater than that set by our risk stop.

Overnight risk is a potentially more dangerous form of trade risk. The only sure way to entirely eliminate this risk is to close out the position every night. That, however, is not always a desirable feature in a trading strategy. Understanding overnight risk, however, provides the strategist with an opportunity to more specifically manage this particular form of risk.

Let us now consider three examples of ways to define the amount to be risked during a trade and is managed by the risk stop.

The most common way to set a risk stop is to use a *dollar amount* that the trading strategist is willing to risk each trade.

Definition: A *dollar risk stop* is an unconditional exit, at a loss, at a point equal to a dollar amount above or below the entry price.

For example, assume a risk stop set at $1,000 (assume $1,000 is equal to 4.00 points) and a long position is entered at 350. The sell risk stop to exit this long position then is 346 (350.00 − 4.00 = 346.00). The sell stop is placed at the time a long position is taken, based on the strategy entry rule. If price subsequently goes against the new position and exceeds (falls to or below) this risk stop, the trading system exits the position with a $1,000 loss plus commissions and any slippage that may occur. A buy risk stop for a short position is calculated opposite to that of a long position.

There are myriad ways to arrive at this dollar amount. The very worst way to set this amount is to base it upon a value arrived at simply by the whim of the strategist. The positive aspect to this form of risk stop is that it is likely to be emotionally comfortable to the trader. The reason why this may be a bad idea is that this method of setting risk is most likely to have absolutely nothing to do with that risk level, which will actually minimize risk while maximizing profit.

The best way to set this risk amount is to base it on a manner that is congruent and in harmony with the rhythm and operation of the trading strategy.

Let us consider another rather typical and generally better way to define trade risk.

Definition: A *volatility risk stop* sets trade risk using some measure of market volatility.

There are many ways to calculate volatility, of course. Let us consider a relatively simple example. The main reason a volatility-based measure of risk is superior to a fixed dollar value is that it will adjust as volatility expands and contracts.

Let us use the daily range (high minus low) as our basic unit of volatility. Let us further assume that we will use a three-day average of daily ranges as our measure of risk. Finally, let us assume that this three-day average volatility on the first day of entry is 5.55 points. Then, a sell risk stop for our long position of 350 set at 5.55 points will be 344.45 (350.00 − 5.55 = 344.45). Buy risk stops for short positions are calculated the opposite way.

Our last example of risk calculation is based on a percentage of trading equity. It is included as an illustration of an oft-cited method of risk calculation. The famous trader and pioneering technical analyst W.D. Gann made famous his Rule of Ten in which he said, "Never risk more than ten percent of your trading capital on any trade."

In actuality, nowadays, most traders would be more inclined to say, "Never risk more than one percent..." It is also worth noting that this rule will only be effective in conjunction with a sizing method that is based in some way on account equity. If size is fixed, otherwise, the effect of this formula will be to increase risk per trade as account size increases.

Let us assume an account size of $100,000. Let us also assume a position size of two contracts per trade and that 1 percent of equity will be risked per trade. Then a sell risk stop for our two contract long positions at 350 set at 1 percent of equity will be at 2.00 points ($100,000 × .01 = $1,000/2 contracts = $500 per contract = 2.00 points per contract), or 348.00 (350.00 − 2.00 = 348.00). Buy risks stops for short positions are calculated the opposite way.

Strategy Risk

Definition: *Strategy risk* is the amount of capital put at risk while using a particular trading strategy so as to be able to realize its return potential.

Another way of putting this is that there is a risk inherent in the use of a specific trading strategy. The best of trading strategies can fail. In other words, any trading strategy can stop producing profit and, instead, produce trading losses that exceed levels set by the strategist before the inception of trading with the strategy. This will be examined in more detail in Chapter 14: Trading the Strategy.

There are various ways to estimate the amount of risk capital necessary to trade a specific trading strategy. It is helpful to view strategy risk as somewhat analogous to a risk stop on the trading strategy, or, a strategy risk stop. Extending this analogy, it is possible to define it based on dollars or as a percentage of equity.

There is an effective formula, however, that is used to calculate the risk of a strategy. It uses risk defined as maximum drawdown combined with an additional sum that serves as a safety buffer or as a margin of error.

Definition: The *maximum drawdown* is the largest drop in equity measured from equity high to a succeeding equity low.

Maximum drawdown is widely considered to be one of the best measures of the overall risk of a trading strategy. As important a measure as maximum drawdown is, however, it is still only an approximation of overall strategy risk. We know from statistics that there is likely to be some degree of variability in all performance statistics calculated by historical simulation, maximum drawdown included.

Given this statistical consideration, and that it is always best in trading to err on the side of caution, then it is best to make an allowance for this statistical variability and add a measure of caution by increasing the size of maximum drawdown in some way.

Definition: The *strategy stop* is strategy risk defined as maximum drawdown multiplied by a safety factor.

Let us use a safety factor multiplier of 1.5 for our example. If we have a maximum drawdown of 40,000, this will make our system stop at $60,000 ($40,000 × 1.5).

We can extend this concept a bit further to arrive at a formulation of required trading capital.

Definition: *Required capital* is the amount of trading capital necessary to accommodate maximum drawdown, margin requirements, and a safety factor so as to successfully trade with a particular strategy.

Let us consider a formula to calculate the account size necessary to trade our strategy. Assume again a maximum drawdown of $40,000 and a safety factor of 1.5. Also assume margin of $15,000. The account size necessary to provide required capital for our strategy then is $75,000 ($40,000 × 1.5 + $15,000).

This is still a fairly risky state of affairs, however. Consider what happens if in the worst case scenario, our strategy produces a $50,000 drawdown. This leaves our trading account at $25,000, which is margin plus a small surplus of $10,000. What would happen if we had a small profitable runup of $15,000, taking our account up to $40,000, and then hit another drawdown of $40,000? We would be wiped out and unable to continue trading without committing new capital.

Let us consider then a more conservative formula, which would allow us to weather this very difficult circumstance. Let us calculate our account size as maximum drawdown times the safety factor times two plus margin.

According to this formula our account size would be $135,000 ([($40,000 ×
1.5) × 2] + $15,000).

Let us examine how our account capitalized in this manner would
weather our back-to-back drawdown scenario. After the first $50,000 draw-
down, our account is at $85,000. After the profitable $15K run, it is at
$100,000. After the second $40,000 drawdown, our account is at $60,000.
Given two drawdowns and a maximum drawdown of $40,000, there is suf-
ficient margin for error.

This is discussed in fuller detail in Chapter 14: Trading the Strategy.

Portfolio Risk

Definition: *Portfolio risk* is the amount of capital put at risk while using a
particular trading strategy or strategies with multiple markets and possibly
multiple time frames so as to be able to realize its return potential.

Just as with strategy risk, there is a risk of ruin inherent in the use of
any trading strategy or strategies with multiple markets in a balanced portfolio. As stated before, even the best of trading strategies can fail. Just as a
strategy can fail, a portfolio of markets trading a strategy can also fail. Extending this further, even the most highly diversified portfolio imaginable
can fail.

The probability of portfolio failure becomes increasingly unlikely as
the number of diversified strategies, multiple time frames, and markets increases. Risk reduction is one of the primary benefits of diversification. As
traders, however, we deal in probabilities and we must always err on the
side of caution. We must consequently consider the possibility of portfolio
failure as well, no matter how improbable.

The formula for the calculation of our portfolio risk stop is analogous
to that of our strategy risk stop. There are a number of differences, of
course, inherent in this process at the portfolio level. The one big difference is the use of the portfolio maximum drawdown in our formula.

Definition: The *portfolio maximum drawdown* is the largest drop in
portfolio equity measured from the portfolio equity high to a succeeding
portfolio equity low.

The calculation of a portfolio risk stop is the same as that of the
strategy risk stop. Because a portfolio equity stream comprises a number of markets, robust statistics would suggest that it is less likely to be
as variable as that of the maximum drawdown of an individual trading
strategy on one market. In addition, the reliability of the portfolio drawdown will rise as the level of diversification rises. Consequently, the reliability of the portfolio drawdown of a highly diversified portfolio incorporating multiple, uncorrelated strategies, multiple time frames, and a basket of as uncorrelated markets as possible will be higher than that of a

single-strategy, single–time frame portfolio of five different interest rate markets.

One of the primary advantages, of course, of a more precise and reliable measurement of portfolio risk is that the portfolio can be more heavily leveraged and with a higher degree of confidence.

Up to this point, our focus on risk management has been primarily defensive. In other words, we have focused on those elements of trading strategy design that protect our trading equity if the trade is simply wrong. There is another entirely different and more pleasant aspect of money management, however, that occurs when a trade has begun to produce a profit in its open equity. This stage of money management might best be called profit management. Let us explore this aspect now.

THE MANAGEMENT OF PROFIT

This area is as potentially complex as is that of risk management. Whereas the focus appears to be different, profit management is also about the preservation of trading capital. The major difference is that it is about the preservation of open trading profit. Its main focus is to capture as much profit as possible from a trade while avoiding the cost of premature exit from a trade that is riding a trend that is still not finished. There are two main methods to preserve open equity profit: the trailing stop and the profit, or target, order.

The Trailing Stop

Definition: A *trailing stop* is a dynamic order that moves up with new highs (long) or down with new lows (short) in the market so as to preserve some predetermined proportion of open trade profit.

The trailing stop is constructed in a manner that continuously advances a stop in the direction of a profitable market move during the life of the trade. A trailing stop to protect a long position will move up as the market advances. A short trailing stop protects a short position in a declining market.

It is also central to the concept of the trailing stop that it does not retreat. In other words, once a new high or low has been established and a new higher or lower trailing stop has been calculated, it is never moved lower or higher if the market moves against the trade.

The ideal trailing stop preserves as much open trading profit as possible while at the same time providing enough breathing room to encompass the market volatility that is a part of all trades. The vast majority of trades do not go straight in one direction without pullback. Ideally, the trailing stop will allow for these natural pullbacks and exit when the main thrust of the trade is ended.

There are endless potential trailing stop variations. Let us look at examples of two relatively common types of trailing stops: dollar and volatility.

Definition: A *trailing dollar profit stop* is an order to exit a position and is set at a fixed dollar value above the most current low price (short) or below the most current high price (long).

For example, assume a dollar trailing stop of $1,000 (where $1,000 is equal to 2 points), a long position of 350, and a current market high of 356.00. The trailing sell stop on this long position is 354 (356.00 – 2.00 = 354.00). If price subsequently goes against the long position and falls through this sell exit trailing stop, the position is exited with a $2,000 profit minus commission and slippage. A trailing buy stop for a short position is the reverse.

Definition: A *trailing volatility profit stop* is an order to exit a position and is set at a point value based upon some measure of market volatility above the most current low price (short) or below the most current high price (long).

Let us assume that:

1. The daily range (high minus low) is our basic unit of volatility
2. We will use 50 percent of volatility for our stop point values
3. A three-day average of daily ranges is our measure of volatility

Given this, assume a three-day average volatility today of 5.50 points. Fifty percent of 5.50 points is 2.75 points.

Assume a long position of 350 and a current market high price of 356.00. The trailing sell stop on this long position then is 353.25 (356.00 – 2.75 = 353.25). If price subsequently goes against the long position and falls through this sell exit trailing stop, the position is exited with a $1,625 profit minus commission and slippage. A trailing buy stop for a short position is calculated in the opposite manner using new lows.

There are many ways to establish trailing stops beyond these basic types. For the sake of illustration, three examples of different types of trailing stops are: the value of a moving average, support and resistance levels, and the percentage retracements of an n-period range.

The key to a successful trailing stop is to find that price level in the life of a trade, which, if penetrated, tells us that the move captured by the profitable trade is over. Of course, there are many ways to do this and it is left to the strategist to find that style of trailing stop most organically suitable to his strategy.

The Impact of Overnight Change on the Trailing Stop

A trailing stop is dynamic, moving up or down as the market moves in favor of the trade. A trailing stop must be placed as a GTC order or entered each day throughout the life of the position in order to be effective. This still does not entirely limit the profit to the level at which the order is set, however. Why? Once again, a large and volatile overnight close to open price change can exceed the price level of the trailing stop. For example, if the market opens at 340, 10 points lower than the trailing stop price of 350, our stop becomes a market order on the open and it will be filled at the opening price. Overnight risk can potentially transform an open profit into a loss. Overnight risk can and does also move in favor of our trade, of course.

Profit Targets

The other way to protect open equity profit is to take profits when a predetermined price level or profit threshold has been reached. There are many ways to calculate such *profit target* thresholds. Profit target orders are set with *price or better* or *price limit* orders.

Definition: A *profit target* is an unconditional exit of a trade with a locked-in profit at some predetermined price or profit level.

The incorporation of a profit target into a trading system is a more proactive and aggressive method of profit management. The most positive aspect of a profit target is that once the desired profit is realized, it is captured immediately. It therefore cannot be lost like it can be with a trailing stop. The negative aspect occurs when a profit is taken and the market continues to move well beyond this target level. These potential additional gains are lost because our profit target has closed out the position.

There are trade-offs with the use of profit targets. Some traders cannot live without them just as some cannot live with them. Trading systems that use profit targets, in contrast to those that do not, can be less profitable overall but can produce a higher percentage of winning trades and a smoother equity curve. Sometimes profit targets reduce per trade, and total risk and overall performance can be more stable.

Not all systems are improved by the use of profit targets. Whether profit targets are beneficial or not very much depends on the style and pace of the trading strategy. In general, active, countertrend trading strategies that trade from overbought and oversold conditions benefit the most from profit target orders. Conversely, slower, trend-following trading strategies generally benefit the least from profit targets.

Another plus to target orders is that price limit orders are generally free of slippage in the strict sense as a poor fill price. In fact, price orders can and do experience positive slippage in this sense. A certain percentage of price limit orders go unfilled, however. This is a form of slippage that can be very costly.

To illustrate, let us examine two different types of profit targets: the dollar target and the volatility target.

Definition: A *dollar profit target* is an unconditional exit of a trade at a profit and at a price level equal to a dollar amount above (long) or below (short) the entry price.

For example, assume a dollar target of $1,000 (where $1,000 is equal to 2.00 points), and a short position at 350.00. The buy target price for this short position is 348.00 (348.00 − 2.00 = 348.00). This buy or better order is placed, GTC, immediately after the initiation of the short position. If price subsequently goes in the direction of the new position and reaches the target, the trading system exits the position with a $1,000 profit minus commission and slippage.

Definition: A *volatility profit target* is an unconditional exit of a trade at a profit and at a price level equal to a value based upon market volatility above (long) or below (short) the entry price.

Let us once again assume that:

1. The daily range is our basic unit of volatility

2. We will use 150 percent of volatility for our target values

3. A three-day average of daily ranges is our measure of volatility

Given this, assume a three-day average volatility today of 5.50 points. One hundred fifty percent of 5.50 points is 8.25 points.

Assume a long position of 350.00. The sell target price for this long position is 358.25 (350.00 + 8.25 = 358.25). This sell or better order is placed, GTC, immediately after the initiation of the long position. If price subsequently goes in the direction of the new position and reaches the target, the trading system exits the position with a $4,125 profit minus commission and slippage.

The Impact of Overnight Change on Target Orders

The profit target order is entered as a price limit order and as good till canceled because it must be in place throughout the life of the position. This does not restrict the profit of a target order to that of its order price, however. Once again, overnight price change is on stage. If the market opens 10 points higher than the price level of our sell price order, it will be filled at the opening price. Here, the overnight gap of 10 points in the direction of the trade adds $5,000 to the profit of the trading system.

POSITION SIZING

The determination of the size of the trading position is the third, and in the eyes of many, the most important component of a trading strategy. Simply stated, trade sizing determines our bet size, or the amount of capital to be risked on each trade.

Definition: A *position sizing* rule determines the number of contracts or shares that are committed to each trade.

It is very easy to see the impact of position sizing at either extreme. If we trade a position size that is too small—for example, one S&P contract per $1,000,000—our trading equity is not being used at optimal levels. Conversely, a position size that is too large—for example, 100 S&P per $100,000—for our capital can increase our risk of ruin to certainty.

Only the most naive and inexperienced of traders will be ensnared by either of these extremes. It is in the area between these two opposite ends of the spectrum, however, where a sizing rule will have the most impact on strategy performance, whether positive or negative.

The best and most efficient sizing principle will be the one that applies our trading capital in an optimal manner so as to achieve maximum returns with an affordable risk.

The problem of efficient position sizing is difficult. There are many mathematically sophisticated approaches to this problem that are beyond the scope of this book.

One of the primary reasons for this difficulty, however, arises from the non-Gaussian (especially fat-tailed) distributions that are typical of financial markets and the returns that are produced by them. Such distributions reduce the effectiveness of traditional statistical estimation methods that are employed in more sophisticated sizing methods.

Another level of difficulty in sizing arises from the lack of statistical robustness of many of the measures that are employed in sizing rules. Last, but not least, position sizing takes on another level of complexity when a trading strategy is incorporated in a portfolio of markets.

These are complex and highly technical issues that are beyond the scope of this book. It is absolutely *essential*, however, to realize that position sizing can make or break a trading strategy.

We will look at four position sizing examples:

1. Volatility adjusted
2. Martingale
3. Anti-Martingale
4. The Kelly method

A volatility adjusted sizing rule uses the size of the account and the size of the risk assumed per contract per trade.

Definition: *Volatility adjusted* position sizing determines the number of contracts or shares per trade as a fixed percentage of trading equity divided by the trade risk.

For example, assume:

1. A risk size of 3 percent of equity
2. A risk per contract of $1,000
3. An account size of $250,000

The trade unit would be seven contracts and is calculated as follows:

Total Equity to Risk = $7,500($250,000 × .03)

Number of Contracts = 7($7,500/$1,000 = 7.5 rounded down = 7)

An example of a well-known money management rule is the Martingale strategy. It is derived from a gambling money-management method.

Definition: The *Martingale sizing* rule doubles the trade size after each loss and starts at one unit after each win.

There are a number of variations on this theme. One such variation is anti-Martingale.

Definition: The *anti-Martingale sizing* rule doubles the number of trading units after each win, and starts at one unit after each loss.

Optimal f (fixed fractional trading) was introduced by Ralph Vince in 1990. It is based on a formula derived from the Kelly method, which was, in turn, applied by Professor Edward Thorpe to gambling and trading.

Let us look at one implementation of the Kelly formula.

Kelly % = (Win % − Loss %)/(Average Profit/Average Loss)

For example, assume a strategy that has a winning percentage of 55 percent, an average win of $1,750, and average loss of $1,250. The Kelly percent will tell us what percentage of our trading capital to risk is on the next trade.

Kelly % = (55 − 45)/($1,750/$1,250)

Kelly % = 10/1.4

Kelly % = 7.14 %

Let us use this to calculate our position size. We have our risk size of 7.14 percent of equity from the Kelly formula, a risk per contract of $1,000, and an account size of $250,000. The trade size would be seventeen contracts and is calculated as follows:

Total Equity to Risk = $250,000 × .0714

Total Equity to Risk = $17,850

Number of Contracts = $17,850/$1,000 = 17.65

Number of Contracts = 17.85 rounded down = 17 contracts

Recall from our earlier discussions that these numbers are often *lacking* in statistical robustness. Another way to look at these numbers is to recognize that they are a bit fuzzy. Because of a limited sample size and large variance, the numbers used in this formula will, in turn, introduce a significant degree of variance in the results of the Kelly formula. It is this very fuzziness that introduces a level of inaccuracy in the use of formulae such as Kelly or Optimal f.

There are many different formulations of position sizing rules. They all share a way of setting the number of contracts or shares per trade. These methods are presented here as examples and not as recommendations. It is worthy of notice that many of these sizing algorithms are derived from the gambling literature.

Position sizing is a critical component in trading system design. The problems that exist should in no way deter the strategist from exploring and evaluating such methods. The trader should be very aware, however, of the statistical limitations of their accuracy and their inherent limitations. There is a large body of work developing in this area, since many involved with trading have finally come to accept that financial markets have a non-Gaussian distribution. Furthermore, some have now come to accept the fractal distribution of these markets.

ADVANCED STRATEGIES

There is an advanced sizing strategy that is widely used among professional traders called scaling into and out of a position. Because of the difficulty of doing it well, this is a method that is often used by skillful discretionary traders. There is no inherent reason, however, why scaling cannot be incorporated into an automated trading strategy.

Definition: *Scaling into a position* adds incrementally to an existing position as the market moves in the profitable direction of the trade.

Definition: *Scaling out of a position* incrementally decreases an existing position.

An example of scaling into a position would be to add one trading unit to a position each time open equity profit increases by $1,000. An example of scaling out of a position would be to remove one trading unit every time open equity increases by $1,000.

An example of both scaling into and out of a position would be to add one trading unit to a position each time open equity profit increases by $1,000 until a maximum open equity profit of $5,000 on the oldest position is reached, and to then remove one trading unit each time open equity increases by an additional $1,000.

SUMMARY

This chapter has presented information about the three primary components of a trading strategy. A trading system can range from extremely simple to quite complex. There is no performance benefit inherent in either extreme. However, simplicity or complexity should not be sought for their own sake.

Rather, as a valued associate and friend once quipped: "The best trading system is one that relies upon an irresistible force of nature for its profits."

In the final analysis there are only two things that matter for a trading strategy: its risk-adjusted rate of return, and its robustness in real-time trading.

CHAPTER 6

The Historical Simulation

We defined the term *simulation* in Chapter 2: The Systematic Trading Edge as a computer model of the trading performance of a trading strategy. The only price data available, of course, for a simulation are historical or past price data.

As was also noted therein, there can be a great deal of different information produced by a historical simulation. This information ranges from detailed information at the trade-by-trade level up to performance data, which summarizes an array of statistical data. Also, if the strategy were optimized, there is a body of data regarding this as well. Finally, if a Walk-Forward Analysis was performed, there are still more data resulting from this more complex process. Examples of all of these different reports and output will each be presented and explained in the respective chapters dedicated to these processes.

In this chapter, we focus on one of the most important, yet often neglected, aspects of the entire trading strategy development process: the accuracy of the historical simulation.

The information produced by a historical simulation is at the very foundation of our acceptance or rejection of the validity of the trading strategy. Beyond the simulation itself, of course, the evaluation of the optimization and the evaluation of the likelihood of real-time profit are also pivotal.

These results, however, are all built upon the simulation. If the historical simulation is inaccurate or flawed by design, consequently, the entire structure of strategy evaluation is proportionately weakened and can crumble, much like a building erected on an unsound foundation.

THE ESSENTIAL REPORTS

There are many types of reports produced by the historical simulations from different software applications. Certain reports are essential, such as the performance summary (see Table 6.1) and the trade listing. Others are extremely valuable, such as performance broken down over various time intervals and a chart of the daily equity curve. There are reports beyond these, but to a large extent, they are not as essential.

The Performance Summary

This report provides key statistics that describe the overall performance of the strategy over the historical period for which the simulation was created. Key statistics are net profit, maximum drawdown, number of trades, percentage of winners, average trade, and the ratio of average win to average loss. The Sharpe Ratio is extremely valuable because it is a key statistic for many professional investors, yet it is not offered by many of these applications.

As you can see from our example, this is a historical simulation of S&P futures for the period of 01/01/1989 to 12/31/2006 for a trading strategy called PTIx. It produced a net profit of $338,625, maximum drawdown of $149,100 with 218 trades, 66.9 percent winning trades, a $6,081 average winning trade, and a profit factor of 1.62.

These statistics will be examined in more detail in Chapter 12: The Evaluation of Performance.

The Trade List

This report is a tabulation of the historical performance of the trading strategy on a trade-by-trade basis. This report typically provides the entry date, entry price, label, exit date, exit price, label, the trade profit or loss, and a cumulative total profit and loss (see Table 6.2).

Table 6.3 examines the entry for one trade.

From this, we can see that our PTIx strategy entered a long trade on 06/16/1998 at a price of 1365.6 on the signal named PTIlo. It exited this position and went short on 06/25/1998 at a price of 1421.1 on the signal named PTIsh. This trade produced a profit of $13,675, providing a cumulative net profit of $84,450 to date.

This report is typically useful during the preliminary stages of the development of the strategy. It is essential then, as a diagnostic, to confirm that trading is proceeding as specified.

The trade list has another more valuable and underused application. That is as a trading simulator, during which the trader can look at each

TABLE 6.1   Performance Summary of PTIx on S&P Futures

Performance Summary: Long Trades

Total net profit	$222,550	Open position P/L	($850.00)
Gross profit	$502,200	Gross loss	($279,650.00)
Total number of trades	110	Percent profitable	72.73%
Number winning trades	80	Number losing trades	30
Largest winning trade	$26,300	Largest losing trade	($41,200.00)
Average winning trade	$6,277.50	Average losing trade	($9,321.67)
Ratio average win/ average loss	0.673431075	Average trade (win & loss)	($2,023.18)
Maximum consecutive winners	11	Maximum consecutive losers	5
Average number bars in winners	8	Average number bars in losers	20
Maximum intraday drawdown	($149,100.00)	Maximum number contracts held	1
Profit factor	1.795816199	Yearly return on account	8.30%
Account size required	$149,100		

Performance Summary: Short Trades

Total net profit	$116,075	Open position P/L	$0.00
Gross profit	$385,650	Gross loss	($269,575.00)
Total number of trades	108	Percent profitable	61.11%
Number winning trades	66	Number losing trades	42
Largest winning trade	$20,175	Largest losing trade	($20,600.00)
Average winning trade	$5,843.18	Average losing trade	($6,418.45)
Ratio average win/ average loss	0.910372388	Average trade (win & loss)	$1,074.77
Maximum consecutive winners	8	Maximum consecutive Losers	5
Average number bars in winners	9	Average number bars in losers	22
Maximum intraday drawdown	($57,050.00)	Maximum number contracts held	1
Profit factor	1.43058518	Yearly return on account	11.31%
Account size required	$57,050		

TABLE 6.2 Trade List of PTIx on S&P Futures

Trades for Session

PTIx.WF_SP SP-9967.TXT 1/1/1989 to 12/31/2006.
System is PTIX()

Buy/Sell	Entry Name	Market	Entry Date	Size	Entry Price	Exit Date	Exit Name	Size	Exit Price	Trade P/L	Running P/L
BUY	PTIlo	SP-9967.TXT	10/28/1996	1	1045.0	11/5/1996	PTIsh	1	1053.1	$1,825.00	$1,825.00
SELL	PTIsh	SP-9967.TXT	11/5/1996	1	1053.1	12/6/1996	PTIlo	1	1073.2	($5,225.00)	($3,400.00)
BUY	PTIlo	SP-9967.TXT	12/6/1996	1	1073.2	12/23/1996	PTIsh	1	1089.1	$3,775.00	$375.00
SELL	PTIsh	SP-9967.TXT	12/23/1996	1	1089.1	1/3/1997	PTIlo	1	1080.9	$1,850.00	$2,225.00
BUY	PTIlo	SP-9967.TXT	1/3/1997	1	1080.9	1/13/1997	PTIsh	1	1101.2	$4,875.00	$7,100.00
SELL	PTIsh	SP-9967.TXT	1/13/1997	1	1101.2	1/28/1997	PTIlo	1	1111.4	($2,750.00)	$4,350.00
BUY	PTIlo	SP-9967.TXT	1/28/1997	1	1111.4	2/3/1997	PTIsh	1	1122.1	$2,475.00	$6,825.00
SELL	PTIsh	SP-9967.TXT	2/3/1997	1	1122.1	2/28/1997	PTIlo	1	1125.2	($975.00)	$5,850.00
BUY	PTIlo	SP-9967.TXT	2/28/1997	1	1125.2	3/10/1997	PTIsh	1	1140.2	$3,550.00	$9,400.00
SELL	PTIsh	SP-9967.TXT	3/10/1997	1	1140.2	3/18/1997	PTIlo	1	1129.2	$2,550.00	$11,950.00
BUY	PTIlo	SP-9967.TXT	3/18/1997	1	1129.2	4/18/1997	PTIsh	1	1096.3	($8,425.00)	$3,525.00
SELL	PTIsh	SP-9967.TXT	4/18/1997	1	1096.3	6/5/1997	PTIlo	1	1168.8	($18,325.00)	($14,800.00)
BUY	PTIlo	SP-9967.TXT	6/5/1997	1	1168.8	6/10/1997	PTIsh	1	1191.7	$5,525.00	($9,275.00)
SELL	PTIsh	SP-9967.TXT	6/10/1997	1	1191.7	6/27/1997	PTIlo	1	1213.5	($5,650.00)	($14,925.00)
BUY	PTIlo	SP-9967.TXT	6/27/1997	1	1213.5	7/3/1997	PTIsh	1	1238.8	$6,125.00	($8,800.00)
SELL	PTIsh	SP-9967.TXT	7/3/1997	1	1238.8	7/22/1997	PTIlo	1	1237.6	$100.00	($8,700.00)
BUY	PTIlo	SP-9967.TXT	7/22/1997	1	1237.6	7/25/1997	PTIsh	1	1263.8	$6,350.00	($2,350.00)
SELL	PTIsh	SP-9967.TXT	7/25/1997	1	1263.8	8/12/1997	PTIlo	1	1259.4	$900.00	($1,450.00)
BUY	PTIlo	SP-9967.TXT	8/12/1997	1	1259.4	9/5/1997	PTIsh	1	1254.8	($1,350.00)	($2,800.00)
SELL	PTIsh	SP-9967.TXT	9/5/1997	1	1254.8	9/12/1997	PTIlo	1	1231.7	$5,575.00	$2,775.00

BUY	PTllo	SP-9967.TXT	9/12/1997	1231.7	1	9/18/1997	PTlsh	1	1262.7	$7,550.00	$10,325.00
SELL	PTlsh	SP-9967.TXT	9/18/1997	1262.7	1	9/29/1997	PTllo	1	1259.7	$550.00	$10,875.00
BUY	PTllo	SP-9967.TXT	9/29/1997	1259.7	1	9/30/1997	BoundExit	1	1266.4	$1,475.00	$12,350.00
BUY	PTllo	SP-9967.TXT	10/20/1997	1258.7	1	11/5/1997	PTlsh	1	1248.2	($2,825.00)	$9,525.00
SELL	PTlsh	SP-9967.TXT	11/5/1997	1248.2	1	11/12/1997	PTllo	1	1219.7	$6,925.00	$16,450.00
BUY	PTllo	SP-9967.TXT	11/12/1997	1219.7	1	11/18/1997	PTlsh	1	1257.7	$9,300.00	$25,750.00
SELL	PTlsh	SP-9967.TXT	11/18/1997	1257.7	1	12/12/1997	PTllo	1	1267.8	($2,725.00)	$23,025.00
BUY	PTllo	SP-9967.TXT	12/12/1997	1267.8	1	1/2/1998	PTlsh	1	1278.8	$2,550.00	$25,575.00
SELL	PTlsh	SP-9967.TXT	1/2/1998	1278.8	1	1/9/1998	PTllo	1	1256.8	$5,300.00	$30,875.00
BUY	PTllo	SP-9967.TXT	1/9/1998	1256.8	1	1/21/1998	PTlsh	1	1275.3	$4,425.00	$35,300.00
SELL	PTlsh	SP-9967.TXT	1/21/1998	1275.3	1	1/27/1998	PTllo	1	1257.3	$4,300.00	$39,600.00
BUY	PTllo	SP-9967.TXT	1/27/1998	1257.3	1	2/2/1998	PTlsh	1	1296.8	$9,675.00	$49,275.00
SELL	PTlsh	SP-9967.TXT	2/2/1998	1296.8	1	3/6/1998	PTllo	1	1338.3	($10,575.00)	$38,700.00
BUY	PTllo	SP-9967.TXT	3/6/1998	1338.3	1	3/10/1998	PTlsh	1	1354.8	$3,925.00	$42,625.00
SELL	PTlsh	SP-9967.TXT	3/10/1998	1354.8	1	3/31/1998	PTllo	1	1394.3	($10,075.00)	$32,550.00
BUY	PTllo	SP-9967.TXT	3/31/1998	1394.3	1	4/3/1998	PTlsh	1	1415.3	$5,050.00	$37,600.00
SELL	PTlsh	SP-9967.TXT	4/3/1998	1415.3	1	4/28/1998	PTllo	1	1386.3	$7,050.00	$44,650.00
BUY	PTllo	SP-9967.TXT	4/28/1998	1386.3	1	5/5/1998	PTlsh	1	1408.8	$5,425.00	$50,075.00
SELL	PTlsh	SP-9967.TXT	5/5/1998	1408.8	1	5/8/1998	PTllo	1	1382.8	$6,300.00	$56,375.00
BUY	PTllo	SP-9967.TXT	5/8/1998	1382.8	1	5/14/1998	PTlsh	1	1403.8	$5,050.00	$61,425.00
SELL	PTlsh	SP-9967.TXT	5/14/1998	1403.8	1	6/16/1998	PTllo	1	1365.6	$9,350.00	$70,775.00
BUY	PTllo	SP-9967.TXT	6/16/1998	1365.6	1	6/25/1998	PTlsh	1	1421.1	$13,675.00	$84,450.00
SELL	PTlsh	SP-9967.TXT	6/25/1998	1421.1	1	7/23/1998	PTllo	1	1443.1	($5,700.00)	$78,750.00
BUY	PTllo	SP-9967.TXT	7/23/1998	1443.1	1	8/20/1998	PTlsh	1	1371.6	($18,075.00)	$60,675.00
SELL	PTlsh	SP-9967.TXT	8/20/1998	1371.6	1	8/28/1998	PTllo	1	1321.6	$12,300.00	$72,975.00
BUY	PTllo	SP-9967.TXT	8/28/1998	1321.6	1	9/15/1998	PTlsh	1	1299.5	($5,725.00)	$67,250.00
SELL	PTlsh	SP-9967.TXT	9/15/1998	1299.5	1	10/2/1998	PTllo	1	1262.0	$9,175.00	$76,425.00

(Continues)

TABLE 6.2 Trade List of PTIx on S&P Futures (Continued)

Trades for Session

PTIx.WF.SP SP-9967.TXT 1/1/1989 to 12/31/2006. System is PTIX()

Buy/Sell	Entry Name	Market	Entry Date	Size	Entry Price	Exit Date	Exit Name	Size	Exit Price	Trade P/L	Running P/L
BUY	PTIlo	SP-9967.TXT	10/2/1998	1	1262.0	10/16/1998	PTIsh	1	1326.0	$15,800.00	$92,225.00
SELL	PTIsh	SP-9967.TXT	10/16/1998	1	1326.0	12/15/1998	PTIlo	1	1407.6	($20,600.00)	$71,625.00
BUY	PTIlo	SP-9967.TXT	12/15/1998	1	1407.6	12/18/1998	PTIsh	1	1443.6	$8,800.00	$80,425.00
SELL	PTIsh	SP-9967.TXT	12/18/1998	1	1443.6	1/14/1999	PTIlo	1	1491.1	($12,075.00)	$68,350.00
BUY	PTIlo	SP-9967.TXT	1/14/1999	1	1491.1	2/1/1999	PTIsh	1	1539.6	$11,925.00	$80,275.00
SELL	PTIsh	SP-9967.TXT	2/1/1999	1	1539.6	2/10/1999	PTIlo	1	1469.1	$17,425.00	$97,700.00
BUY	PTIlo	SP-9967.TXT	2/10/1999	1	1469.1	2/24/1999	PTIsh	1	1529.1	$14,800.00	$112,500.00
SELL	PTIsh	SP-9967.TXT	2/24/1999	1	1529.1	3/1/1999	PTIlo	1	1487.1	$10,300.00	$122,800.00
BUY	PTIlo	SP-9967.TXT	3/1/1999	1	1487.1	3/8/1999	PTIsh	1	1530.1	$10,550.00	$133,350.00
SELL	PTIsh	SP-9967.TXT	3/8/1999	1	1530.1	3/24/1999	PTIlo	1	1514.6	$3,675.00	$137,025.00
BUY	PTIlo	SP-9967.TXT	3/24/1999	1	1514.6	3/31/1999	PTIsh	1	1560.6	$11,300.00	$148,325.00
SELL	PTIsh	SP-9967.TXT	3/31/1999	1	1560.6	4/19/1999	PTIlo	1	1569.6	($2,450.00)	$145,875.00
BUY	PTIlo	SP-9967.TXT	4/19/1999	1	1569.6	4/23/1999	PTIsh	1	1603.1	$8,175.00	$154,050.00
SELL	PTIsh	SP-9967.TXT	4/23/1999	1	1603.1	4/30/1999	PTIlo	1	1594.1	$2,050.00	$156,100.00
BUY	PTIlo	SP-9967.TXT	4/30/1999	1	1594.1	5/13/1999	PTIsh	1	1613.6	$4,675.00	$160,775.00
SELL	PTIsh	SP-9967.TXT	5/13/1999	1	1613.6	5/26/1999	PTIlo	1	1532.1	$20,175.00	$180,950.00
BUY	PTIlo	SP-9967.TXT	5/26/1999	1	1532.1	6/7/1999	PTIsh	1	1567.6	$8,675.00	$189,625.00
SELL	PTIsh	SP-9967.TXT	6/7/1999	1	1567.6	6/14/1999	PTIlo	1	1539.6	$6,800.00	$196,425.00
BUY	PTIlo	SP-9967.TXT	6/14/1999	1	1539.6	6/18/1999	PTIsh	1	1576.1	$8,925.00	$205,350.00

SELL	PTlsh	SP-9967.TXT	6/18/1999	1	1576.1	6/25/1999	PTllo	1	1560.6	$3,675.00	$209,025.00
BUY	PTllo	SP-9967.TXT	6/25/1999	1	1560.6	7/1/1999	PTlsh	1	1607.6	$11,550.00	$220,575.00
SELL	PTlsh	SP-9967.TXT	7/1/1999	1	1607.6	7/22/1999	PTllo	1	1608.1	($325.00)	$220,250.00
BUY	PTllo	SP-9967.TXT	7/22/1999	1	1608.1	8/17/1999	PTlsh	1	1571.1	($9,450.00)	$210,800.00
SELL	PTlsh	SP-9967.TXT	8/17/1999	1	1571.1	8/31/1999	PTllo	1	1555.6	$3,675.00	$214,475.00
BUY	PTllo	SP-9967.TXT	8/31/1999	1	1555.6	9/8/1999	PTlsh	1	1569.9	$3,375.00	$217,850.00
SELL	PTlsh	SP-9967.TXT	9/8/1999	1	1569.9	9/17/1999	PTllo	1	1553.3	$3,950.00	$221,800.00
BUY	PTllo	SP-9967.TXT	9/17/1999	1	1553.3	10/7/1999	PTlsh	1	1548.8	($1,325.00)	$220,475.00
SELL	PTlsh	SP-9967.TXT	10/7/1999	1	1548.8	10/15/1999	PTllo	1	1475.3	$18,175.00	$238,650.00
BUY	PTllo	SP-9967.TXT	10/15/1999	1	1475.3	11/1/1999	PTlsh	1	1581.3	$26,300.00	$264,950.00
SELL	PTlsh	SP-9967.TXT	11/1/1999	1	1581.3	1/6/2000	PTllo	1	1597.0	($4,125.00)	$260,825.00
BUY	PTllo	SP-9967.TXT	1/6/2000	1	1597.0	1/18/2000	PTlsh	1	1657.5	$14,925.00	$275,750.00
SELL	PTlsh	SP-9967.TXT	1/18/2000	1	1657.5	1/26/2000	PTllo	1	1608.5	$12,050.00	$287,800.00
BUY	PTllo	SP-9967.TXT	1/26/2000	1	1608.5	2/3/2000	PTlsh	1	1616.0	$1,675.00	$289,475.00
SELL	PTlsh	SP-9967.TXT	2/3/2000	1	1616.0	2/11/2000	PTllo	1	1612.5	$675.00	$290,150.00
BUY	PTllo	SP-9967.TXT	2/11/2000	1	1612.5	3/2/2000	PTlsh	1	1574.0	($9,825.00)	$280,325.00
SELL	PTlsh	SP-9967.TXT	3/2/2000	1	1574.0	3/9/2000	PTllo	1	1558.2	$3,750.00	$284,075.00
BUY	PTllo	SP-9967.TXT	3/9/2000	1	1558.2	3/20/2000	PTlsh	1	1659.2	$25,050.00	$309,125.00
SELL	PTlsh	SP-9967.TXT	3/20/2000	1	1659.2	3/31/2000	PTllo	1	1684.2	($6,450.00)	$302,675.00
BUY	PTllo	SP-9967.TXT	3/31/2000	1	1684.2	5/16/2000	PTlsh	1	1642.2	($10,700.00)	$291,975.00
SELL	PTlsh	SP-9967.TXT	5/16/2000	1	1642.2	5/23/2000	PTllo	1	1576.7	$16,175.00	$308,150.00
BUY	PTllo	SP-9967.TXT	5/23/2000	1	1576.7	6/2/2000	PTlsh	1	1660.2	$20,675.00	$328,825.00
SELL	PTlsh	SP-9967.TXT	6/2/2000	1	1660.2	6/13/2000	PTllo	1	1618.8	$10,150.00	$338,975.00
BUY	PTllo	SP-9967.TXT	6/13/2000	1	1618.8	6/15/2000	PTlsh	1	1648.8	$7,300.00	$346,275.00
SELL	PTlsh	SP-9967.TXT	6/15/2000	1	1648.8	6/26/2000	PTllo	1	1620.8	$6,800.00	$353,075.00

(Continues)

TABLE 6.2 Trade List of PTIx on S&P Futures (*Continued*)

Trades for Session

PTIx_WF_SP SP-9967.TXT 1/1/1989 to 12/31/2006. System is PTIX()

Buy/Sell	Entry Name	Market	Entry Date	Size	Entry Price	Exit Date	Exit Name	Size	Exit Price	Trade P/L	Running P/L
BUY	PTIlo	SP-9967.TXT	6/26/2000	1	1620.8	7/11/2000	PTIsh	1	1638.8	$4,300.00	$357,375.00
SELL	PTIsh	SP-9967.TXT	7/11/2000	1	1638.8	7/25/2000	PTIlo	1	1635.3	$675.00	$358,050.00
BUY	PTIlo	SP-9967.TXT	7/25/2000	1	1635.3	8/8/2000	PTIsh	1	1633.3	($700.00)	$357,350.00
SELL	PTIsh	SP-9967.TXT	8/8/2000	1	1633.3	9/13/2000	PTIlo	1	1624.7	$1,950.00	$359,300.00
BUY	PTIlo	SP-9967.TXT	9/13/2000	1	1624.7	11/3/2000	PTIsh	1	1567.2	($14,575.00)	$344,725.00
SELL	PTIsh	SP-9967.TXT	11/3/2000	1	1567.2	11/10/2000	PTIlo	1	1521.2	$11,300.00	$356,025.00
BUY	PTIlo	SP-9967.TXT	11/10/2000	1	1521.2	12/28/2000	PTIsh	1	1452.9	($17,275.00)	$338,750.00
SELL	PTIsh	SP-9967.TXT	12/28/2000	1	1452.9	1/9/2001	PTIlo	1	1423.4	$7,175.00	$345,925.00
BUY	PTIlo	SP-9967.TXT	1/9/2001	1	1423.4	1/16/2001	PTIsh	1	1438.4	$3,550.00	$349,475.00
SELL	PTIsh	SP-9967.TXT	1/16/2001	1	1438.4	2/9/2001	PTIlo	1	1443.4	($1,450.00)	$348,025.00
BUY	PTIlo	SP-9967.TXT	2/9/2001	1	1443.4	3/8/2001	PTIsh	1	1371.1	($18,275.00)	$329,750.00
SELL	PTIsh	SP-9967.TXT	3/8/2001	1	1371.1	3/13/2001	PTIlo	1	1294.1	$19,050.00	$348,800.00
BUY	PTIlo	SP-9967.TXT	3/13/2001	1	1294.1	4/11/2001	PTIsh	1	1288.1	($1,700.00)	$347,100.00
SELL	PTIsh	SP-9967.TXT	4/11/2001	1	1288.1	5/15/2001	PTIlo	1	1348.6	($15,325.00)	$331,775.00
BUY	PTIlo	SP-9967.TXT	5/15/2001	1	1348.6	5/18/2001	PTIsh	1	1385.1	$8,925.00	$340,700.00
SELL	PTIsh	SP-9967.TXT	5/18/2001	1	1385.1	5/30/2001	PTIlo	1	1357.6	$6,675.00	$347,375.00
BUY	PTIlo	SP-9967.TXT	5/30/2001	1	1357.6	7/3/2001	PTIsh	1	1328.3	($7,525.00)	$339,850.00
SELL	PTIsh	SP-9967.TXT	7/3/2001	1	1328.3	7/9/2001	PTIlo	1	1283.3	$11,050.00	$350,900.00
BUY	PTIlo	SP-9967.TXT	7/9/2001	1	1283.3	7/31/2001	PTIsh	1	1294.3	$2,550.00	$353,450.00

SELL	PTish	SP-9967.TXT	7/31/2001	1	1294.3	8/8/2001	PTllo	1	1285.8	$1,925.00	$355,375.00
BUY	PTllo	SP-9967.TXT	8/8/2001	1	1285.8	10/2/2001	PTish	1	1121.8	($41,200.00)	$314,175.00
SELL	PTish	SP-9967.TXT	10/2/2001	1	1121.8	10/19/2001	PTllo	1	1149.8	($7,200.00)	$306,975.00
BUY	PTllo	SP-9967.TXT	10/19/2001	1	1149.8	10/29/2001	PTish	1	1180.5	$7,475.00	$314,450.00
SELL	PTish	SP-9967.TXT	10/29/2001	1	1180.5	11/1/2001	PTllo	1	1144.8	$8,725.00	$323,175.00
BUY	PTllo	SP-9967.TXT	11/1/2001	1	1144.8	11/6/2001	PTish	1	1181.8	$9,050.00	$332,225.00
SELL	PTish	SP-9967.TXT	11/6/2001	1	1181.8	12/12/2001	PTllo	1	1220.3	($9,825.00)	$322,400.00
BUY	PTllo	SP-9967.TXT	12/12/2001	1	1220.3	12/20/2001	PTish	1	1229.5	$2,100.00	$324,500.00
SELL	PTish	SP-9967.TXT	12/20/2001	1	1229.5	1/11/2002	PTllo	1	1238.6	($2,475.00)	$322,025.00
BUY	PTllo	SP-9967.TXT	1/11/2002	1	1238.6	2/12/2002	PTish	1	1185.5	($13,475.00)	$308,550.00
SELL	PTish	SP-9967.TXT	2/12/2002	1	1185.5	2/20/2002	PTllo	1	1165.5	$4,800.00	$313,350.00
BUY	PTllo	SP-9967.TXT	2/20/2002	1	1165.5	2/27/2002	PTish	1	1194.0	$6,925.00	$320,275.00
SELL	PTish	SP-9967.TXT	2/27/2002	1	1194.0	3/15/2002	PTllo	1	1237.3	($11,025.00)	$309,250.00
BUY	PTllo	SP-9967.TXT	3/15/2002	1	1237.3	3/20/2002	PTish	1	1242.3	$1,050.00	$310,300.00
SELL	PTish	SP-9967.TXT	3/20/2002	1	1242.3	3/22/2002	PTllo	1	1230.8	$2,675.00	$312,975.00
BUY	PTllo	SP-9967.TXT	3/22/2002	1	1230.8	5/15/2002	PTish	1	1168.8	($15,700.00)	$297,275.00
SELL	PTish	SP-9967.TXT	5/15/2002	1	1168.8	5/23/2002	PTllo	1	1165.3	$675.00	$297,950.00
BUY	PTllo	SP-9967.TXT	5/23/2002	1	1165.3	6/19/2002	PTish	1	1106.9	($14,800.00)	$283,150.00
SELL	PTish	SP-9967.TXT	6/19/2002	1	1106.9	6/25/2002	PTllo	1	1077.4	$7,175.00	$290,325.00
BUY	PTllo	SP-9967.TXT	6/25/2002	1	1077.4	7/31/2002	PTish	1	976.9	($25,325.00)	$265,000.00
SELL	PTish	SP-9967.TXT	7/31/2002	1	976.9	8/30/2002	PTllo	1	987.2	($2,775.00)	$262,225.00
BUY	PTllo	SP-9967.TXT	8/30/2002	1	987.2	9/12/2002	PTish	1	977.8	($2,550.00)	$259,675.00
SELL	PTish	SP-9967.TXT	9/12/2002	1	977.8	9/16/2002	PTllo	1	963.5	$3,375.00	$263,050.00
BUY	PTllo	SP-9967.TXT	9/16/2002	1	963.5	10/15/2002	PTish	1	942.3	($5,500.00)	$257,550.00
SELL	PTish	SP-9967.TXT	10/15/2002	1	942.3	11/12/2002	PTllo	1	956.8	($3,825.00)	$253,725.00

(Continues)

TABLE 6.2 Trade List of PTIx on S&P Futures (Continued)

Trades for Session

PTIx.WF.SP SP-9967.TXT 1/1/1989 to 12/31/2006. System is PTIX()

Buy/ Sell	Entry Name	Market	Entry Date	Size	Entry Price	Exit Date	Exit Name	Size	Exit Price	Trade P/L	Running P/L
BUY	PTIlo	SP-9967.TXT	11/12/2002	1	956.8	11/19/2002	PTIsh	1	971.8	$3,550.00	$257,275.00
SELL	PTIsh	SP-9967.TXT	11/19/2002	1	971.8	12/9/2002	PTIlo	1	980.3	($2,325.00)	$254,950.00
BUY	PTIlo	SP-9967.TXT	12/9/2002	1	980.3	1/6/2003	PTIsh	1	985.2	$1,025.00	$255,975.00
SELL	PTIsh	SP-9967.TXT	1/6/2003	1	985.2	1/21/2003	PTIlo	1	981.7	$675.00	$256,650.00
BUY	PTIlo	SP-9967.TXT	1/21/2003	1	981.7	2/21/2003	PTIsh	1	915.7	($16,700.00)	$239,950.00
SELL	PTIsh	SP-9967.TXT	2/21/2003	1	915.7	3/6/2003	PTIlo	1	900.2	$3,675.00	$243,625.00
BUY	PTIlo	SP-9967.TXT	3/6/2003	1	900.2	3/17/2003	PTIsh	1	905.8	$1,200.00	$244,825.00
SELL	PTIsh	SP-9967.TXT	3/17/2003	1	905.8	4/1/2003	PTIlo	1	926.8	($5,450.00)	$239,375.00
BUY	PTIlo	SP-9967.TXT	4/1/2003	1	926.8	4/4/2003	PTIsh	1	958.8	$7,800.00	$247,175.00
SELL	PTIsh	SP-9967.TXT	4/4/2003	1	958.8	5/21/2003	PTIlo	1	994.3	($9,075.00)	$238,100.00
BUY	PTIlo	SP-9967.TXT	5/21/2003	1	994.3	5/29/2003	PTIsh	1	1031.3	$9,050.00	$247,150.00
SELL	PTIsh	SP-9967.TXT	5/29/2003	1	1031.3	6/25/2003	PTIlo	1	1060.5	($7,500.00)	$239,650.00
BUY	PTIlo	SP-9967.TXT	6/25/2003	1	1060.5	7/2/2003	BoundExit	1	1062.0	$175.00	$239,825.00
BUY	PTIlo	SP-9967.TXT	8/6/2003	1	1040.5	8/19/2003	PTIsh	1	1080.3	$9,750.00	$249,575.00
SELL	PTIsh	SP-9967.TXT	8/19/2003	1	1080.3	9/26/2003	PTIlo	1	1080.6	($275.00)	$249,300.00
BUY	PTIlo	SP-9967.TXT	9/26/2003	1	1080.6	10/3/2003	PTIsh	1	1112.6	$7,800.00	$257,100.00
SELL	PTIsh	SP-9967.TXT	10/3/2003	1	1112.6	10/24/2003	PTIlo	1	1104.1	$1,925.00	$259,025.00
BUY	PTIlo	SP-9967.TXT	10/24/2003	1	1104.1	10/30/2003	PTIsh	1	1133.2	$7,075.00	$266,100.00
SELL	PTIsh	SP-9967.TXT	10/30/2003	1	1133.2	11/12/2003	PTIlo	1	1127.1	$1,325.00	$267,425.00
BUY	PTIlo	SP-9967.TXT	11/12/2003	1	1127.1	11/26/2003	PTIsh	1	1137.9	$2,500.00	$269,925.00

									P/L	Balance
SELL	PTish	SP-9967.TXT	11/26/2003	1137.9	1	PTilo	1	1218.8	($20,425.00)	$249,500.00
BUY	PTilo	SP-9967.TXT	2/24/2004	1218.8	1	PTish	1	1239.5	$4,975.00	$254,475.00
SELL	PTish	SP-9967.TXT	3/8/2004	1239.5	1	PTilo	1	1223.3	$3,850.00	$258,325.00
BUY	PTilo	SP-9967.TXT	3/10/2004	1223.3	1	PTish	1	1208.6	($3,875.00)	$254,450.00
SELL	PTish	SP-9967.TXT	3/31/2004	1208.6	1	PTilo	1	1212.9	($1,275.00)	$253,175.00
BUY	PTilo	SP-9967.TXT	4/16/2004	1212.9	1	PTish	1	1223.3	$2,400.00	$255,575.00
SELL	PTish	SP-9967.TXT	4/26/2004	1223.3	1	PTilo	1	1199.6	$5,725.00	$261,300.00
BUY	PTilo	SP-9967.TXT	4/30/2004	1199.6	1	PTish	1	1202.3	$475.00	$261,775.00
SELL	PTish	SP-9967.TXT	5/27/2004	1202.3	1	PTilo	1	1203.8	($575.00)	$261,200.00
BUY	PTilo	SP-9967.TXT	7/6/2004	1203.8	1	PTish	1	1181.6	($5,750.00)	$255,450.00
SELL	PTish	SP-9967.TXT	7/30/2004	1181.6	1	PTilo	1	1153.9	$6,725.00	$262,175.00
BUY	PTilo	SP-9967.TXT	8/6/2004	1153.9	1	PTish	1	1162.6	$1,975.00	$264,150.00
SELL	PTish	SP-9967.TXT	8/18/2004	1162.6	1	PTilo	1	1191.8	($7,500.00)	$256,650.00
BUY	PTilo	SP-9967.TXT	9/24/2004	1191.8	1	PTish	1	1202.5	$2,475.00	$259,125.00
SELL	PTish	SP-9967.TXT	10/1/2004	1202.5	1	PTilo	1	1207.6	($1,475.00)	$257,650.00
BUY	PTilo	SP-9967.TXT	10/11/2004	1207.6	1	PTish	1	1206.0	($600.00)	$257,050.00
SELL	PTish	SP-9967.TXT	10/28/2004	1206.0	1	PTilo	1	1260.6	($13,850.00)	$243,200.00
BUY	PTilo	SP-9967.TXT	12/9/2004	1260.6	1	PTish	1	1281.1	$4,925.00	$248,125.00
SELL	PTish	SP-9967.TXT	12/14/2004	1281.1	1	PTilo	1	1267.6	$3,175.00	$251,300.00
BUY	PTilo	SP-9967.TXT	1/6/2005	1267.6	1	PTish	1	1271.1	$675.00	$251,975.00
SELL	PTish	SP-9967.TXT	2/2/2005	1271.1	1	PTilo	1	1268.6	$425.00	$252,400.00
BUY	PTilo	SP-9967.TXT	2/23/2005	1268.6	1	PTish	1	1285.9	$4,125.00	$256,525.00
SELL	PTish	SP-9967.TXT	3/2/2005	1285.9	1	PTilo	1	1283.3	$450.00	$256,975.00
BUY	PTilo	SP-9967.TXT	3/14/2005	1283.3	1	PTish	1	1265.8	($4,575.00)	$252,400.00
SELL	PTish	SP-9967.TXT	4/1/2005	1265.8	1	PTilo	1	1235.9	$7,275.00	$259,675.00

(Continues)

TABLE 6.2 Trade List of PTIx on S&P Futures (Continued)

Trades for Session

PTIx.WF_SP SP-9967.TXT 1/1/1989 to 12/31/2006. System is PTIX()

Buy/Sell	Entry Name	Market	Entry Date	Size	Entry Price	Exit Date	Exit Name	Size	Exit Price	Trade P/L	Running P/L
BUY	PTIlo	SP-9967.TXT	4/15/2005	1	1235.9	4/25/2005	PTIsh	1	1236.0	($175.00)	$259,500.00
SELL	PTIsh	SP-9967.TXT	4/25/2005	1	1236.0	5/16/2005	PTIlo	1	1232.2	$750.00	$260,250.00
BUY	PTIlo	SP-9967.TXT	5/16/2005	1	1232.2	5/19/2005	PTIsh	1	1264.9	$7,975.00	$268,225.00
SELL	PTIsh	SP-9967.TXT	5/19/2005	1	1264.9	6/27/2005	PTIlo	1	1265.9	($450.00)	$267,775.00
BUY	PTIlo	SP-9967.TXT	6/27/2005	1	1265.9	7/12/2005	PTIsh	1	1293.6	$6,725.00	$274,500.00
SELL	PTIsh	SP-9967.TXT	7/12/2005	1	1293.6	8/9/2005	PTIlo	1	1302.1	($2,325.00)	$272,175.00
BUY	PTIlo	SP-9967.TXT	8/9/2005	1	1302.1	9/8/2005	PTIsh	1	1304.2	$325.00	$272,500.00
SELL	PTIsh	SP-9967.TXT	9/8/2005	1	1304.2	9/22/2005	PTIlo	1	1280.4	$5,750.00	$278,250.00
BUY	PTIlo	SP-9967.TXT	9/22/2005	1	1280.4	10/4/2005	PTIsh	1	1297.9	$4,175.00	$282,425.00
SELL	PTIsh	SP-9967.TXT	10/4/2005	1	1297.9	10/6/2005	PTIlo	1	1266.8	$7,575.00	$290,000.00
BUY	PTIlo	SP-9967.TXT	10/6/2005	1	1266.8	10/26/2005	PTIsh	1	1261.5	($1,525.00)	$288,475.00
SELL	PTIsh	SP-9967.TXT	10/26/2005	1	1261.5	12/21/2005	PTIlo	1	1327.6	($16,725.00)	$271,750.00
BUY	PTIlo	SP-9967.TXT	12/21/2005	1	1327.6	1/6/2006	PTIsh	1	1344.3	$3,975.00	$275,725.00
SELL	PTIsh	SP-9967.TXT	1/6/2006	1	1344.3	1/25/2006	PTIlo	1	1330.9	$3,150.00	$278,875.00
BUY	PTIlo	SP-9967.TXT	1/25/2006	1	1330.9	1/31/2006	PTIsh	1	1343.4	$2,925.00	$281,800.00
SELL	PTIsh	SP-9967.TXT	1/31/2006	1	1343.4	2/6/2006	PTIlo	1	1323.6	$4,750.00	$286,550.00
BUY	PTIlo	SP-9967.TXT	2/6/2006	1	1323.6	2/16/2006	PTIsh	1	1340.3	$3,975.00	$290,525.00
SELL	PTIsh	SP-9967.TXT	2/16/2006	1	1340.3	3/7/2006	PTIlo	1	1333.4	$1,525.00	$292,050.00
BUY	PTIlo	SP-9967.TXT	3/7/2006	1	1333.4	3/16/2006	PTIsh	1	1362.6	$7,100.00	$299,150.00
SELL	PTIsh	SP-9967.TXT	3/16/2006	1	1362.6	3/31/2006	PTIlo	1	1355.8	$1,500.00	$300,650.00

BUY	PTIlo	SP-9967.TXT	3/31/2006	1355.8	1	4/6/2006	PTIsh	1	1363.4	$1,700.00	$302,350.00
SELL	PTIsh	SP-9967.TXT	4/6/2006	1363.4	1	4/11/2006	PTIlo	1	1352.3	$2,575.00	$304,925.00
BUY	PTIlo	SP-9967.TXT	4/11/2006	1352.3	1	4/20/2006	PTIsh	1	1362.1	$2,250.00	$307,175.00
SELL	PTIsh	SP-9967.TXT	4/20/2006	1362.1	1	5/15/2006	PTIlo	1	1336.4	$6,225.00	$313,400.00
BUY	PTIlo	SP-9967.TXT	5/15/2006	1336.4	1	6/2/2006	PTIsh	1	1336.6	($150.00)	$313,250.00
SELL	PTIsh	SP-9967.TXT	6/2/2006	1336.6	1	6/8/2006	PTIlo	1	1299.4	$9,100.00	$322,350.00
BUY	PTIlo	SP-9967.TXT	6/8/2006	1299.4	1	7/3/2006	PTIsh	1	1319.5	$4,825.00	$327,175.00
SELL	PTIsh	SP-9967.TXT	7/3/2006	1319.5	1	7/14/2006	PTIlo	1	1284.4	$8,575.00	$335,750.00
BUY	PTIlo	SP-9967.TXT	7/14/2006	1284.4	1	7/28/2006	PTIsh	1	1310.2	$6,250.00	$342,000.00
SELL	PTIsh	SP-9967.TXT	7/28/2006	1310.2	1	8/14/2006	PTIlo	1	1313.8	($1,100.00)	$340,900.00
BUY	PTIlo	SP-9967.TXT	8/14/2006	1313.8	1	8/17/2006	PTIsh	1	1332.4	$4,450.00	$345,350.00
SELL	PTIsh	SP-9967.TXT	8/17/2006	1332.4	1	9/8/2006	PTIlo	1	1333.3	($425.00)	$344,925.00
BUY	PTIlo	SP-9967.TXT	9/8/2006	1333.3	1	9/14/2006	PTIsh	1	1351.1	$4,250.00	$349,175.00
SELL	PTIsh	SP-9967.TXT	9/14/2006	1351.1	1	11/3/2006	PTIlo	1	1400.2	($12,475.00)	$336,700.00
BUY	PTIlo	SP-9967.TXT	11/3/2006	1400.2	1	11/8/2006	PTIsh	1	1406.9	$1,475.00	$338,175.00
SELL	PTIsh	SP-9967.TXT	11/8/2006	1406.9	1	11/29/2006	PTIlo	1	1417.1	($2,750.00)	$335,425.00
BUY	PTIlo	SP-9967.TXT	11/29/2006	1417.1	1	12/5/2006	PTIsh	1	1437.4	$4,875.00	$340,300.00
SELL	PTIsh	SP-9967.TXT	12/5/2006	1437.4	1	12/27/2006	PTIlo	1	1443.3	($1,675.00)	$338,625.00
BUY	PTIlo	SP-9967.TXT	12/27/2006	1443.3	1	12/29/2006	Still Open		1440.7	($850.00)	$337,775.00

TABLE 6.3 Individual Trade of PTIx on S&P Futures

Buy/ Sell	Entry Name	Market	Entry Date	Size	Entry Price	Exit Date	Exit Name	Size	Exit Price	Trade P/L	Running P/L
BUY	PTIlo	SP-9967.TXT	6/16/1998	1	1365.6	6/25/1998	PTIsh	1	1421.1	$13,675.00	$84,450.00

trade and its behavior on a price chart to get an intuitive feel for what it will be like to trade with this strategy in real time when he will be watching these trades on a daily, and perhaps far more frequent, basis. Even the best of trading strategies will have their unpleasant moments of drawdown and of losing periods. The trade list is the ideal tool with which the strategist can familiarize himself with the daily dynamic of the trading strategy on a more intimate basis. The value of this exercise cannot be underestimated.

The Equity Curve

This is typically a graphical report that displays the cumulative profit and loss of the trading strategy. It is typically plotted as line chart in a window below a price chart of the market on which the strategy was simulated (see Figure 6.1).

We can see from our example that on 04/07/2005 the equity curve for PTI on the SP was $76,675. One of the primary benefits of the equity curve is a quick indication of its relative smoothness and consistency, or the lack thereof. Another extremely valuable benefit of the equity curve is the

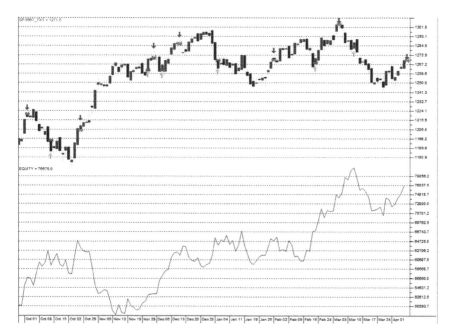

FIGURE 6.1 Bar Chart and Equity Curve of PTIx on S&P Futures

insight that it provides as to the performance of the market under different conditions. Of particular value is to examine market action during periods of suboptimal performance, particularly during maximum drawdown. The evaluation of the equity curve will be treated in more detail in Chapter 12: The Evaluation of Performance.

Performance by Period

This is a report that provides some essential information about the tradability and robustness of the trading strategy. It breaks down trading performance on an interval basis. For most strategies, typically, we are interested in performance on an annual basis.

We can see from our example (Table 6.4) that this report provides key performance statistics on a year-by-year basis. As with the equity curve, this report gives us a measure of the relative consistency of trading performance distributed over time. We are always looking for the trading strategy that performs most consistently. Alternatively, if we find a strategy that has the bulk of its profitability in one or two intervals, this is cause for concern. More on this in Chapter 12: The Evaluation of Performance.

TABLE 6.4   Performance on an Annual Basis of PTIx on S&P Futures

Annual Breakdown Report

PTIx_WF_SP SP-9967.TXT 1/1/1989 to 12/31/2006. System is PTIX()

Period	Trades	Winning Trades	Win %	Open Trade	Net Profit	Return %	Running %
1996	4	3	75.00%	1	$3,100.00	3.48%	3.48%
1997	24	16	66.67%	1	$21,500.00	24.14%	27.62%
1998	23	16	69.57%	1	$42,375.00	47.58%	75.20%
1999	26	21	80.77%	1	$174,175.00	195.56%	270.76%
2000	22	16	72.73%	1	$99,775.00	112.02%	382.78%
2001	20	11	55.00%	1	($16,425.00)	−18.44%	364.34%
2002	19	9	47.37%	1	($75,925.00)	−85.25%	279.09%
2003	18	12	66.67%	1	$7,475.00	8.39%	287.49%
2004	18	10	55.56%	1	($11,425.00)	−12.83%	274.66%
2005	19	13	68.42%	1	$22,875.00	25.68%	300.34%
2006	25	19	76.00%	1	$70,275.00	78.90%	379.25%
Total	218	146			$337,775.00		

THE IMPORTANCE OF ACCURACY

All of the established trading strategy development tools are capable of producing a relatively accurate historical simulation. This means that they are capable of creating trades and the analysis thereof in a standard and reliable manner. There is always the issue of software bugs, of course, and these can affect the accuracy of a simulation. Bugs are an unpleasant fact of computing life, however, and if you have encountered one that has had a negative impact, you know that this needs to be addressed in the best possible manner.

The testing of a trading strategy by computer is the creation and evaluation of a simulation or model of the trading performance of the strategy. As with all simulations, it can be accurate or inaccurate. An accurate simulation is one that trades historical data as closely as possible to the way it will trade in real time.

The more accurate the simulation, the better the real-time trading results are likely to be. An inaccurate or overly optimistic simulation will lead to false conclusions about the trading strategy. Such a false conclusion will most likely lead to real-time trading losses. This chapter covers those considerations necessary to achieve the most complete simulation possible to accurately test a trading system.

The creation of the most perfect simulation possible requires two things: a thorough knowledge and understanding regarding the implications of software limitations and data issues, and the use of conservative assumptions regarding costs and slippage in its various forms.

SOFTWARE LIMITATIONS

These are subtle matters, and unless the strategist is aware of these issues, she is likely to be led into a sense of false security or excessive optimism regarding the reliability of her historical trading simulation.

Rounding Issues

As technical and as innocuous as this may sound, the use of rounding—or its absence—to the proper tick price of data and of entry and exit orders can have the cumulative effect of exaggerating trading performance. It can even lead to another area of error, which is the inclusion or omission of trades that would not be triggered in actual trading.

What is this rounding of which we speak? All markets trade in increments of minimum fluctuations, or *ticks*. For example, soybeans trade in ticks of .25 cents, T-bonds in .03125s and the S&P trades in .10 of a point. Obviously, when placing an order, they are always placed at a price reflecting the proper tick such as 1535.60 for the S&P, 109.08 for T-bonds and 812.5 for soybeans.

Why is this a problem for simulation software? Some applications will round both the data and the orders to their proper tick value. This is called doing tick math. Others do not. What does this mean exactly? It can lead to two types of errors, one worse than the other. If proper tick math is not used in simulations, it can result in orders that are filled and should not have been or not filled that should have been. The second source of error is that it can lead to a subtle, small, and persistent over- or understatement of profits.

Consider the following example, which shows how the lack of rounding can lead to an order not being filled. Instead of using order prices in a T-bond simulation of 109.08, it will use an imprecise decimal value of 109.24997. And, instead of comparing the correct order price of 109.08 to an actual market price of 109.08, it may use an imprecise decimal value of 109.249999. (Because of technical reasons concerning rounding math in computer languages and processors, there can be these type of extremely close near hits.) Of course, this is absurdly close for the sake of illustration. The point is that if the order was correctly rounded to its proper market tick value of 109.08 and the price was correctly rounded to its proper tick value of 109.08, this buy stop would have been executed as it would be in actual trading. Instead, the buy stop in this simulation is not executed and this trade entry or exit is not recorded.

Consider the following example which shows how simulation profits and losses can be overstated by inaccurate rounding. Let us consider an example where, because of rounding errors, a profit is overstated by a tick. Consider a buy, which if properly rounded, would be 1525.20 but is in decimal form 1525.15123, and a sale, which if properly rounded, would be at 1527.90 but is in decimal form at 1527.94999.

The proper profit of this trade done in tick math is $675 (1527.90 − 1525.20 = 2.70 × 250). However, because of incorrectly rounded order prices, the trade profit recorded for this simulation is $699.69 (1527.94999 − 1525.15123 = 2.7988 × 250), which is overstated by $24.69.

One might think that a difference this small really should not matter. Before we jump to this convenient conclusion, however, consider two things. If we are considering a valid trading strategy that has an average trade of $100, then a consistent error of this size might actually make the difference between a usable and unusable strategy. Consider a more robust strategy with an average trade of $250. Against this more robust strategy, this error looks even less significant. In essence, however, it may lead to an overstatement of profit of 10 percent or thereabouts.

The bottom line is that it really isn't all that difficult for trading simulation software to do tick math. The absence of tick math in a simulation can lead to errors significant enough to transform an apparently profitable strategy into an unprofitable one. As a consequence, tick math should be done as a matter of course.

It is up to the strategist to determine whether the software he uses for simulation has this math capability. If it does not, the strategist has no recourse other than to factor this distortion into his evaluation of the trading simulation.

Rounding errors will have a more significant impact on a trading strategy that trades frequently for small profits per trade. It will generally have less impact on a slower trading system, unless a rounding error leads to the inclusion or omission of a big win or loss that either should or should not be included.

Phantom Trades

This is another one of those problem areas that deal with the hidden, inner operations of simulation software. It arises in the way that simulation software handles the order of execution of two contingent orders that are placed on the same price bar. For example, consider a trading strategy that trades on daily bars and has an entry order based on the open plus minus some value. If this entry is executed, the strategy places a covering risk stop that can, if hit, be executed on the same bar of entry.

Assume a trading system enters one order per day before the open. The simulation software must test to see if it is triggered only by the open. If not, the next check is to determine whether it is within the daily range, in which case it is considered to be executed. If either condition is true, the order is filled without ambiguity. If both are false, the order is not filled.

Consider a trading system, however, that produces an entry order and a contingent risk stop. If the prices of both orders are within the daily range, the results can be inaccurate. This is due to the way in which some applications check order execution. Consider the simplest case when the simulation checks the entry order and determines that is filled on the open. It then checks the contingent risk stop against the daily range. It is determined that the order is within the daily range. This is where an element of ambiguity and error can enter into the simulation. Why? Because this level of checking cannot accurately determine whether the entry order is filled during the day. That is because whether or not the risk stop is filled depends on whether the high or the low came first.

For example, consider a buy entry stop price of 352, a contingent sell stop at the fill price minus 2.00 points, a high of 354, a low of 350 and a close of 353. With these prices, clearly the entry stop at 352 is filled. However, here is where it becomes uncertain. If the high came first, then the risk stop at 350 will also be filled and the trade is stopped out. However, if the low came first, the simulation will assume that the entry order was filled on the way up to the close from the low earlier in the day and the risk stop was not hit.

To generalize, this problem can arise from the simulation of a trading strategy that uses any two orders that can be filled on the same bar. Using daily bars alone, the simulation cannot know for sure the proper order of execution nor whether the second order was or was not executed. This information can be provided only by reference to a smaller time frame parallel data set to determine the proper sequence of order execution and whether the second order is filled or not. For example, a simulation of a strategy trading on the daily time frame may consult five-minute bars to determine the proper sequence when both orders are within the daily range.

However, some simulation software allows a strategy with two potential orders in a bar to be traded based upon the best guess as to whether the high or the low came first in the establishment of the daily range.

Most such guesses are made based on the somewhat reasonable assumption that if either the high or low is nearer to the opening price, then it came first in the order of the day and the other came later. The problem arises with bars where, for example, the open is closest to the high, but, in fact the more distant low came first and the high came later.

This is generally a reasonable guesstimation except in those cases when the guess is wrong. The result of this erroneous guess by the simulation software, once again, is the inclusion or exclusion of the execution of an order that would have been filled in real-time trading. These are referred to as tracking errors.

For many strategies, the difference in performance caused by such tracking errors may be insignificant. Once again, however, a faster strategy with close stops and smaller average trades can be heavily affected by these tracking errors. It can potentially be enough to change a profitable strategy into an unprofitable one. At minimum, it introduces an element of unquantified risk into the simulation. It is best if trading simulations with tracking errors are avoided. If tracking errors cannot be eliminated, then the strategist must factor in, once again, this added cost and risk in some way into his evaluation of the strategy.

Price Orders

This issue is the last of the problems resulting from the inner operations of simulation software. Price or limit orders (formally defined in the next section) are placed under (to buy) and over (to sell) the market. They are most typically used as entry orders in countertrending systems that buy dips and sell rallies and with profit target orders. Unlike a stop or market order, however, an execution is not guaranteed if the price of the order is touched or exceeded.

Herein lies the problem. Most strategy simulation software automatically assumes a fill on any price limit order if the limit price is touched. Perry Kaufman maintains that as many as 30 percent of all limit orders go unfilled.[1] This form of slippage is addressed later in this chapter.

Where the software limitations come to play in this matter lies in the treatment of this matter. Whereas there is no guarantee of an execution of a price limit order, one can enhance the probability of execution by adding an additional requirement to simulation of limit orders in trading. The additional requirement is to allow the strategist to set the amount by which the price needs to be penetrated for it to be considered as filled.

Consider the following example: A limit order to buy S&P futures is set at 1525.50 or better. The strategist specifies in the simulation software that this order will not be executed unless the limit price is exceeded by eight ticks (.80) or some other value that exceeds the level of what might be considered a small price fluctuation. In other words, during the simulation, this order will not be filled unless the price reaches 1524.70 (1525.50 – .80). Whereas this is still no guarantee that all orders treated in this manner will be filled, it is a far more realistic assumption than expecting every price limit order is filled if touched.

This is a very significant consideration for the strategist that employs price limit orders. The more they are used in the strategy and the faster the pace of trading, the more significant this issue becomes.

REALISTIC ASSUMPTIONS

In the creation of a trading simulation, a number of seemingly innocuous assumptions need to be made. These assumptions, however, are not innocuous and invalid decisions will lead to questionable to highly questionable simulation results. The most overt and important assumptions are all related to the various forms of slippage to which a trading strategy is subject.

Price and Trade Slippage

Each trade has a fixed and a variable transaction cost composed of commission and slippage.

Definition: *Commission* is the transaction expense charged by a brokerage firm to execute a trade.

While no one questions commissions—they are a fixed cost set by the brokerage firm—many strategists dramatically underestimate the cost of slippage.

Definition: *Price slippage* is the transaction expense charged by poor quality executions. It is the difference between the order price and the actual execution or fill price.

Slippage is a significant cost of trading. It is quite real. Part of the difficulty in developing a full appreciation for slippage, particularly in this era of highly efficient electronic order entry, is that its biggest impact occurs on those trades when the slippage is extremely large. A strategy may trade for some time during orderly and relatively quiet markets and have little or no slippage. But, comes the day when an unexpected event triggers a huge move in a fast market and the order is filled with slippage 10 times your average. The net effect of these large slippage events offsets the preceding period of zero slippage in a hurry. The various ways in which adverse market action can contribute to slippage are discussed in the following sections.

The slippage also depends on the type of order placed, the size of the order, and the liquidity of the market.

Definition: A *market order* is an order to buy or sell at the current market price.

Definition: A *sell stop order* is placed at a price below the current market and becomes a market order to sell when the market trades at or below it.

Definition: A *buy stop order* is placed at a price above the current market and becomes a market order to buy when the market trades at or above it.

Stop orders can be used for market entries and exits. Buy stop orders are placed above the market and sell stops are placed below it. Stop orders are often filled at prices worse than their stop price. This is because when a stop price is touched, it becomes a market order with no further restriction on the fill price. This matter is often further exacerbated because of the market location at which many breakout type strategies and traders place stop orders. In reality, many trading strategies place stops that are in the location of many other stops—bunched orders—from other strategies and market players.

When such groupings of stops are touched, they can lead to an exaggerated price movement leading to even poorer fills and more slippage. There are many reasons why stops do not get filled at their price. It is sufficient to know that this form of stop order slippage is a reality of trading and to use a conservative and sufficient measure of slippage that will accommodate this and more.

Definition: A *sell price limit order* is placed at a price above the current market and must be filled at or above its price.

Definition: A *buy price limit order* is placed at a price below the current market and must be filled at or below its price.

Buy price limit orders are placed below the market and sell limit orders are placed above the market. Price limit orders operate opposite to and different from stop orders in that a fill is not guaranteed. If a price limit is to be filled, it will be filled at or better than its price. Price limit orders, consequently, cannot experience price slippage. Because a price limit order is not guaranteed a fill, however, their usage can and will lead to a form of slippage that is the result of profitable trades that do not occur because the entry order went unfilled. It can also lead to another form of slippage, which is the result of missed exits leading to smaller profits on a trade.

Definition: *Trade slippage* is the cost of missed trades that are never entered or trades that are exited at a worse price because of price limit orders that are not filled.

Definition: A *sell Market If Touched (MIT) order* is placed at a price above the current market and becomes a market order to sell when the market trades at its price.

Definition: A *buy MIT order* is placed at a price below the current market and becomes a market order to buy when the market trades at its price.

Buy Market If Touched (MIT) orders are placed in a falling market and sell MIT orders are placed in a rising market. The MIT order combines the best of the price limit order and the stop order. The price limit order seeks a potentially more desirable price by buying on dips and selling on rallies. The stop order guarantees a fill at some price once the market has traded in the vicinity of a price that your strategy has identified as desirable. Just like the stop order, however, the MIT order is subject to price slippage.

Opening Gap Slippage

All markets have price gaps from the prior day's close to the next day's open. More often than not, these gaps are not all that large and their impact on trading is consequently not all that great. There are occasions, however, when these gaps are large because of significant economic or political events that occur when the markets are closed. Opening gaps can and will create a form of price slippage for GTC orders of all kinds. Opening prices that exceed stop orders, of course, will create negative price slippage. Opening gaps that exceed limit orders will create positive slippage.

Since all simulation software will execute GTC orders correctly, this form of slippage will never be recorded as such. It will either be recorded as a worse entry or exit in the case of stop orders or as a better entry or exit in the case of limit orders. The strategy designer, however, should be sufficiently alert to this type of trading action so as to determine whether the trading strategy is benefiting from or being adversely affected by the impact of opening gaps.

If a strategy has an unusual number of adverse fill prices from resting stops filled on the open, the strategist might consider this as a design weakness and potential area for improvement.

Conversely, if a strategy is the beneficiary of a significant amount of positive slippage because of resting price limit orders exceeded by opening prices, the strategist might consider this to be a hidden strength of the strategy and something that may be enhanced through additional design.

In any case, the strategist should be aware of this subtle form of slippage and should be mindful of the information it provides regarding potentially hidden weaknesses or strengths.

Opening and Closing Range Slippage

This is another form of silent slippage. It is silent in that it will never be noticed as slippage unless it is sought out by the strategist. It is slippage in that it *will* add an additional cost compared to that recorded by the simulation when the strategy is traded in real time.

Consider that the opening price included in most price databases is either the first tick of the day or the midpoint of the opening range. This means that in the simulation, an order executed at the market on the open will be recorded at this price. In actual trading, however, a market order on open will be filled within the opening range, and it is fairly typical that it will be filled at or near the most undesirable price possible. This difference between the historical open and the price that will be obtained in trading is a deviation from the simulation, and in reality, is a form of unrecorded and typically undetected slippage. In all likelihood, most of the time it will not be all that dramatic. It is a cost, however, and it can and will add up over time and should not be ignored.

The exact same phenomenon occurs with Market On Close (MOC) and Stop Close Only (SCO) orders. In the case of the close, though, it will probably be worse. The closing price (for daily data) available in most statistical databases are either the settlement price (the price within the last 30 or 60 seconds of trading determined by the exchange to be most representative) or the average of the high and low of the last 30 to 60 seconds of trading.

Once again, as with the open, the simulation will take the closing price recorded in the database as the price of the fill for a MOC or SCO order. In real trading, executions will more likely be at the adverse end of the closing range. Again, this unrecorded and typically unnoticed form of slippage will add unaccounted costs to real-time trades.

Without belaboring the point, the fill prices for Market On Open (MOO), MOC, and SCO orders used in the historical simulation will not be the same as those arrived at in real-time trading. In all likelihood, market and stop orders filled within the opening or closing ranges will probably be filled at about the worst (lowest sell, highest buy) price possible. This form of silent slippage can add up and take the strategist by surprise because she did not even know it existed.

Slippage Due to Size

The size of an order will have an impact on slippage as well. The greater the size of the order, the greater the slippage is likely to be. A stop order to buy five S&P 500 futures is easy to execute and standard slippage will provide an accurate cost. A stop order to buy 500 S&P 500 futures, however, becomes a different story. A larger slippage should be applied to such an order. Order size has an impact on any type of order. It is likely to prove very costly to price limit orders.

Slippage is likely to grow significantly as order size grows. The strategist who is designing for this scale of trading would be well-advised to explore design options that allow for the full execution of the desired order size yet does it in a staggered or scaled manner.

The Significance of Slippage

The significance of the added transaction costs due to price slippage is often not that significant for a long-term and less frequent trading strategy that aims for larger average trading. Consider a system that trades for four years, makes 10 trades, and earns $20,000 in profit before transaction costs. Deduct transaction costs of $125 ($25 for commission and $100 for slippage) per trade from the $20,000 profit. This leaves $18,750 profit ($20,000 – ($125 × 10)). These relatively small transaction costs are of little significance in this case.

The impact of price slippage transaction costs is much more apparent, however, in a very active, short-term trading system. Transaction costs can have a dramatic impact on the performance of such a system. Assume a strategy that trades for one year, makes 200 trades, and earns a net profit of $10,000. Let us now deduct transaction costs of $125 per trade from the $10,000 profit. After costs, we are left with a loss of the $10,000 profit into a $15,000 loss ($10,000 – ($125 × 200)). In this case, typical transaction costs have transformed a profitable strategy into a significantly unprofitable one.

The impact of trade slippage, however, that is, losses due to unfilled trades, is likely to have an effect on both types of trading strategies. A missed trade, ironically, may have an even worse impact on a strategy that trades infrequently in that it may be the one or two big trades that make or break the strategy that is missed. Trade slippage will also have quite an impact on the strategy that trades more frequently in that it is likely to result in the loss of a significant number of trades that, to make matters worse, are likely to be profitable ones.

LIMIT MOVES

Many futures contracts have daily trading limits. This daily limit is set by the exchange and it determines the maximum or minimum price level to which many futures and options markets are allowed to rise or fall in a day. These limit bands are calculated using the previous day's settlement price.

For example, the current daily limit for soybeans is 50 cents above or below the previous day's settlement price. Assume a settlement price of 635. This means that the next trading day prices can rally to 685 (635 + 50, limit up) but no higher. Conversely, prices can fall to 585 (585 – 50, limit down) but no lower. Trading can continue at these extremes, but not higher or lower.

The exchanges set limits so as to limit risk but not impede the flow of trade. There are rare circumstances, but they do exist, when a market can open limit up or limit down and remain at this price level throughout the entire trading day. This is called locked limit. Statistically, a locked-limit day has an equal open, high, low, and close. When a market is locked limit, the volume of trading is minimal to none. Consequently, for all intents and purposes, it should be considered nearly impossible to buy into a limit-up market or sell into a limit-down market. A trading simulation should not allow entries or exits on locked-limit days.

There can also be days when there is a small amount of trading before the market locks at the limit. To create a reliable historical simulation, these types of days should not be considered as tradable either. Special care should be taken to identify these types of days. A day that locks limit at the high is identified by an equal high and close with a high that is equal to the previous day's close plus the daily limit. A day that locks limit at the low is identified by an equal low and close with a low that is equal to the previous day's close minus the daily limit.

MAJOR EVENTS AND DATES

Major scheduled economic reports, rollovers, and contract and option expiration dates can cause unusual and potentially explosive market movements. These movements are oftentimes so dramatic that it has led to the creation of trading strategies that seek to exploit these events. Such a style of trading has come to be known as event trading.

Some traders and strategies exit positions on the eve of significant economic reports or expiration days as a result of these often dramatic movements. Some traders also make it a practice not to enter trades within some predetermined time band around the time of the release of key economic reports. As observed in the section on price slippage, massive price slippage can and will occur on orders that are filled during these sometimes massive and very rapid market movements. It is a point of debate among traders and strategists as to the best way to manage such events. It is easy to see that these events can and will have different effects on different strategies.

Some traders will also choose to suspend trading in a market after a cataclysmic political or economic event, such as the outbreak of war or an unanticipated economic shock that generates extreme price movement and hypervolatility. For example, such traders might have chosen to suspend trading in oil on the day after the first American air strikes in Iraq in March 2003.

Other trades and strategies thrived on this volatility. It is difficult to correctly anticipate price movement in very sensitive, news-driven markets. If a trading strategy is on the right side of such a movement, windfall profits are the result. Conversely, if the strategy is on the adverse side of these movements, extremely large losses can occur. Such market events become known as a *black swan event*.

It is the view of many systematic traders that a well-tested trading strategy should be able to weather such event-driven storms successfully. As in all things trading, however, there are those who take an opposite view.

It is important that the strategist be aware of the existence of such extreme event-driven market action and that she craft her strategy so as to do all that is possible to ensure the survival and success of this strategy in the face of such events.

It is wise and prudent to evaluate the historical simulation with and without the trades caused by these large and unusual market moves. For example, any trading system that caught the stock market mini-crash of October 27, 1997, would have made a windfall profit. Conversely, any trader long through this crash may have experienced unusually large losses. Such events are rare and largely unpredictable and should not be assumed to be readily repeatable trading behavior. In other words, the windfall profits should be enjoyed but not expected to be repeated so as to sustain profitable trading. Alternatively, the risk must be accommodated by the strategy. It is essential to evaluate the performance of the trading strategy with the trades produced by such events removed from the simulation.

HISTORICAL DATA

It goes without saying that a trading simulation should be based upon the most accurate and reliable historical data possible. Futures and options all have a finite life and end at their expiration. This continuous expiration in these instruments causes two problems and makes them more difficult to test than the equities or cash markets.

STOCK PRICES

Unlike futures and options, the history of a security does not expire or end (except in the case of bankruptcy, acquisition, or delisting). Its price data consequently avoid the complication of futures and options with their finite lives. All listed stocks traded on the different organized stock exchanges such as the New York Stock Exchange or the London Stock Exchange are readily available from data vendors.

There is an important complication to stock prices that pay a dividend. Stock prices need to be accurately adjusted to reflect these dividend payments. Stock prices must also be adjusted for splits.

There is also a minor problem worth noting. Many stock price histories do not provide an accurate opening price. To compound matters, some use the previous day's close price for the next day's opening price field. Data of these types cannot be used to simulate a trading strategy that relies on the open price.

CASH MARKETS

All futures markets have a corresponding, underlying cash or spot market. There is the S&P 500 index on which the S&P index futures are based. Soybean futures are based on the cash soybean markets. Crude oil futures are based on the cash crude market. The degree of formality and centralized access for cash markets vary from market to market from that of the decentralized cash grain markets to the highly organized cash currency markets, which many traders use interchangeably with futures.

Historical price data for many cash markets are generally available. There are underlying cash instruments for all futures markets. Cash markets are continuous and do not expire. Cash markets, however, typically behave differently from instruments derived from them and they should not be considered as a substitute for futures prices.

FUTURES MARKETS

A futures market consists of a series of contracts to be delivered at different forward dates. All futures contracts have a finite life. They are delivered or settled on the last day of contract trading, which is their expiration date. Trading ceases in that contract at the end of trading on its expiration day and the contract formally ends.

For example, S&P futures contracts are offered in four expirations per year: March, June, September, and December. They expire on the third Friday of the spot month. The March 2006 S&P futures contract expired on March 16, 2006. On March 19, 2006, the June 2006 contract became the first expiration.

Because of this expiration, all futures contracts go through a continuous change in the way they behave as they progress through their life cycle. The lead contract, or first expiration, is typically the most heavily traded. There are some markets, like the energy markets and the interest rate products, which have more volume and liquidity in the more distant expirations because of the way that traders and commercials employ them.

Consider an illustration. In January 2006, the September 2006 S&P futures contract was the third deferred delivery and because of this it was more thinly traded than the March 2006 first expiration. The majority of speculative interest in S&P futures is generally on the first expiration. Because of this lessened focus by traders, the September 2006 contract had less trading activity. This was evidenced by lower volume and open interest. The effect of this lower trading interest on price action was most easily seen as gappy price action and lower volatility, that is, smaller daily ranges.

Figures 6.2 and 6.3, respectively, show daily price bars for the March 2006 and September 2006 S&P futures contracts each from June 2005 to March 2006. The difference is quite apparent. Each chart is marked with rectangles labeled with their respective expiration position to indicate where in the expiration cycle they are from the reference point of March 2006.

The S&P September 2006 contract at the start of June 2005 is the fifth expiration. This is evident from the large number of close-to-open gaps and small range bars. These characteristics progressively diminish as this contract moves to the fourth and then third expiration positions.

The S&P March 2006 contract at the start of June 2005 is the third expiration. This is evident again from the large number of close-to-open gaps and small range bars. These characteristics progressively diminish as this contract moves to the second and then completely vanishes as it becomes the first or spot expiration.

FIGURE 6.2   S&P 09-2006 Contract

FIGURE 6.3   S&P 03-2006 Contract

Consider the next stage in the life cycle of the S&P futures December 2006 expiration. When the March 2006 contract expired, the September 2006 contract moved up from the third expiration to the second expiration. As a result, it attracted a little more trading from speculators and spreaders. As a result of this increase in volume and speculative activity, its price action takes on a slightly different complexion.

The final increase in trading volume occurred when the June 2006 contract expired and the September 2006 contract became the first expiration, or delivery month.

The general pattern of this futures contract expiration life cycle begins with gappy, low volatility price action because of low volume and open interest to ends with normal lead contract volatility, volume, and open interest.

It is this finite life and this continuously developing volatility and volume that make the use of actual futures contracts unsuitable for the purposes of trading strategy simulations. Typically, speculative trading will take place in the most liquid contract, which is also most reflective of the price movement of the underlying cash market. This is usually the first expiration. As we will consequently see in the sections that follow, historical simulations are best constructed on the basis of a special type of futures price history, which features the front expiration on a continuous basis.

Also, this process of regular contract expiration and trading interest moving to the new front expiration creates a need in actual trading to roll open positions from the expiring contract to the new front contract.

For example, assume a long position in the S&P March 2006 contract. Further assume that the strategy chooses to roll positions on the fifth trading day in the spot expiration. This happened to be March 5, 2006. On that day, the trader simultaneously liquidates his long positions in the March 2006 contract and puts on a new and equal position in the S&P June 2006 contract.

There is typically some difference in the prices between the expiring March 2006 contract and the new June 2006 front contract. This is the rollover gap. The price gaps that occur at rollover, that is, the transition from the expiring contract to the current active contract, generally do not have that great of an impact on trading. The strategist must be mindful, however, of the existence of the rollover. There can be circumstances, such as in the energy futures, which have expirations every month, and where the frequency of rollovers might have an impact on real-time performance.

Ideally, the simulation should actually include this rollover trade. In this way, the impact, if any, of the roll gap, slippage, and commissions would be accurately represented in the simulation.

Most trading simulation software, however, is unable to do accurate simulations of rollover trades. The strategist, consequently, must be mindful and consider whether the roll will have any impact on his strategy. If he determines this to be the case, one simple way to deal with this is to add in the estimated cost of the roll as additional slippage.

In the majority of cases, however, the roll is not much of a factor one way or another on the performance of most trading strategies.

In summary, actual futures price contracts are unsuitable for long-term testing for two reasons: They are too short and their volume and volatility are not representative of that which is typically traded. Also, the expiration of futures contracts requires the long-term strategy to perform rollover trades to keep long-term positions intact.

A number of data solutions have been offered to solve the problems that futures contracts present to the testing of strategies. The majority of these solutions involve merging a patchwork of prices from the first expirations into some form of continuous contract for the purposes of testing. We will consider these various methods in the next sections.

THE CONTINUOUS CONTRACT

One solution to this problem is the continuous contract. This contract is a sequential patchwork of successive individual futures contracts. For example, in January of 2006, the continuous S&P contract had price data from the March 2006 contract. In April of 2006, it had price data from the June 2006 S&P contract. The continuous contract concatenates price data from the most active front contract price expiration into a single price history file.

The continuous contract solves two of the three major problems. It can be as long as required. It has the front expiration contract prices and accurately reflects the natural trading vehicle of most speculative traders. It has one problem, however: The rollover price gap between the last close of the expiring contract and the opening price of the new contract sometimes appears as a large opening gap. This can result in a windfall profit or loss in the simulation, when, in fact, that situation never existed in real trading. If the strategist chooses to use the continuous contract for testing, this roll gap must be taken into consideration.

THE PERPETUAL CONTRACT

Another popular solution is the perpetual contract. This contract is very different from the continuous contract. It consists of a mathematical transformation of price data which are, consequently, *not* real price data. Price data in a perpetual contract are actually created with an interpolation formula that attempts to create the three-month forward values of the commodity in a manner similar to the London Metals Exchange forward pricing. The design of the extrapolation formula is intended to create a price history that is close to the targeted three-month contract.

The perpetual contract solves two of the three major problems: It can be as long as necessary and it eliminates the rollover price gaps. Whereas its price and volatility structure is similar to that of the front contract price data, it is not exactly like the actual prices of the front contract that it attempts to model. This difference will introduce subtle discrepancies between simulated performance and real-time trading performance.

The perpetual contract introduces three unique problems. First, it does not contain real price history. Every price is transformed. Second, it introduces a new distortion of its own and it tends to somewhat artificially dampen actual price volatility by behaving differently from the actual price data themselves. Third, entry orders for real-time trading derived from it must be transformed. If used to create daily trading signals, these signal prices will need to be adjusted so as to be usable in real-time trading.

This added price distortion may be of little consequence, with a very slow system that trades for the big moves. This distortion, however, may prove to be a serious problem with a very active trading system that targets small moves and is highly sensitive to short-term changes in volatility.

ADJUSTED CONTINUOUS CONTRACTS

The *adjusted continuous contract* combines the best of all of the preceding alternatives. It merges front expiration price data into a continuous price history. It mathematically removes all of the price roll gaps, however. It can be done in two ways. Contracts can be adjusted, keeping the most recent data unchanged and adjusting all preceding data up or down an amount equal to the roll gaps. This is a back-adjusted continuous contract (see Figure 6.4).

A front-adjusted continuous contract adjusts from the beginning of the file to the end. This leaves the most distant data in their natural form and the most current data are adjusted.

The neutral data transform preserves the relative differences between prices. It introduces a distortion with any calculations that use percentages of price. It cannot be used with charting applications that use absolute prices for support and resistance. Back-adjusted contracts can also have negative prices because of the gap adjustments.

FIGURE 6.4   S&P Futures Continuous Back-Adjusted Contract

A back-adjusted continuous contract solves all three of the major problems for most systems: It can be as long as necessary, it faithfully represents the data to be traded, and it eliminates the rollover gap. If the price data extend far back in time, prices can become unusually large or even negative, which will introduce a distortion in calculations using a percentage of price. Back-adjusted continuous contracts, therefore, are not without problems testing some types of trading strategies.

THE SIZE OF THE TEST WINDOW

A simulation of a trading strategy is performed on a segment of historical data of some length or another. For example, a historical simulation of a moving average system is constructed on S&P 500 futures historical price data from 1/1/1995 through 12/31/2006.

Definition: The *test window* is the length of the historical price data on which a trading strategy is evaluated by historical simulation.

Two main considerations must be satisfied when deciding the size of the test window: statistical soundness and relevance to the trading system and to the market.

These two requirements do not stipulate the size of a particular test window in days, weeks, or months. Instead, they specify a set of guidelines that can be followed to determine the correct window size for a particular trading strategy and market. One size does *not* fit all when it comes to size of the test window.

The size of the test window will have a significant impact upon the outcome and reliability of the historical simulation. Its size will influence parameter selection and trading pace. It will also go a long way toward determining the statistical reliability, or lack thereof, of the simulation.

Statistical Requirements

The test window must be large enough to generate statistically sound results and also include a broad sample of data conditions. *Statistically sound* means two things. There must be a sufficiently large number of trades so as to be able to draw meaningful conclusions. The test window must also be large enough to allow enough degrees of freedom for the number and length of the variables employed by the trading strategy. If these guidelines are not followed, the results of the historical simulation are likely to be deficient in statistical robustness, and are therefore suspect.

Sample Size and Statistical Error

The standard error is a mathematical concept used in statistical analysis. We can use an application of this statistic to provide us with some helpful insight regarding the impact of the trade sample size produced by our historical simulation on the robustness and precision of the resulting performance statistics. A large standard error would indicate that the data points are far from the average and a small standard error indicates that they are clustered closely around the average. The smaller the standard error the less an individual winning trade will vary from the average winning trade.

Standard Error = Standard Deviation/Square Root of the Sample Size

We are going to calculate three standard errors of the average winning trade based on three different numbers of winning trades.

Let us specify the values to be used in our application of this formula to calculate the standard error of the mean or average win:

$$AWt = \text{Average Win}$$
$$StDev = \text{Standard Deviation}$$
$$SqRt = \text{Square Root}$$
$$Nwt = \text{Number of Winning Trades}$$
$$StandardError = StDev(AWt)/SqRt(Nwt)$$

Standard error will provide us a measure of reliability of our average win as a function of the number of winning trades, that is, the sample size. For example, if the average win is $200 and has a standard error of $50, then the typical win will be within a range of $150 to $250 ($200 +/– $50.) The wise strategist will always err to the side of conservatism, so he will assume that the average win is likely to be $150 (the pessimistic side of the range of expected wins).

To get an idea of how this plays out with different sample sizes, consider three examples of standard error based on different trade sample sizes of 10, 30, and 100. We will assume a standard deviation for our winning trades of $100.

When our number of wins is 10, the standard error is:

$$\text{Standard Error} = 100/SqRt(10)$$
$$\text{Standard Error} = 100/3.16$$
$$\text{Standard Error} = 31.65$$

With a sample of 10 trades, the standard error is 31.65 rounded to $32. Plugging this value into our formula, the range of wins is $200 +/– $32 or $168 to $232. With a sample of 30 winning trades, the standard error is $18. ($18.25 rounded). The expected range then of wins is $200 +/– $18 or $182 to $218. Finally, with a sample of 100 wining trades, the standard error is $10. The expected range then of wins is $200 +/– $10 or $190 to $210.

From these examples, it is clear that the larger the trade sample size, the lower the standard error or variance of winning trades. Whereas we selected the average winning trader for our analysis, this relationship of larger sample size to smaller standard error will hold true for all performance statistics produced by a historical simulation. The larger the trade sample, the smaller the standard error.

HOW MANY TRADES?

How many trades are enough? Based on the information presented in the previous section, we can see that more are always better. The analysis of a historical simulation is a statistical analysis of its trades. Statisticians are always of a mind that the larger the sample, the more reliable the forecast. As traders with significant sums of capital on the line each day, the more reliable our forecast, that is, trading strategy, the better. The bottom line is that it should be very hard for a prudent trader to trust a trading strategy with a small sample of trades.

Yet, for a variety of reasons, it is not always possible to get as many trades as we might like. This desire for a large trade sample can lead to a problem in the testing of long-term trading systems that trade infrequently. The best way to attempt to get a sufficient number of trades when testing a slower trading strategy is to make the test window as large as possible.

Statisticians seem fond of the number 30 as the smallest sample size that can be evaluated statistically with confidence. Yet, for the strategist, it is not always possible to obtain 30 trades. The number of trades is also related to the size of the test window and to the style and pace of the trading strategy.

If a simulation contains fewer than 30 trades, consequently, extra caution must be exercised in its evaluation. For example, the strategy must be theoretically sound, that is, be based on logical principles of market action that provide additional confidence. If the strategy has optimizable variables, then robustness across a wide range of these variables is even more important. Additionally, the performance of the strategy across a broad range of different markets adds to its statistical validity.

STABILITY

The *stability* of a trading system refers to the overall consistency of its trading performance. The more consistent a trading system is in each of its performance dimensions, the more stable and reliable it tends to be in real-time trading. Chapter 8: The Evaluation of Performance presents the principles used to evaluate the performance of a trading model. A few highlights, however, will prove helpful here.

Trades should be relatively evenly distributed throughout the test window. The smaller the standard deviation of the size and the length of wins and losses, the more stable the strategy is likely to be. Likewise, it is better to have a smaller standard deviation of the size and the length of winning runs and losing runs. It is also better to have consistent trading performance on a quarter-by-quarter and year-by-year basis. The more consistent trading performance is from parameter set to parameter set, the more robust the strategy. These measures of trading consistency are important indications of the stability of the strategy. Stability in historical simulation is one of the more important predictors of reproducibility in real-time trading.

DEGREES OF FREEDOM

It is a fundamental principle of statistics that for a statistical test to produce reliable conclusions, it must begin with *sufficient degrees of freedom.*

> *The term* degrees of freedom *is quite descriptive, in the sense that it is the number of observations in the data collection that are* free *to vary after the sample statistics have been calculated.*[2]

Consider *degrees of freedom* as the simulation sample size adjusted for the number of conditions and rules placed upon it. The simulation test space is reduced in proportion to the number of degrees of freedom that are consumed by the rules and variables of the trading strategy.

Consider the following simple example as an illustration. Assume a trading strategy uses a single moving average with a length of 30 days and a test window size of 100 days. It is said that one degree of freedom is consumed by each data point that is used in its calculation. Our 30-day moving average then uses 30 degrees of freedom. To understand the relevance of this in a more practical way, we determine the remaining degrees of freedom according to the following formula.

$$DF = \text{Degrees of Freedom}$$
$$Udf = \text{Used Degrees of Freedom}$$
$$Odf = \text{Original Degrees of Freedom}$$
$$Rdf\% = \text{Remaining Percentage of Degrees of Freedom}$$
$$Rdf = 100 \times [1 - (Udf/Odf)]$$
$$Rdf = 100 \times [1 - (30/100)]$$
$$Rdf = 70\%$$

The degrees of freedom left in our example are 70 percent, which is not that attractive. As a rule of thumb, we would prefer that the remaining degrees of freedom exceed 90 percent. Therefore, there is no point in performing this simulation as stipulated.

On the other hand, consider a trading system that again uses a single moving average with a period of 10 days and a test window size of 1,000 days.

$$Rdf\% = 100 \times [1 - (10/1,000)]$$
$$Rdf = 99\%$$

This simulation can proceed with 99 percent degrees of freedom. This will produce a more statistically reliable historical simulation.

Consider two other applications of this principle. In the first, a trading strategy has 100 rules and a simulation with one hundred 100 days of data is considered. Applying our formula, we see that this leaves us with no degrees of freedom. It is easy to see that this test is absurd. In contrast, consider a simulation of a trading strategy with 1 rule and 100 days of data. Even though it is a small data sample, the 99 percent degrees of freedom is acceptable.

FREQUENCY OF TRADING

It is an interesting aspect of the trading simulation process that the size of the test window will exercise a somewhat disproportionate influence on the pace of trading. A smaller test window is capable of producing an adequate trade sample for a short-term, more active trading strategy. It is somewhat inherent in the nature of the process that the faster trading parameters will tend to rise to the top. Also, there is no inherent reason why a short-term system will not perform well over a large test window as well. This is not always the case, however.

Very fast trading strategies on volatile markets such as the S&P index typically benefit from smaller test window sizes. For example, a fast countertrending strategy exploiting a short (three-day) price swing may well benefit from short windows such as one to three years.

Conversely, a small test window is generally not capable of producing an adequate trade sample for a longer-term system with a slower trading pace. It is a function of the slower pace of trading and of the disproportionate consumption of degrees of freedom by longer indicators typical of slower-paced strategies.

Slower trend-following strategies trading in markets that are more highly trend-persistent like the yen will typically benefit from longer windows in the three-to-six year (and beyond) range.

Because of this tendency for market trends and volatility levels to make large shifts over time, the periodic reoptimization offered by Walk-Forward Analysis can be preferable.

More on this topic is presented, of course, in Chapter 11: Walk Forward Analysis *and in particular* the section of this chapter called The Theory of Relevant Data.

TYPES OF MARKETS

Even the casual observer of trading markets will be aware that markets go through different phases. There are four different types of markets:

1. The bull
2. The bear
3. The cycling
4. The congested

Besides also being able to intermingle with one another, they can exhibit a high degree of variability regarding factors such as intensity, range, and duration.

For example, congestion phases of short duration can occur during a corrective phase of a bull market. Shorter bear market swings will occur during corrective phases in bull market. A cycling market can overlay a bull movement.

The potential combinations and variations of these four basic market types are endless.

The Bull Market

Bull markets are advancing markets. It features prices that are going up for a sustained time. There are typical bull markets. A regression line drawn through a typical bull market will have a slope between roughly 15 and 50 degrees. Such a market will advance at a relatively gradual pace, is sustainable, and can last for months or even years (see Figure 6.5).

There can be roaring bull markets as well. A line of regression drawn through such a market may have an angle between 50 and 70 degrees and sometimes beyond. Such a market looks as if it is exploding. Roaring bull markets are rarer than typical bull markets. They are also less sustainable and therefore relatively short-lived (see Figure 6.6).

Bull markets are among the most effective markets for most strategies.

FIGURE 6.5   Chart of Typical Bull Market

FIGURE 6.6   Chart of Very Strong Bull Market

The Bear Market

Bear markets are declining markets; it will feature prices that are falling for a sustained time. There are also typical bear markets. A line of regression drawn through a typical bear market will have a slope between 15 and 40 degrees. Such a market will decline at a relatively gradual pace, is sustainable and can last for months or even years (see Figure 6.7).

There can be panic bear markets as well. A line of regression drawn through such a market may have an angle between 50 and 70 degrees and sometime beyond even that. Such a market looks like it is in freefall. They are usually the result of mass hysteria in the financial markets. The hysterical bear market is frequently violent and thankfully short-lived.A bear market like this is often referred to as a panic. The stock market crashes of 1929 and 1987 were such bear panics (see Figure 6.8).

Bear markets are among the better types of markets to trade, but even though it is an opposite trend to the bull market, it is not usually as profitable to trade for many systems because of differing market dynamics.

FIGURE 6.7 Chart of Typical Bear Market

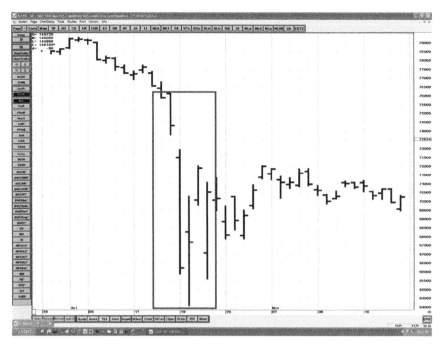

FIGURE 6.8 Chart of Stock Market Crash of 1987

The Cyclic Market

The cyclic market—also known as a trading range market—is clear to see although less well known to the nonprofessional. As the name implies, a cyclic market oscillates with shorter bull and bear movements within a price or trading range. A market hits a cycle low and then rallies to the top of the trading range. It forms an interim cycle high and then breaks to the bottom of the trading range. The primary characteristic of a cyclic market when viewed over time is that of a more or less regular oscillation between the top and bottom of a price range (see Figure 6.9). The cyclic market can also be essentially trendless in the context of longer time horizons.

A cyclic market can also exist within a larger trend. There can be a mild bullish or bearish tilt to the trading range (see Figure 6.10). If the trading range is large enough, such markets are eminently tradable.

The broad cycling market is among the very best markets to trade. The cycling bull market is the best market for most strategies to trade.

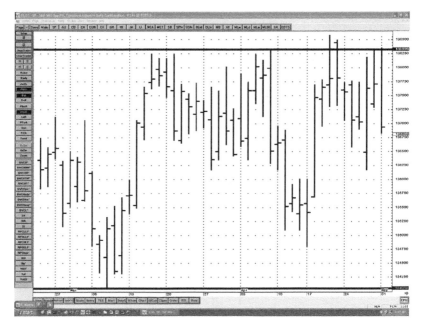

FIGURE 6.9   Chart of Trading Range with top and bottom of range indicated

FIGURE 6.10   Chart of Cycling Bull Market

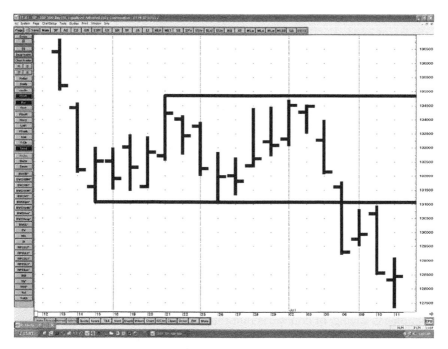

FIGURE 6.11 Chart of Congestion with top and bottom of range indicated

The Congested Market

The congested or consolidating market is typically characterized by an absence of trend, volatility, and tradable price movement. A congested market consists of very short-lived, one to two bars, fluctuations between the top and bottom of a generally narrow trading range (see Figure 6.11). They are typically untradable and are areas where most trading strategies will experience some degree of drawdown. If market congestion continues for an extended time, even a good trading strategy will experience a large—if not its maximum—drawdown.

The congested market is the worst type of market to trade for most strategies. It offers good trading mostly for the very short-term trader who is scalping the market for small profits. Even for them, however, the congested market can be difficult.

EFFICIENT MARKETS

The Efficient Market Hypothesis (EMH), developed by Eugene Fama, has enjoyed a great deal of support in the academic community. It is the current view of many, however, that the EMH is no longer accepted as an accurate theory of market action. It is difficult to talk about market efficiency without at least a brief mention of it, though.

EMH states that the market is informationally efficient. This means that all information that can have an effect on the price level of a market is equally available to all players and is therefore very quickly assimilated and reflected in the current market price.

EMH holds that because the market is so efficient at processing relevant information—almost instantaneously—that one trader cannot obtain a persistent advantage over another. The EMH states, in effect, that all forms of trading advantages, such as market analysis and automated trading strategies, are essentially illusions and cannot be profitable in the long run.

There are obviously many who have made fortunes trading and investing and this alone tends to discredit the EMH.

The Nobel Laureate Myron Scholes provided further support for this view in the form of a revealing quote made while touting his former hedge fund (the now defunct Long-Term Capital Management): "The fund will succeed," he told one skeptical investor, "because of fools like you."[3] What Scholes is saying, of course, is that the geniuses at LTCM would efficiently exploit the inefficiencies of "foolish" market participants. And so they did for a number of highly profitable years. But little did Scholes know that the fatal "inefficiencies" of LTCM as a professional money manager would add further "fuel to the fire of market inefficiencies" for others to exploit this time at their expense![4] The "unwinding" of LTCM's positions—among other things—nearly caused a stock market crash.

Let us examine the idea of market efficiency in a more practical way, however.

It is true that free open-outcry markets, which are rapidly being replaced by far more efficient electronic markets, are the most efficient markets in the world. Information about a market is distributed, assimilated, and more or less accurately reflected by the price of the market in short order. Prices are set as quickly, although perhaps not all that accurately, as the opinions of the community of traders can be expressed in the form of trades in the market.

The markets, however, especially today as their globalization continues at a rapid pace, are vast and getting vaster. They also operate within a wide range of time horizons, from one-minute time horizons up to monthly time frames and everything in between. This has a multiplier effect in that many of these different time horizons really attract totally different groups of market participants. A market can have a range of participants from thousands to millions all wanting different things from the market and each pursuing their own often narrow self-interest.

Certainly, anyone who has been around traders will know that every trader has his own opinion about the market. Find me a trader who does not! Professional traders and money managers have access to more or less the same information at more or less the same time. They all filter this information through their own belief system and strategies and then trade accordingly.

Different traders have different uses and needs for the market. The floor scalper wants to profit by a few ticks per trade. The floor day trader wants to capture the middle of an interday move. The hedger wants to insure against adverse price moves in the futures market after buying or selling a cash product. The arbitrageur wants to take advantage of small price deviations between two related products. The highly mechanized statistical arbitrageur trades huge positions for tiny fluctuations that can be detected only by the power of their advanced algorithms and captured by the speed of computers. The speculator just wants to make money any way possible. Speculators trade from minute to minute, day to day, week to week, or month to month.

As more has been learned about market action, it becomes increasingly clear how little is truly known. The structure of price action is obviously imperfectly understood. A large and growing body of knowledge in the area of technical analysis has been accumulated over the years. Yet, this information cannot really be said to be codified into a body of precise and formal mathematical knowledge. Furthermore, many advanced mathematical methods have been successfully used to extract profit from the markets with statistical arbitrage.

At the same time, computing power, high-speed communications, and electronic order entry have all been eroding market inefficiencies. This combination of increasingly sophisticated knowledge and powerful technologies has made the markets just that much more efficient.

Time and time again, market opportunities—inefficiencies—have existed, been discovered, been exploited, and have ceased to exist as they became more widely known. A market inefficiency, once discovered, will generally not remain for long. As new methods and technologies arise, however, new inefficiencies will be uncovered, exploited, and erased. It is most likely that this ongoing dance of inefficiency and efficiency will continue without end.

Yes, the market is efficient. However, the market is not omniscient. Nor is it perfectly efficient, nor is it ever likely to be. Furthermore, all that can be known about a market can never known by even one participant, let alone all participants; it is simply not possible.

As a matter of fact, quite the opposite is true. The bigger the market becomes, and the more players it attracts, the more complicated it will become. Consequently, there will always be market opportunities to be discovered and exploited. The smarter the participants and the greater the technological power brought to bear on the market, however, the more original must the strategy be.

Given this ongoing assimilation of traders, technique, and technology to the markets, is it any wonder why a trading model or strategy may have a limited life?

THE LIFE CYCLE OF A TRADING STRATEGY

It is obvious that the title of this section harbors a fundamental belief about parameter sets and trading strategies—that they have a life cycle, a beginning, middle, and perhaps an end.

More plainly, the operating assumption is that any given set of values for the model parameters of a trading strategy will be of limited utility. This assumption also extends to the belief that a trading strategy itself may be of limited duration.

These assumptions are impossible to prove in the space available here. They are based, however, upon years of experience in strategy research, consulting, and trading. In addition, there has been much of a more anecdotal nature in the literature over the years supporting this view. I have also personally heard many stories from a variety of traders over the years that lend a great deal of weight to these concepts.

Last, but not least, in recent years, it has almost become a matter of commonly accepted belief by many in the hedge fund and commodity trading adviser communities, and, in particular, among those who invest in these vehicles, that money needs to be spent continuously to research, adapt, and refine strategies.

This is a subject that has been debated by developers of trading strategies for years and will probably continue to be debated for many more years to come.

There are two schools of thought on this subject. The first school maintains that the only good trading strategy is a trading strategy that need not and does not vary over time. Inherent in this belief is that the best trading strategy will work without optimization and on all markets with the same rules and parameters. It certainly goes without saying that this would be an excellent trading strategy. If, in fact, you have one like this, you do not need this book. Go now and make your fortune.

The alternative view is that to achieve optimal trading performance over long periods of time with a trading strategy, it will need to be updated, at least occasionally. It is also part of this view that it is perfectly acceptable for a trading strategy to employ different parameters for different markets. This is, in fact, preferable, in that it adds an additional level of portfolio diversification.

Making this case in the necessary detail is an argument beyond the scope of this book. Suffice it to say that I have seen a lot of trading strategies over the years and I have yet to see a trading strategy of the forever and one-size-fits-all markets, trends, and conditions.

In fact, it has even been said by Richard Dennis, of Market Wizard and Turtle Traders fame, that the principal driver of the Turtle Trading system no longer works.[3] But worthy of mention on this note is that the Turtle Trading system and variants thereof are reputed to have produced hundreds of millions of dollars in trading profits in the years when it *did* work.

Also, I have seen profitable real-time trading strategies that do use different parameter values for different markets and do benefit from periodic reoptimization. In fact, the models employed by the commodity trading advisor Pardo Capital Limited fit this profile. Its performance is a matter of public record for those who are interested.

I suspect that if you were able to look behind the scenes at a number of professional money managers, you might be surprised at the degree to which their models and strategies have changed and developed over time.

As a matter of note, the current climate among large institutional investors is that a money manager should be constantly looking to change, adapt, and develop his strategies. Quite a change from the one-size-fits-all crowd of a decade ago.

It is the operating assumption of this book that models and even strategies will benefit from modification from time to time. It is also one of the reasons that Walk-Forward Analysis was originally created.

WINDOW SIZE AND MODEL LIFE

We assume that the parameter sets of the majority of trading strategies will require and benefit from the adjustments produced by reoptimization. We now must examine the relationship between the size of the test window and the duration of its use. And by usage, we mean two things. The first application is an out-of-sample window in a Walk-Forward Analysis. The second application is the length of time a model can be traded in real time before requiring reoptimization.

Many trading strategies, particularly those that are nonadaptive, which benefit from optimization, will require some type of periodic reoptimization. The effect of this reoptimization is to adjust the trading model to current market action by locating the best model parameters for current market conditions.

Experience has shown, and common sense agrees, that a trading strategy optimized on a larger test window is likely to last longer between reoptimizations. Conversely, strategies optimized on shorter test windows are more likely to require reoptimization more often. Models built on smaller windows are said to have a shorter life. Those built on bigger windows are said to have a longer life.

The main reasons for this are structural. The time between reoptimizations has generally been found to be some smaller portion of the original test window size. This is highlighted by Walk-Forward Analysis, which is presented in Chapter 11: Walk-Forward Analysis. A good rule of thumb for the determination of the size of the trading window is to set it at between one-eighth and one-third of the test window size.

For example, if a 24-month test window is used to optimize the trading strategy, then it can safely be traded out-of-sample or in real time for between three ($24/8 = 3$) and six ($24/3 = 8$) months with minimal likelihood of adverse performance. Let us try to provide some intuitive concept for this principle. Consider the following example. A strategist optimizes a strategy on two years of data. Would he be confident trading this model for the next six months? Probably. Would he be confident trading this same model for next three years? Maybe not and with good reason.

This is somewhat analogous to the application of a similar statistical modeling procedure. It is known that statistical forecasts are the most accurate for the next period forward and less accurate for forecasts made further out in time. Let us assume, for example, that we are using a polynomial regression model to forecast the closing price of oil. The forecast made for the next period out will be more accurate (and with narrower confidence bands) than a forecast made five periods out. This will be discussed in more detail in the next section.

The main reason a trading system must be reoptimized is that markets change with some frequency. They do not change, however, with great regularity. If market conditions remain the same, a new reoptimization of the trading system will most likely arrive at the same parameter values that were identified by the previous optimization. Conversely, if market conditions change, especially dramatically, reoptimization will most likely identify new parameter values.

So, what is the main reason why a short test window is most likely to be tradable for some minor fraction of its size? Primarily, because a small test window is unlikely to include a comprehensive sampling of market types and volatility levels. Consider that a small window where the majority of market activity is a strong bull market can be said to have seen only one type of market. Review Figure 6.12 for an illustration of this concept. Also, if it has been a fairly consistent bull market, it is relatively likely that trading volume and volatility have been relatively consistent as well.

FIGURE 6.12   Chart of a strong one year bull market

When a trading strategy has been optimized on a test window with a steady bull market and stable volatility, it can be said that this model has been adapted to this type of market and set of conditions. In fact, one could say that the model has been particularly well adapted to such conditions. Perhaps the strategy is *too* well adapted. The strategy will perform well under similar conditions but it is unlikely to continue to perform well if the market trend changes from a steady bull market to a choppy bear market.

When market type and volatility change into something that the strategy has not seen in its life, there is no guarantee that it will continue to perform as it did during its previous optimization. Reoptimization empowers the trading strategy with the capability to adapt to just this type of changing market and unfolding conditions. A smaller window, by definition, has just such a limited view of market type and volatility conditions. It is this limited view that requires more frequent reoptimization.

Conversely, a longer test window will likely incorporate a greater range and variety of types of markets and a broader set of volatility and volume levels. By definition, it has a much broader view of the market and is adapted to function effectively in this larger domain. With a larger knowledge base, such a trading strategy is more likely to be able to trade effectively in more types of market types and conditions (see Figure 6.13).

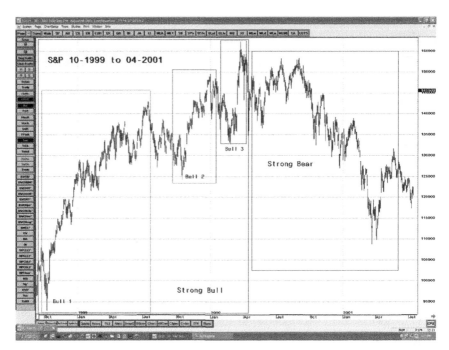

FIGURE 6.13 Chart of a strong bull and a strong bear market over a three-year time period

In general, a shorter window requires more frequent reoptimization, is more responsive, that is, more profitable, to current price action and is less capable of adapting effectively to dramatic changes in trend and volatility.

Conversely, and in general, a longer window requires less frequent reoptimization, is less responsive, that is, less profitable, to current price action and is more able to adapt effectively to large shifts in trend and volatility.

CHAPTER 7

Formulation and Specification

N ow that we have completed our review of the necessary background material, we can begin a detailed presentation of the eight stages of strategy development with the first step: formulation and specification.

A trading idea begins as an idea. The trading idea may be quite precise in which case the balance of this stage will unfold in a straightforward manner. Or the idea may be vague. In this case, the formulation process becomes more involved. Without a clear and precise formulation of the strategy, the development process ends before it starts. If the strategy is vague, then it first needs to be made precise.

The first stage in the strategy development process, in a nutshell, is the translation of a trading idea into a scripted form understandable to a trading strategy development application in order to produce a historical trading simulation. As we have seen in the previous chapter, the historical simulation is the lifeblood of the strategy evaluation process.

FORMULATE THE TRADING STRATEGY

As previously stated, a trading strategy begins as an idea or set of related ideas. In its totality, it will comprise various formulae, indicators, rules, order prices, and so on. Each of these different components of the strategy must be specified individually and in detail. The interconnections of these components also must be made specific.

145

A strategy can be very simple or extremely complex. The simplicity or complexity of the strategy is of no consequence in itself. What does matter, however, is that the strategy be specified accurately, completely, and consistently.

Consider the clarity of this simple trading strategy, for example. Go long on a stop when the market rallies to a price level that is equal to or more than yesterday's close plus 125 percent of yesterday's daily range. Go short on a stop when the market falls to a price level that is equal to or less than yesterday's close minus 145 percent of yesterday's daily range. Exit and reverse positions on opposite entry signals.

It goes without saying that exact and precise specification of a trading strategy in all of the necessary detail is essential to success in this process. That being said, the incomplete specification of each and every rule, formula, and detail of a strategy is one of the most common mistakes that is made in strategy development. This is especially true of traders new to the strategy development process.

No successful trader would begin trading without being completely prepared. In the same way, every successful trading strategy developer must cross every t and dot every i. In the trading strategy development process, like in so many other intricate processes, the devil is in the details.

The ease or difficulty with which the strategist will perform this first stage is highly variable. The more organized, thorough, logical, and clear-thinking strategist will have little difficulty with this process. The strategist lacking in these qualities, however, will find it a more formidable task. As with all skills, this process becomes easier with practice and repeated application.

The process of organizing and specifying a trading strategy is much like the planning and organization required to proceed with any project or design. All the pieces—formulae, rules, and indicators—must first be assembled. Their accuracy must be verified. All of the pieces of the puzzle must then be placed in the correct order. In other words, we must calculate and obtain all of the information necessary. We must follow the trading decision process through all of its steps and in order. The decision tree must be in correct logical order. Thorough organization and attention to detail are the keys to successful strategy specification.

After all of the trading formulae and rules have been assembled and organized, it is best to write out the trading strategy in some form of abbreviated English. In programming, this process is called *pseudocoding*. The more detailed and specific the pseudocode, the better. This pseudocode will then be translated into a scripting test language. The more detailed the specification, the easier the translation.

One of the greatest advantages of the pseudocoding process is that it is a very effective means of determining whether all the elements have been assembled and that all of the steps in the process have been identified.

SPECIFICATION—TRANSLATE THE IDEA INTO A TESTABLE STRATEGY

The following fictional dialogue presents an extreme example of the type of vagueness with which a trading idea can be surrounded. The dialogue is between Joe Trader, a highly intuitive, nonanalytical, and successful trader and Alex Programmer who is a highly analytical, logical, and organized programmer. His specialty is the interview process, whereby he engages in a structured dialogue with a trader and extracts all of the methods that the trader uses to form his trading decisions. Alex then organizes this information into a precisely formulated trading strategy suitable for translation into a scripting language.

Before Alex takes this step, however, he and Joe review his formulation and correct any errors and misunderstandings. Alex then incorporates these corrections, additions, deletions, and so on and once again has it reviewed by Joe. This back-and-forth process will continue until the strategy is in the form that Joe thinks best represents his trading strategy and Alex thinks can be coded for testing.

Please note that this dialogue is a bit tongue in check and has been exaggerated for the sake of illustration. Traders obviously come from all types of different backgrounds, especially in the highly competitive contemporary trading environment, and will range in organizational and analytic ability anywhere from that of Joe Trader to the mindset of a highly trained Ph.D. That being said, let us continue with our dialogue.

Joe Trader uses a trading strategy that employs moving averages in a quasi-systematic manner. He has enjoyed some degree of success employing moving averages in a somewhat unique manner. Joe believes he would be able to make more money trading if he understood more about how they worked and why they were effective. In pursuit of this information, he hired Alex Programmer to write a computer program that will allow him to formulate and test his trading strategy. The following conversation ensued as Joe explained his methods.

"I buy when the moving averages look good and I sell when the averages look bad," says Joe Trader.

"Hmm, that's pretty interesting. Does it work?" says Alex Programmer.

"Sometimes," says Joe T.

"Interesting," says Alex P. "But we are going to need to be a little more specific to test this idea. Do you mind if I ask you a few questions?"

Joe: "I guess not, but I hope it won't take too long."

Alex: "Okay. Can you first tell me what you mean by the averages looking good?"

Joe: "Yeah, but I think it's pretty obvious. The averages look good when the short one just blasts through the long one."

Alex: "Well, it may be obvious to you, but it is not to me nor will it be to the computer. By 'blasts through' do you mean that the faster moving average—MA1—crosses from under to over the slower moving average—MA2?"

Joe: "Yep."

Alex: "Good. Does it matter how much MA1 crosses over MA2?"

Joe: "Sometimes yes, sometimes no. It all depends."

Alex: "On what?"

Joe: "It's hard to say."

Alex: "Well, then, maybe we should leave how much it crosses over for future improvements. Let's just get the basic system formulated first. We know that we will go long if MA1 crosses from under to over MA2. Now, what do you mean by 'the averages look bad'?"

Joe: "That should be obvious, too. They just fall apart, go to hell in a handcart."

Alex: "Well, since we go long when MA1 comes from under to over MA2, am I correct in assuming that we go short when MA1 crosses from over to under MA2?"

Joe: "Uh-huh, you got it, Alex."

Alex: "Good. This looks like we are always in a position. Is that correct?"

Joe: "Most of the time."

Alex: "When are you not in a position?"

Joe: "When the whole thing just falls apart."

Alex: "What do you mean by that?"

Joe: "When the market isn't moving, moving averages just cut me to pieces."

Alex: "What do you mean when you say 'the market isn't moving'?"

Joe: "There is just no action. Lots of little swings, but no big swings."

Alex: "Does that mean that this moving average strategy is really only able to catch big swings?"

Joe: "Yes."

Alex: "What is a big swing, then?"

Joe: "That depends."

Alex: "On what?"

Joe: "The market."

Alex: "I see. Does this vary from market to market and from year to year?"

Joe: "You got it."

Alex: "Do different length moving averages have an impact on this?"

Joe: "Yeah."

Alex: "How do you determine which ones to use?"

Joe: "I play around with different moving averages in my charting program and use the ones that look good."

Alex: "Well, you don't know anything about the profit and risk performance of these averages that 'look pretty good,' do you?"

Joe: "No I don't. That's why I hired you. You're supposed to figure this all out for me."

Alex: "Well, I will do my best. How do you control your risk when you take a position?"

Joe: "It depends. If one average just blows through the other like a bat out of hell, I usually make some money right away and it's no problem. But sometimes the market just looks pretty lame, and I put in a close stop on the position."

Alex: "You mean sometimes you use a stop, and sometimes you don't?"

Joe: "Uh-huh."

Alex: "That sounds inconsistent and could be dangerous as well. Do you want to test the strategy with and without a risk stop?"

Joe: "Yes, that's a good idea."

Alex: "Okay. I will build this in as an option. What do you do when you have a winner?"

Joe: "If I get a couple of grand in it, I usually ring the cash register and take profits."

Alex: "Do you mean that you take a profit after you have made a certain amount of money in position?"

Joe: "Yep."

Alex: "How much is enough?"

Joe: "It depends."

Alex: "On what?"

Joe: "The market. How I have been doing lately. How I feel. A lot of stuff."

Alex: "Well should I build in some kind of profit idea as an option in the program?"

Joe: "That would be great."

Alex: "Let us see what we have here. Our basic trading model uses two different-length moving averages. The model is always either long or short unless our optional risk or profit management exits a trade. We go long if the faster average goes from under to over the slower average. We go short when the faster average goes from above to below the slower average. Is that correct?"

Joe: "So far, so good."

Alex: "There are two variations on this basic model. A risk stop and a profit target order. The use of either of these will lead to an alteration of the model. If a position is exited using a risk stop or a profit or better target order, then the model will not always be in the market. Is that okay?"

Joe: "Let's just play it by ear and find out."

Alex: "Okay. I will set up this program to have user-definable moving average lengths. It will have an option to use a risk stop, a target profit, or both. The program will be capable of testing a batch of different-length moving average combinations. Do you think this will do it?"

Joe: "It's a start. Let's see what happens."

MAKE A VAGUE IDEA PRECISE

This little melodrama serves to highlight the vagueness that can surround a trading strategy at the inception of the development process. Joe Trader may seem a bit extreme. The number of ways in which a trading strategy can lack clarity, however, are too numerous to list. And, in truth, Alex Programmer was a lot better communicator and far more accommodating than many programmers.

You may engage yourself in this type of dialogue or you may enlist outside help. However, the collection, organization, and exact specification of the trading strategy, which are done next, and as were illustrated in this dialogue, are the essential first steps.

A trading strategy is a set of precise rules and formulae, no matter how simple or complex. If the trading idea cannot be expressed in a way that is precise and logical, then it is not a trading strategy.

The trading strategy discussed in the dialogue above can be described in three ways: ordinary English, precise rules and formulae, and computer code. The English version is pseudocode. The formulae represent a more exact representation of pseudocode on its way to becoming computer-testable code. The strategy expressed as C code is in a form that a computer can understand.

As English language pseudocode, this moving average trading strategy can be expressed as follows:

1. Calculate a fast moving average
2. Calculate a slow moving average
3. Go long when yesterday the fast moving average was below the slow moving average and today the fast moving average is above the slow moving average
4. Once long, stay long until a sell entry occurs
5. Go short when yesterday the fast moving average was above the slow moving average and today the fast moving average is below the slow moving average
6. Once short, stay short until a buy entry occurs

This strategy pseudocode can be converted to the following set of definitions, formulae, and logic rules:

1. $C(t)$ is the close of the tth day with $t = 1$, the present day
2. X is the length of moving average one (MA1)
3. Y is the length of moving average two (MA2)
4. $MA1 = [C(t) + C(t + 1) + \ldots + C(t + X - 1)]/X$
5. $MA2 = [C(t) + C(t + 1) + \ldots + C(t + Y - 1)]/Y$
6. Y is never less than 2 times X
7. If we have no position and $MA1(t) > MA2(t)$ and $MA1(t - 1) < MA2(t - 1)$, then go long.
8. If we are short and $MA1(t) > MA2(t)$ and $MA1(t - 1) < MA2(t - 1)$, then go long.

9. If we have no position and MA1 (t) < MA2 (t) and MA1 (t − 1) > MA2 (t − 1), then go short.

10. If we are long and MA1(t) < MA2(t) and MA1(t − 1) > MA2(t − 1), then go short.

Such ideas look quite a bit different in the C programming language. The C code to calculate the value of a moving average is displayed in Example 1.

```
int SMA(int day,int period,int type,float *value)
{   register int i;
    float total;
    *value = 0.0;
    if ( period <= 0 )
       period = 1;
    if (day < period)
       return(−1);
    total = 0.0;
    for ( i = 0; i < period; i++ )
       total += get_price_data( type, day-i );
    *value = total/(float) period;
    return(1);
}
```

Of course, there is no need to understand this C code unless you are a programmer. It is simply included as an illustration of the degree of precision that is required at this level of programming. To complete this example, the final version of this trading strategy in C takes care of every last detail and is 8,187 lines long. In this form, it can be tested precisely against price data.

For those not proficient in C, or some other programming language, such as Visual Basic, there are more user-friendly trading applications that have been specifically designed for the nonprogramming trader.[1] These applications enable the strategist to describe and test trading ideas without programming proficiency. This is not to say that proper results can be expected from an incorrectly specified system. They cannot. These programs do, however, have a number of built-in functions and operations that make the specifications of a computer-testable trading strategy a great deal easier.

Examples in this book will use *Metastock*, *TradeStation*, and *Traders-Studio* interchangeably. Any trading strategy development application must give the user the same abilities to express rules precisely and to test and optimize these rules.

We will refer to any coded expression of a trading idea as a *script*. An EasyLanguage script (TradeStation's scripting language) that expresses the earlier-specified two moving-average trading strategy looks like this:

```
{ EOTS-MA © 2007 Robert Pardo All Rights Reserved }
{ This is the sample code from TradeStation EasyLanguage }
Input:        MA1_Period(10),MA2_Period(30);
Vars:MA1_Today(0),MA1_Yesterday(0),
   MA2_Today(0),MA2_Yesterday(0);
IF currentbar > MA2_Period then begin
{ Calculate MA values }
MA1_Today    =      average(close,MA1_Period);
MA1_Yesterday    =      average(close,MA1_Period)[1];
MA2_Today    =      average(close,MA2_Period);
MA2_Yesterday    =      average(close,MA2_Period)[1];
{ Set buy entry }
if MA1_Today > MA2_Today then begin
   if MA1_Yesterday < MA2_Yesterday then begin
      buy("LOen") next bar on open;
   end;
end;
{ Set sell entry }
if MA1_Today < MA2_Today then begin
   if MA1_Yesterday > MA2_Yesterday then begin
      sell("SHen") next bar on open;
   end;
end;
END;
```

A script expressing this trading strategy in Metastock looks as follows:

```
BUY---
  Fast:=10;
  Slow:=30;
  Fm:=Mov(C,Fast,S);
  Sm:=Mov(C,Slow,S);
  Y:=Cross(Fm,Sm);
  Ref(Y,-1)
SELL---
  Fast:=10;
  Slow:=30;
  Fm:=Mov(C,Fast,S);
  Sm:=Mov(C,Slow,S);
  Y:=Cross(Sm,Fm);
  Ref(Y,-1)
```

```
SHORT---
  Fast:=10;
  Slow:=30;
  Fm:=Mov(C,Fast,S);
  Sm:=Mov(C,Slow,S);
  Y:=Cross(Sm,Fm);
  Ref(Y,-1)
COVER---
  Fast:=10;
  Slow:=30;
  Fm:=Mov(C,Fast,S);
  Sm:=Mov(C,Slow,S);
  Y:=Cross(Fm,Sm);
  Ref(Y,-1)
```

A script expressing this trading strategy in TradersStudio looks as follows:

```
'EOTS-MA (c) 2007 Robert Pardo All Rights Reserved
'This is the sample code from TradersStudio Basic
Sub EOTS_MA(MA1_Period, MA2_Period)
  Dim MA1_Today As BarArray
  Dim MA1_Yesterday As BarArray
  Dim MA2_Today As BarArray
  Dim MA2_Yesterday As BarArray
  If BarNumber=FirstBar Then
    'MA1_Period = 10
    'MA2_Period = 30
    MA1_Today = 0
    MA1_Yesterday = 0
    MA2_Today = 0
    MA2_Yesterday = 0
  End If
If CurrentBar > MA2_Period Then
'Calculate MA values
    MA1_Today = Average(Close, MA1_Period, 0)
    MA1_Yesterday = Average(Close, MA1_Period, 1)
    MA2_Today = Average(Close, MA2_Period, 0)
    MA2_Yesterday = Average(Close, MA2_Period, 1)
'Set Long Entry
  If MA1_Today > MA2_Today Then
    If MA1_Yesterday < MA2_Yesterday Then
       Buy("LOen", 1, 0, Market, Day)
    End If
  End If
'Set Short Entry
```

```
   If MA1_Today < MA2_Today Then
     If MA1_Yesterday > MA2_Yesterday Then
       Sell("SHen", 1, 0, Market, Day)
     End If
   End If
End If
End Sub
```

As you can see, these three different scripts are a lot easier to understand than the C code. They are more condensed than the English version and it looks a lot like the definition and formula version. The EasyLanguage script sets the value for the variable "MA1_Period" as the number 10 and for "MA2_Period" as 30. It further sets "MA1_Today" as a simple moving average of length 10 for the current day [that is, *average(close,MA1_Period)*], and so on for other values of the moving average on close prices.

The *buy* condition is set in what is called an "i" statement. An if statement is a way of setting a condition, that is, "if this is true, then do this; if it is false, then do something else." When these conditions are met—in this case when the MA1 crosses over MA2—an order is set to buy and reverse the current short position with the open of the next bar. The sell condition is also set in a different "if" statement. When its conditions are met, an order is set to sell and reverse the current long position with an order placed at the open of the next bar.

These scripts will do the exact same thing as the C code with a lot less effort and in a lot less time because of all the built-in features that are included in these different trading strategy development applications.

A comparison of these three different script versions of the moving average trading strategy reveals two main things. First, they all accomplish the same thing, but each in their own way. Second, they are, in essence, programming languages and they each have their strong points, weak points, and idiosyncrasies.

As we indicated in Chapter 4: The Strategy Development Platform, it is essential to the success of any trading strategy development process that the strategist choose that application that has the features required and the ease of use desired.

Even if the application has the needed capabilities, however, it is up to the strategist to be certain that the trading strategy has been correctly specified and programmed in the scripting language of choice.

CHAPTER 8

Preliminary Testing

W e have now completed the first stages of strategy development—its conceptualization, design, specification, and scripting in a testable form. Now, all of this work must be verified. In other words, we must now confirm that all of this code works correctly and as intended and that it is consistent with your trading strategy.

The second stage of the strategy development process is the preliminary testing of the trading model. This round of testing accomplishes five things. The first three are more concerned with scripting issues. The last two provide preliminary insight into performance.

Preliminary testing will:

1. Verify that all of the formulae and rules are calculated correctly
2. Determine whether the formulae, rules, and their combinations behave as designed
3. Confirm that the trading strategy is performing consistently with theoretical expectations
4. Provide a preliminary estimate of profitability
5. Give preliminary insight to its robustness

Robustness is an important concept in trading strategy development. In ordinary usage the term carries the connotation contained in its formal definition. The same sense applies to a robust trading strategy.

The *New Oxford American Dictionary* provides the following definition of *robust* for processes, particularly economic ones: "Able to withstand or overcome adverse conditions."

This is particularly apropos when applied to the concept of a robust trading strategy. For the robust trading strategy is that which is most likely to continue producing strong profit even under changing and difficult market trends and conditions. In other words, a robust trading strategy is tough and long lasting.

The four main features of a robust trading strategy are that it is profitable over:

1. A broad range of contiguous parameter sets
2. A wide-ranging basket of diverse markets
3. A wide range of market types and conditions
4. Long and short trades

As in so many things related to trading, of course, there are many degrees of robustness. We always seek the most robust strategy possible. And we do so because a robust strategy is our best insurance of positive outcome in the highly uncertain world of trading. As defined, it is easy to see that the robust strategy is one that will continue to perform profitably when markets change. And since markets are in a relatively constant state of flux to some degree or another, the more robust the strategy, the greater the chances of lasting profit.

Larry Hite, a money manager profiled in *Market Wizards*, by Jack Schwager, said, "We are not looking for the optimum method; we are looking for the hardiest method."

Replace *hardiest* with *robust* and we see the importance this accomplished trader places on this aspect of a trading strategy. A trading model that makes money only in the T-bond market during a high volatility, roaring bull market and is profitable only over a small parameter set is a trading model that is not too likely to survive long term, trading a broad basket of markets with multiple trends and varying degrees of volatility.

I discuss different aspects of the robustness of a trading strategy in Chapters 8, 10, 11, 12, and 13.

VERIFICATION OF CALCULATIONS AND TRADES

To verify the design of a trading system, its calculations and trades must be individually verified. Even the most experienced and proficient programmers and trading strategy designers must perform this crucial stage of testing.

To determine the accuracy of the scripted implementation of the trading strategy, it is usually sufficient to create one historical simulation on a sample of historical price data. The historical sample must be large enough so that every formula and rule of the trading model produces at least a handful of buy-and-sell signals. Use values for the model that are reasonable on the basis of theory or experience; these values don't really matter much, however, as long as they yield an acceptable sample of trades. To ensure the accuracy of the calculations and the coding of the trading rules, the trading signals are hand checked on a significant sample of signals on a bar-by-bar basis.

With simpler strategies, this is often a relatively quick and painless process. The trading signals are inspected on a chart, a trade listing, or in some other type of report. This type of reporting is quite variable from platform to platform.

If the system is more complex, it will require a more time-consuming examination of the different signals, indicators, orders, and so on. This requires more skill and patience on the part of the developer. This level of validation typically requires the design and creation of some type of custom reporting or formatted print statements for a review of this information at the appropriate level of detail (see Figure 8.1).

Calculations

A detailed review of all of the variables, rules, entry, and exit orders must prove that the trades are being generated correctly by the strategy's formulae and rules. The only way that this can be accomplished is to compare hand calculations or calculations done with a spreadsheet with those generated by the trading strategy application. It is usually sufficient to spot check these calculations. The spot check should include at least a few instances of each possible calculation. In Table 8.1, the values for a 5-day moving average are presented along with the daily closes.

There is generally no reason to check the calculations produced by the functions and indicators supplied by the scripting language of the trading strategy application. It is just part of good scripting, however, to verify the results of any formulae that are created by the trading strategist.

Trading Rules

It is also an essential part of good scripting to verify that the trading rules are behaving as intended, designed, and scripted. As the complexity of the trading strategy rises, so rises the time and effort necessary to validate their performance. This becomes considerably more intricate as a function of the complexity of the trading strategy decision tree branching.

Consider a simple moving average trading strategy consisting of two moving averages and a two-day time filter. The two-day time filter requires the signal to be true for the length of time set by the filter. In this example, the moving average crossover must remain intact for two days. The model buys at the open of the third day when MA1 (a three-day close moving

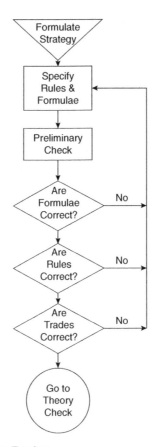

FIGURE 8.1 Preliminary Testing

TABLE 8.1 Moving Average Values

Daily Closes	5-Day Moving Average
Close = 62.11	5-Day MA = 62.5880
Close = 61.45	5-Day MA = 62.3419
Close = 61.50	5-Day MA = 62.0900
Close = 61.63	5-Day MA = 61.8759
Close = 62.37	5-Day MA = 61.8120
Close = 61.72	5-Day MA = 61.7340
Close = 61.85	5-Day MA = 61.8139
Close = 61.12	5-Day MA = 61.7379
Close = 62.89	5-Day MA = 61.9899
Close = 62.89	5-Day MA = 62.0940

average) crosses over and remains over MA2 (a 12-day midpoint moving average) for two days. Conversely, the model sells at the open of the third day when MA1 has remained lower than MA2 for two days.

If MA1 and MA2 are calculated by a built-in average function, it is assumed they are correct. It should be verified that they are calculated on the desired price fields and at the correct length. Since these are scripted by the strategist, however, it is more important to validate the buy and sell signals. It must be verified that the buy entries occur at the opening price on the correct day and after the MA1 has been over MA2 for two days. The reverse conditions must be verified as being the cause of a sell entry.

A trade list report is a spreadsheet-like report with the date, price, typically the signal name (usually), and profit or loss by trade and cumulatively for every buy and sell. The trade list and a chart marked with buy and sell signals is the perfect tool to perform this diagnosis. It is also helpful to have available any indicators or other calculations relevant to the trading strategy that can be plotted on a chart. This will enable the strategist to ascertain that the model is buying and selling when it should and at the correct price levels. This larger, more macroscopic review of trading performance will reveal any other anomalies that may have eluded the more microscopic hand check of a small sample of buy and sell signals. Figure 8.2 shows a chart of S&P with a plot of buy and sell signals for XT06ct.

Table 8.2 shows the Trade List of S&P signals for XT06ct that correspond to the signals plotted in Figure 8.2.

FIGURE 8.2   S&P Chart

TABLE 8.2 Trade List of S&P

Trade Number	Date	Time	Type	Cnts	Price	Signal Name	Entry P/L	Cumulative
1191	7/27/2004		Buy	10	1119.50	LOen		
	8/3/2004		LExit	10	1124.40	LOex	10,250.00	2212150.00
1192	8/5/2004		Sell	10	1116.80	SHen		
	8/6/2004		SExit	2	1097.30	SHpt1	9350.00	2221500.00
	8/6/2004		SExit	2	1097.30	SHpt2	9350.00	2230850.00
	8/6/2004		SExit	2	1087.90	SHpt3	14050.00	2244900.00
	8/10/2004		SExit	4	1103.00	SHex	13000.00	2257900.00
1196	8/16/2004		Buy	10	1097.70	LOen		
	8/17/2004		LExit	2	1108.30	LOpt1	4900.00	2262800.00
	8/17/2004		LExit	2	1109.90	LOpt2	5700.00	2268500.00
	8/18/2004		LExit	2	1117.40	LOpt3	9450.00	2277950.00
	8/25/2004		LExit	2	1129.50	LOpt4	15500.00	2293450.00
	8/30/2004		LExit	2	1129.80	LOex	15650.00	2309100.00
1201	8/31/2004		Sell	10	1121.40	SHen		
	9/1/2004		SExit	2	1130.00	SHps1	(4700.00)	2304400.00
	9/1/2004		SExit	8	1130.20	SHrs1	(19200.00)	2285200.00
1203	9/15/2004		Sell	10	1151.90	SHen		
	9/17/2004		SExit	2	1157.30	SHps1	(3100.00)	2282100.00
	9/22/2004		SExit	2	1145.00	SHpt1	3050.00	2285150.00
	9/22/2004		SExit	2	1140.80	SHpt2	5150.00	2290300.00
	9/23/2004		SExit	2	1133.90	SHpt3	8600.00	2298900.00
	9/24/2004		SExit	2	1139.80	SHex	5650.00	2304550.00

	Date	Type	Qty	Price	Signal		
1208	9/28/2004	Buy	10	1138.70	LOen		2310000.00
	10/1/2004	LExit	2	1150.40	LOpt1	5450.00	2319100.00
	10/1/2004	LExit	2	1157.70	LOpt2	9100.00	2334050.00
	10/6/2004	LExit	2	1169.40	LOpt3	14950.00	2354450.00
	10/7/2004	LExit	4	1159.90	LOex	20400.00	
1212	10/8/2004	Sell	10	1149.00	SHen		2360950.00
	10/14/2004	SExit	2	1135.20	SHpt1	6500.00	2379350.00
	10/15/2004	SExit	8	1139.00	SHex	18400.00	
1214	10/26/2004	Buy	10	1128.70	LOen		2384800.00
	10/27/2004	LExit	2	1140.40	LOpt1	5450.00	2393850.00
	10/27/2004	LExit	2	1147.60	LOpt2	9050.00	2408750.00
	11/1/2004	LExit	2	1159.30	LOpt3	14900.00	2433000.00
	11/4/2004	LExit	2	1178.00	LOpt4	24250.00	2471350.00
	11/16/2004	LExit	2	1206.20	LOex	38350.00	
1219	11/19/2004	Sell	10	1205.30	SHen		2475750.00
	11/22/2004	SExit	2	1195.70	SHpt1	4400.00	2477550.00
	11/22/2004	SExit	8	1203.60	SHex	1800.00	

Correct any inaccurate calculations. Modify any incorrect trading rules. Repeat this round of testing with these new formulae and trading rules and continue this check and adjustment process until all calculations and rules are working as intended. When it has been determined that all formulae and trading rules are functioning perfectly, it is safe to proceed to the next round of testing.

In Summary

At the conclusion of this round of testing, we know two things about our trading strategy: The formulae are producing accurate results and the trading rules are entering and exiting the markets correctly and as intended.

THEORETICAL EXPECTATIONS

The performance of the trading model must now be evaluated in light of its theoretical expectations (see Figure 8.3). We must now determine whether the results of preliminary testing are in line with the theoretical foundation of the trading strategy.

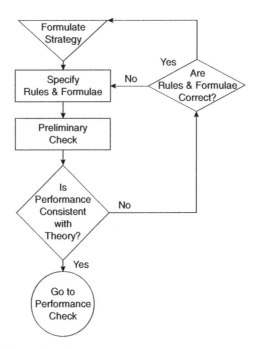

FIGURE 8.3 Theory Check

What do we mean by this? This means that the trading results of this first historical simulation should be in general overall alignment with the assumed behavior of the trading strategy.

Consequently, if we are looking at a long-term and slower-paced trading strategy, we assume that it is not going to be making three trades a week. Rather, it should be making trades at a pace more like once a month. If we are looking at a trend following trading strategy, we would expect to see trades being made in the direction of a longer-term trend and perhaps only after there has been some degree of confirmation of the existence of a trend.

Conversely, assume that the theoretical objective of the trading strategy is to trade swings of intermediate degree (5 to 10 days in length) at a short lag so as to reduce false signals. Such a model should have a few obvious characteristics: a moderate number of trades (two to four a month), limited whipsaws, and moderately large average profits.

We must then determine at this stage whether trading performance roughly conforms to that of its anticipated theoretical trading profile. If we are comfortable that it does, we can proceed with the next round of testing. Keep in mind that this is preliminary testing and that this evaluation is just a rough estimation.

If trading performance deviates dramatically from its theoretical profile the cause must be determined. Was the trading theory wrong? If this is the case, does the unusual profitability of this mutated trading system warrant further evaluation as an entirely different, unanticipated trading strategy?

When doing trading strategy research, keep in mind that the history of science includes many significant discoveries that were the results of mistakes or of other unforeseen branches in the research process. Trading strategy research done correctly is a form of scientific research and consequently subject to all of the same caveats.

If the performance of this unexpected trading strategy is attractive, if the theory is sound, if the scripting is error-free, then it makes sense to explore this as an entirely new and unanticipated strategy. The history of science is littered with many such happy accidents. And so is the evaluation of trading strategies.

If the performance is unattractive, however, and its behavior is radically different from theoretical expectations, it may be time to reassess the strategy. Redesign the apparently flawed trading strategy, if possible, keeping theoretical expectations in mind. Repeat the testing process in its entirety.

It is also important when a trading strategy is performing far outside the range of theoretical expectation to rule out unusual market action as the cause.

In this context, it is important to note whether the price history used for this simulation was hostile or unusually adverse to the underlying trading theory. Such price data can be the cause of large deviations between theoretical expectation and simulated results.

For example, was a trend-following system tested on a segment of price data that included an extended period of congestion as well as a large period of nondirectional and highly choppy data? Such data will cause a slower trend-following model to trade far more actively and far less profitably than it would in a more favorable trending period.

If the price data used in the simulation can be determined to be a likely cause, it might obviate the need for outright rejection or radical restructuring of the trading model. It still can be reason for rejection if the theory suggests different performance in difficult conditions. What is really happening in this case is an examination of the performance of the trading strategy under adverse conditions. If performance adheres to theoretical expectations under these types of conditions, consequently, we can move to the next round of testing.

At this point, we now know three things about our trading strategy and its scripting: all formulae are calculated correctly, all trading rules are performing as designed, and it is behaving consistently with its theoretical expectations.

PRELIMINARY PROFITABILITY

Our next step is to determine some rough estimate of the profitability of the trading strategy (see Figure 8.4). To do this, we first calculate profit and loss on a current piece of price history of reasonable length. This will vary as a function of the style of the trading strategy. A short-term system can be tested on one to two years of data, an intermediate-term on two to four years, and a long-term on four to eight years. These are general guidelines, of course, and there can be quite a bit of variance in these window lengths depending on the strategy, the market, and the conditions.

This test will provide a preliminary estimate of profit and risk. A general rule is to expect an annual profit equal to the margin required to trade the market. Risk should not exceed annual profit. Because of its very limited scope, however, it would not be a good idea to ascribe tremendous significance to profit performance at this early stage.

The main purpose of this test is to arrive at a rough idea of performance. Since it is likely that this strategy evolved from thinking about current market conditions and that the strategist will be testing this on a market for which it was designed, it is not unreasonable to expect that its

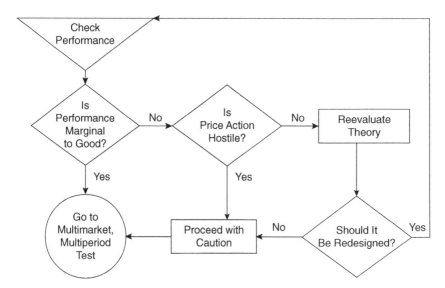

FIGURE 8.4 Performance Check

performance at this stage should be reasonable. In other words, performance should be either mildly profitable or at least not horribly unprofitable. Table 8.3 shows the moving average strategy on S&P with acceptable performance.

Performance is deemed acceptable if it yields a marginal gain or loss. Marginal performance depicts returns that are at or modestly below preliminary expectations. If this test yields a very high profit and accuracy with a very low risk, this of course, is very promising, especially if its performance profile conforms closely to theoretical expectations. In both of these cases, this test would be considered a success.

Performance yielding an unusually high loss, however, should be viewed as a preliminary warning sign. Table 8.4 shows the moving average strategy on pork bellies, with questionable performance. As discussed earlier, this can occur because of very hostile market conditions. If this is determined to be the case, go on to the next round of testing.

If this large loss occurs under market conditions that are not terribly unusual, or even worse, ideal for the trading model, it might be worth considering that this strategy should be abandoned. This suggests that the theory clearly has problems.

For example, a moving average model that loses money in a strongly trending market is a poor model. The only reason to not completely abandon the model at this stage is due to the narrow range of the scope of this test. If there is reason to believe this is an anomaly, go on to the next round

TABLE 8.3 Moving Average Strategy

TradeStation Strategy Performance Report—Mov Avg Crossover SP 67/99—Daily

Performance Summary: All Trades

Total net profit	$19,750.00	Open position P/L	$0.00
Gross profit	$91,550.00	Gross loss	($71,800.00)
Total number of trades	33	Percent profitable	30.30%
Number winning trades	10	Number losing trades	23
Largest winning trade	$17,050.00	Largest losing trade	($6,450.00)
Average winning trade	$9,155.00	Average losing trade	($3,121.74)
Ratio average win/ average loss	2.93	Average trade (win & loss)	$598.48
Max consecutive winners	2	Max consecutive losers	8
Average number bars in winners	17	Average number bars in losers	5
Maximum intraday drawdown	($26,325.00)		
Profit factor	1.28	Maximum number contracts held	1
Account size required	$26,325.00	Return on account	75.02%

TABLE 8.4 Moving Average Strategy on Pork Bellies

TradeStation Strategy Performance Report—Mov Avg Crossover PB 67/99—Daily

Performance Summary: All Trades

Total net profit	($5,804.00)	Open position P/L	$0.00
Gross profit	$11,556.00	Gross loss	($17,360.00)
Total number of trades	32	Percent profitable	28.13%
Number winning trades	9	Number losing trades	23
Largest winning trade	$3,580.00	Largest losing trade	($1,712.00)
Average winning trade	$1,284.00	Average losing trade	($754.78)
Ratio average win/ average loss	1.70	Average trade (win & loss)	($181.38)
Max consecutive winners	3	Max consecutive losers	13
Average number bars in winners	12	Average number bars in losers	5
Maximum intraday drawdown	($13,392.00)		
Profit factor	.67	Maximum number contracts held	1
Account size required	$13,392.00	Return on account	−43.34%

of testing. If there is not, however, it may be wise to abandon this trading strategy or at least return to the design stages for a possible redesign.

Regardless of whether or not the strategy produces extraordinary profits or gut-wrenching losses it would be premature to assume that this is telling us a great deal. In any case, the strategist should take this strategy to the next round of testing unless there is some very strong reason to believe that these results are more broadly predictive.

THE MULTIMARKET AND MULTIPERIOD TEST

This multimarket and multiperiod test is an expansion of the preliminary performance check in the dimensions of markets and history (see Figure 8.5). A batch of historical simulations is produced. These historical simulations comprise a selected set model of parameters for the trading strategy applied to a small basket of diversified markets over a number of different historical periods.

The purpose of this test is to obtain a quick and preliminary idea of model robustness and a broader view of trading. It is a relatively tough test for a trading strategy and it can be accomplished quickly and with little effort.

Whereas this round of testing is neither exhaustive nor conclusive, it can provide valuable insight into the potential merit of the trading strategy. A trading strategy that does extremely well is certainly likely to do better in the later stages of development. This is grounds for cautious optimism.

Conversely, a trading strategy that does extremely poorly across the board is quite likely one that should be abandoned. In the middle, where most strategies will fall, we find unfilled potential. A strategy that falls into this category is certainly one that warrants further research and examination.

A test of the trading strategy on a basket of markets assumes that the strategy is intended to trade on many different markets. There are valid trading models, of course, that are intended to work on specific markets or on markets for a particular market sector, such as the stock index futures. If this is the case, the multiperiod test should be done, but the multimarket test on a diversified market basket can be skipped.

Selecting the Basket

If the trading strategy is designed to trade a basket of markets, it is best to select a basket of highly diversified markets. At this stage, we are seeking a relatively quick and easy validation of the trading strategy. It is

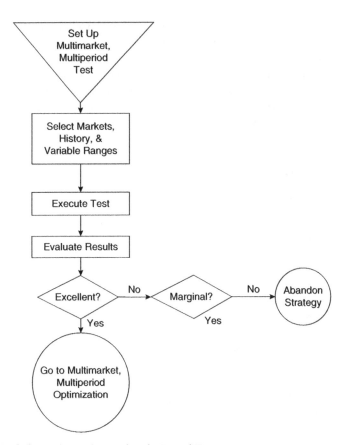

FIGURE 8.5 Multi-Market and Multi-Period Test

consequently sufficient to select a smaller market basket. It certainly can and should be more limited than the full portfolio to which the proven trading strategy will ultimately be tested. This round of testing is more like a quick performance sketch.

Given that this testing basket will be of limited scope by design, it is that much more important to seek the greatest possible market diversification. Obviously, selecting the S&P, the Russell Index, and the NASDAQ offers little overall diversity. A selection of General Motors, Ford, and Mercedes Benz would be rejected for the same reason. Alternatively, a minibasket of S&P, yen, T-bonds, crude oil, and coffee offers nice futures diversification. A minibasket of Microsoft, Home Depot, United Airlines, Ford, and Citigroup offers nice big cap equities diversification.

There are two main criteria that provide a measure of the degree of difference between markets. They are statistical correlation and fundamental diversity (which should be supported by a lack of correlation.) A calculation of the correlation coefficient between the closing prices of two markets will measure the degree of similarity between them. If the correlation coefficient is +1, they are perfectly correlated and one should be rejected. If their coefficient correlation is negative (–1 is a perfect inverse correlation), they are inversely correlated and both can and should be included. A correlation coefficient between –0.5 and +0.5 suggests little correlation, and such markets can also be included.

Given that the number of markets in this basket should be in the range of 5 to 10, however, performing a correlation matrix analysis is generally unnecessary.

Knowledge of the fundamentals of the markets composing this test basket is easier and generally sufficient. Coffee, cattle, and the stock market are governed by different fundamental conditions. As such, they would be excellent candidates for the same minibasket.

A good futures test basket could include coffee, cotton, crude oil, gold, pork bellies, soybeans, the S&P 500, sugar, yen, and T-bonds. A smaller test basket might include coffee, cotton, crude oil, the S&P 500, and T-bonds.

Determining the Length of the Test Period

The next step is to determine the optimum number of years of price history per market on which to test the trading model. Generally, the more price history used, the better are the test results. Ten years of history for each market creates a solid test. As a rule of thumb, five years (daily data) is the minimum. It is highly preferable that the period of price history to be used include at least one of each major market types: bull, bear, and sideways.

Obviously, the first question that must be answered is whether there are enough data available for the size test window that has been chosen. With the growth of futures trading in the last 10 years, there are a large number of relatively newer markets with limited price history. For example, Dow futures began trading in 1997, providing only 10 years of history. Most agricultural futures have price data back to the 1970s and the 1980s, which are sufficient for most purposes. The S&P 500 futures have the longest history of the stock index markets, and it began trading in 1982. Many financial futures only began trading in the mid 1980s. Many newer markets began trading in the 1990s, and this can present testing problems.

The availability of price history is a factor in all rounds of testing. Given the limited size of our test basket, however, there should be no problem selecting enough markets with sufficient price history to proceed.

Segmenting the Data

Another question that must be answered is whether to test the strategy on one piece or in a set of smaller pieces. Testing the strategy on one segment of price history would seem to be the most statistically sound. This is true in that this is more likely to create a statistically significant sample of trades. This approach, however, can mask some very significant information. It is extremely important that a trading strategy perform with some degree of consistency from one historical period to another.

A trading strategy simulation that produces a profit of $100,000 in a 10-year period may look very impressive at first glance. What if this profit, however, is all produced in one or two very good years and the other eight years it loses or performs marginally? Does it still look as good? It does not, of course, in view of this information.

Consequently, for the purposes of this round of testing, it is better to test the entire historical period divided into a number of equal, smaller intervals. For example, a 10-year test divided into five two-year segments is good. If the trading model is longer-term, however, and generates a statistically invalid sample in two-year intervals, it may prove necessary to use three- or four-year data segments. It also may prove necessary to use a longer overall test period to provide a sufficient number of data segments. This is discussed in more detail in Chapter 10: Optimization.

The Test

To proceed then, we must select a basket of markets, the length of our history look back "window," and the number of historical segments on which to conduct our test. Our test basket will consist of coffee, cotton, crude oil, the S&P 500 and T-bonds. This basket provides excellent fundamental diversification. The length of our testing period will be 10 years from 1997 to 2006. This period of history includes a significant selection of different market types and conditions. This 10-year test period will be divided into five two-year periods for each market. Five segments each of two-year length provide us with enough of a breakdown to supply some degree of statistical reliability.

Now that we have a basket, a historical period, and segments, we can create our test. The same reasonable value parameter set used in the first test is also used for this round of testing. A historical simulation with these same strategy parameters is produced for the five time periods for each of the five markets in the basket. Performance for each time and for each market is recorded and organized into a report.

This report will provide an overview of the profit and risk of the trading strategy. What should be expected at this stage of testing?

It should not be expected that an optimizable trading strategy will produce peak performance for all of the markets in our test basket and for all of the time periods in our history with only one reasonable set of strategy parameters. If, in fact, this test does produce exceptional performance overall, this is an extremely promising sign. We should expect that a robust and sound strategy will perform moderately well under such a test. A strategy that performs poorly overall at this point should be rejected.

A fairly even mix of small profits and small losses randomly distributed throughout the market basket and the different time segments would be considered marginal or acceptable performance at this stage. It is not grounds for celebration, nor is it grounds for rejection.

It also suggests that the strategy has components that depend on an adaptation to particular market conditions to achieve optimal performance. This would be indicated by a strategy that shows good performance in historical periods with conditions that are favorable to it and by losses in historical periods with conditions that are adverse to it. Such a strategy is worth further examination.

This type of testing profile, however, might be suggestive of a different interpretation. If there is no pattern between positive performance and favorable conditions and negative performance and adverse conditions, it is possible that this is a poor strategy. Such a strategy should probably be rejected at this point. If there is some plausible reason for this type of behavior, however, it might be worth taking the strategy to the next round of testing. But if performance shows large losses throughout the basket and history, even if there is an occasional strong showing, the trading strategy is poor and should be abandoned at this point.

Conversely, trading strategy performance with exceptional profit and low risk throughout the basket and history is extremely promising. For this shows not only good performance, but a relatively high degree of robustness. Such excellent early results are grounds for optimism. Further testing is required, of course.

Let us examine a sample multimarket and multiperiod test. We will use the simple moving average crossover system and test it on the following markets and price data segments (see Table 8.5).

TABLE 8.5 Markets and Historical Periods for Multimarket & Multiperiod Test

From To	1/1/1997 12/31/1998	1/1/1999 12/31/2000	1/1/2001 12/31/2002	1/1/2003 12/31/2004	1/1/2005 12/31/2006
Coffee	X	X	X	X	X
Crude oil	X	X	X	X	X
S&P	X	X	X	X	X
T-bonds	X	X	X	X	X
Yen	X	X	X	X	X

TABLE 8.6 Round One Test of MA Trading System with Questionable Results

MA 5x20 R1Test

From 1/1/1990	To 12/31/2006	CL	JY	KC	SP	TQ	Total	Average	Max	Min
1/1/1997	12/31/1998	(10,080.00)	8,775.00	6,350.00	(16,600.00)	2,481.25	(9,073.75)	(1,814.75)	8,775.00	(16,600.00)
1/1/1999	12/31/2000	(2,320.00)	7,875.00	5,706.25	88,350.00	(14,737.50)	84,873.75	16,974.75	88,350.00	(14,737.50)
1/1/2001	12/31/2002	(2,440.00)	(12.50)	(12,762.50)	(57,175.00)	(8,543.75)	(80,933.75)	(16,186.75)	(12.50)	(57,175.00)
1/1/2003	12/31/2004	(4,090.00)	(9,125.00)	(525.00)	59,150.00	(4,325.00)	41,085.00	8,217.00	59,150.00	(9,125.00)
1/1/2005	12/31/2006	6,300.00	3,075.00	(4,131.25)	29,650.00	(4,543.75)	30,350.00	6,070.00	29,650.00	(4,543.75)
Total		(12,630.00)	10,587.50	(5,362.50)	103,375.00	(29,668.75)	66,301.25			
Average		(2,526.00)	2,117.50	(1,072.50)	20,675.00	(5,933.75)	13,260.25			
Max		6,300.00	(9,125.00)	6,350.00	88,350.00	2,481.25	84,873.75			
Min		(10,080.00)	8,775.00	(12,762.50)	(57,175.00)	(14,737.50)	(80,933.75)			

TABLE 8.7 Round One Test of RSIct Trading System with Typical to Good Results

RSIct R1Test
1/1/1990   12/31/2006

From	To	CL	JY	KC	SP	TQ	Total	Average	Max	Min
1/1/1997	12/31/1998	3,110.00	25,650.00	(637.50)	(7,100.00)	20,500.00	**41,522.50**	8,304.50	25,650.00	(7,100.00)
1/1/1999	12/31/2000	80.00	312.50	36,187.50	26,475.00	6,468.75	**69,523.75**	13,904.75	36,187.50	80.00
1/1/2001	12/31/2002	230.00	18,537.50	0.00	37,475.00	6,406.25	**62,648.75**	12,529.75	37,475.00	0.00
1/1/2003	12/31/2004	31,500.00	6,737.50	2,437.50	61,600.00	14,093.75	**116,368.75**	23,273.75	61,600.00	2,437.50
1/1/2005	12/31/2006	0.00	(412.50)	(5,906.25)	48,900.00	843.75	**43,425.00**	8,685.00	48,900.00	(5,906.25)
Total		**34,920.00**	**50,825.00**	**32,081.25**	**167,350.00**	**48,312.50**	***333,488.75***			
Average		6,984.00	10,165.00	6,416.25	33,470.00	9,662.50	66,697.75			
Max		31,500.00	(412.50)	36,187.50	61,600.00	20,500.00	116,368.75			
Min		0.00	25,650.00	(5,906.25)	(7,100.00)	843.75	41,522.50			

TABLE 8.8 Round One Test of XTct Trading System with Excellent Results

XTct R1Test

From 1/1/1990	To 12/31/2006	CL	JY	KC	SP	TQ	Total	Average	Max	Min
1/1/1997	12/31/1998	9,200.00	32,437.50	95,325.00	154,775.00	23,062.90	**314,800.40**	62,960.08	154,775.00	9,200.00
1/1/1999	12/31/2000	3,810.00	(8,637.50)	48,956.25	185,450.00	1,500.10	**231,078.85**	46,215.77	185,450.00	(8,637.50)
1/1/2001	12/31/2002	19,160.00	7,462.50	11,287.50	129,825.00	27,437.30	**195,172.30**	39,034.46	129,825.00	7,462.50
1/1/2003	12/31/2004	27,240.00	3,125.00	10,781.25	(9,850.00)	23,406.05	**54,702.30**	10,940.46	27,240.00	(9,850.00)
1/1/2005	12/31/2006	14,690.00	11,925.00	25,406.25	9,850.00	8,062.60	**69,933.85**	13,986.77	25,406.25	8,062.60
Total		**74,100.00**	**46,312.50**	**191,756.25**	**470,050.00**	**83,468.95**	**865,687.70**			
Average		14,820.00	9,262.50	38,351.25	94,010.00	16,693.79	173,137.54			
Max		27,240.00	(8,637.50)	95,325.00	185,450.00	27,437.30	314,800.40			
Min		3,810.00	32,437.50	10,781.25	(9,850.00)	1,500.10	54,702.30			

This test batch consists of: 25 different tests, on 5 different markets over a 10-year time span divided into two-year data segments. The moving average strategy will be simulated with parameters of 5 and 20 days.

The Results of the Test

The results of the 25 different tests are summarized in Tables 8.6, 8.7, and 8.8.

As stated earlier, the main objective of this test is to determine whether the trading strategy is worthy of further development. A trading strategy that produces exceptional results at this stage of testing is certainly one worthy of further development without reservation. Conversely, a trading strategy that produces deplorable results is likely to not be worthy of further development. There are exceptions to this, however, and this is preliminary testing. If the strategist has reasons to think it may improve with further development, then proceed. If not, conclude research on this strategy. Last, if the results are average, further development is also warranted.

CHAPTER 9

Search and Judgment

T he next stage in the evaluation of a trading strategy is optimization, which is presented in the next chapter. Before we can proceed with a presentation of these methods, however, we need to explore a little understood but extremely important aspect of this process: the search of the optimization space.

To fully understand the most effective way optimization can be applied to a particular trading strategy, we need to understand the contours of this seemingly innocuous area. And before we can fully understand how we can arrive at those trading strategy parameters that are most likely going to produce real-time and lasting trading profits, we need to understand the all-important impact of what has typically been known as the *optimization criterion*. In optimization theory this is also known as the *fitness function*, *objective function*, *search criteria*, and *search function*. In conformity with contemporary usage, we will use the term *objective function* as synonyms for all of these other terms.

To elaborate, the *optimization space* is simply the set of all possible strategy parameters, or *candidates*, for which a historical simulation can be created. An optimization must be performed on multiple pairs of different moving average lengths to determine the most profitable combination of moving averages for our moving average example. To do this, for example, an optimization is set to scan, or create, a simulation for every combination of moving average lengths for MA1 from 2 to 10 at steps of 1 and for MA2 from 20 to 40 at steps of 2. This optimization will create a total of 99 different combinations of the two moving average lengths. This is all explained in more detail later in this chapter.

After all of these historical simulations have been created, however, the best parameter combination must still be selected. The *objective function* is the principle used during the optimization process in making this selection.

The objective function can be simple or complex. Regardless of complexity, however, the objective function is that algorithm that the optimization process employs to rank and to ultimately select the best combination of parameters for the trading strategy. The search function, then, is judge and jury for the trading strategy.

For example, if net profit is our objective function (which by the way, is not recommended, but since it is widely used and understood, it is helpful as an example), then that strategy parameter pair that produced the largest net profit will be selected as best.

Understanding the impact of the search method and of the objective function are more esoteric and less understood dimensions of the testing and optimization process. They appear dry and mundane. Yet their impact on testing and on the understanding of the results is extremely significant.

It is important to keep in mind that the field and literature of optimization theory is extensive and rapidly growing. The current state of the optimization art in contemporary trading strategy development applications is, to a large degree, actually quite primitive when contrasted to recent developments in optimization theory. Most applications still use brute force grid search methods coupled with outdated and inefficient search functions such as net profit.

There are add-ins that provide some advanced functionality in this area such as genetic optimization and Walk-Forward Analysis;[1] there is promise of more to come.

It is important, however, that the strategist understand that these resources exist and can be brought to bear on a development project. It is also important to understand that these various advanced search procedures can and should replace these standard grid search methods, which are currently so prevalent and that these advanced search methods also have an application in Walk-Forward Analysis.

SEARCH METHODS

All optimization processes use some type of search method, be it simple or highly sophisticated. The search method will determine the number of tests to be performed and therefore the amount of processing time required to complete the process. It will also determine how we will go about searching for those solutions with the highest performance. In some of the more sophisticated search methods, such as a genetic optimization algorithm, the search function(s) are tightly tied in with the process itself. They guide which of the many combinations of parameters are actually examined in situations where there are too many candidates to be able to examine them all.

Ultimately then, a search method is a way of progressing in an orderly manner through the different combinations of parameters and then selecting the best set of strategy parameters as defined by the objective function.

In other words, in any optimization, a series of tests are done on historical price data. There may not be time to examine every possible combination of parameters, and so intelligence on the part of the search method is used to guide the search in productive directions. This is one of the reasons why there are different methods of searching the *optimization space*.

An individual *test* is one trading simulation on one piece of historical data with one set of strategy parameters. A *trading simulation* calculates all of the trades using the strategy variables and produces a number of performance statistics, including the strategy's fitness as defined by the objective function. An *optimization* or test run is a batch or set of tests. A successful result of such a process is a set of models that meet minimum performance criteria such as "net profit is greater than zero" or "maximum drawdown is less than 20 percent." An unsuccessful test run may result in no models that satisfy minimum performance criteria.

There is an extensive literature on the subject of optimization. Extremely sophisticated optimization methods with colorful names such as *simulated annealing*, *hill climbing*, and *particle swarm* have been created in this very specialized knowledge domain.

It is once again, however, a somewhat sad commentary that this wealth of knowledge in the optimization domain has not been tapped (except by those very sophisticated quants who keep racking up profits) in the common strategy development applications. Many of these more sophisticated approaches to optimization, of course, would have little real use in simple optimization problems like our moving average example. More advanced search methods, however, will provide increasing utility as the complexity and scope of the optimization process rises.

The Grid Search

This is the simplest form of search method. It is considered a brute force method in that it simply calculates and then ranks every historical simulation specified by the optimization process.

Consider a test of a two moving average crossover trading strategy on S&P futures from 01/01/1995 through 12/31/2005. The first moving average

(MA1) will be tested over a range of values from 3 days in length to 15 days in length at steps of 2 days. In the parlance, the moving average will be scanned from 3 to 15 by 2.

Seven different values will be tested for Moving Average 1: 3, 5, 7, 9, 11, 13, 15.

The second moving average (MA2) will be tested from 10 to 100 in steps of 10. Ten different values will be tested for Moving Average 2: 10, 20, 30, 40, 50, 60, 70, 80, 90, 100.

The entire test run will consist of 70 possible combinations of these two scan ranges (7 × 10 = 70). The test run is conducted as follows. Each potential value for MA1 is tested with the first potential value for MA2 as follows:

MA1:	3	5	7	9	11	13	15
MA2:	10	10	10	10	10	10	10

After this test cycle is completed, the test procedure advances, that is, it goes to the second potential value for MA2. Each possible value of MA1 is then tested with this second possible value for MA2. In other words:

MA1:	3	5	7	9	11	13	15
MA2:	20	20	20	20	20	20	20

This process is continued until each potential value of MA1 is tested with the last potential value for MA2. The final tests are:

MA1:	3	5	7	9	11	13	15
MA2:	100	100	100	100	100	100	100

A historical simulation of trading performance is created for each of these variable pairs of MA1 and MA2. The trading performance for each of these parameter sets is measured and ranked by the objective function. The top strategy—those parameter values that best meet the evaluation criteria—is picked. The illustration in Figure 9.1 depicts the search of this variable grid space. The intersection of each line in the grids in the illustrations to follow represents a pair of parameters to be examined during the optimization process.

The search method described here is known as a *grid search*. The two variable ranges define a grid of variable combinations. Performance at each combination is evaluated. In other words, the entire grid is searched. This is

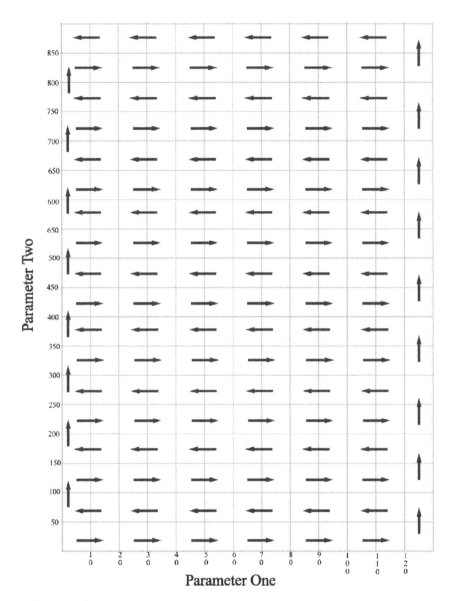

FIGURE 9.1 A Grid Search

the most common type of search method. The advantage of the grid search is its thoroughness. If every possible parameter combination is evaluated, it is impossible to miss the best one—that is, unless the search method or objective function is unsound. This is discussed in the next section.

The drawback of the grid search is its speed, or shall we say, its lack thereof. In small tests such as the previous example, processing time is insignificant. Assuming even a slow speed of one second per test, a grid search of 70 parameter candidates would take only 70 seconds.

Consider, however, what happens with a 4-variable test. Assume a test of two different moving averages (MA1 and MA2) and two volatility bands (VB1 and VB2), one around each moving average.

A reasonable optimization of these parameters would include the following four scan ranges:

MA1:	1 to 15	at steps of 2 = 8 steps
MA2:	5 to 100	at steps of 5 = 20 steps
VB1:	25 to 525	at steps of 25 = 21 steps
VB2:	25 to 525	at steps of 25 = 21 steps

To determine the total number of candidates (potential parameter sets), we multiply the number of steps by each other. This calculation tells us that this test run will have 70,560 ($8 \times 20 \times 21 \times 21 = 70,560$) candidates. At one second per test, this optimization run will take 19.6 [(70,560 tests/60 seconds)/60 minutes = 19.6 hours] hours! That is a long time.

To make matters worse, these variable scans are a bit rough. It would not be entirely unreasonable to scan these four variables in smaller steps such as:

MA1:	1 to 15	at steps of 1 = 15 steps
MA2:	5 to 101	at steps of 2 = 49 steps
VB1:	0 to 500	at steps of 10 = 51 steps
VB2:	0 to 500	at steps of 10 = 51 steps

This defines an optimization run of 1,911,735 ($15 \times 49 \times 51 \times 51 = 1,911,735$) steps. At one second per test, this run will take 531 hours [(1,911,735 tests/60 seconds)/60 minutes = 531 hours]! This is equivalent to 22.13 days (531/24 = 22.13).

This, of course, is entirely impractical and highlights the main drawback of the grid search. Compound this with many markets, different time frames and many strategies, and the strategist will be scrambling for a supercomputer.

Also, once an optimization space exceeds two dimensions (our example here is four dimensions), the examination of the results ranges from difficult to nearly impossible.

To make larger scan ranges and three, four, and more variable tests feasible, therefore, advanced search methods must be used. An advanced search method is an optimization technique (remember our colorfully named examples) that is able to select some of the best variable combinations in a vast optimization space (like our 1,911,735 space) without testing every combination. As processing speed is gained, however, a certain degree of thoroughness is sacrificed. This is where an advanced search method combined with more sophisticated objective functions becomes increasingly important.

The Prioritized Step Search

The *prioritized step search* scans one parameter at a time while holding a selected value constant for each of the other parameter ranges, in order of descending impact on performance. Consider the previous 4-variable optimization space.

MA1:	1 to 15	at steps of 1 = 15 steps
MA2:	5 to 101	at steps of 2 = 49 steps
VB1:	0 to 500	at steps of 10 = 51 steps
VB2:	0 to 500	at steps of 10 = 51 steps

Recall that the time required to perform a grid search on this space was untenable. A prioritized step search of this parameter space is quite manageable, however. At minimum, it will consist of only 166 tests (15 + 49 + 51 + 51 = 166). Because of the iterative nature of this process, it may take a few iterations. Even if it required ten iterations, however, this would still be only 1,666 tests. This is a minimal time requirement, of course.

Let us assume, for example, that variable one is the most impactful parameter. It is scanned first with a constant value for each of the other three parameter ranges. The constants for the other three variables can be chosen at random, or as, for example, the midpoint of the range. The first scan then will be:

MA1:	1	2	3	4	5	...	13	14	15
MA2:	53	53	53	53	53	...	53	53	53
VB1:	250	250	250	250	250	...	250	250	250
VB2:	250	250	250	250	250	...	250	250	250

In the first scan, all of the possible values of MA1 are then evaluated using constant values for MA2 (53,) VB1 (250), and VB2 (250.) Let us assume that this scan produced a value of 5 as best for MA1 with these other parameters.

The next step then will consist of a scan of the second variable, MA2, using constant values for MA1 (5,) VB1 (250) and VB2 (250). MA1 is held constant at 5:

MA1:	5	5	5	5	5	...	5	5	5
MA2:	5	7	9	11	13	...	97	99	101
VB1:	250	250	250	250	250	...	250	250	250
VB2:	250	250	250	250	250	...	250	250	250

This scan will in turn produce an optimal value for MA2. Let us assume that it was 29. The third step will consist of a scan of the third variable, VB1, using constant values for MA1 (5,) MA2 (29,) and VB2 (250). It will look like:

MA1:	5	5	5	5	5	...	5	5	5
MA2:	29	29	29	29	29	...	29	29	29
VB1:	0	10	20	30	40	...	480	490	500
VB2:	250	250	250	250	250	...	250	250	250

This scan will in turn produce an optimal value for VB1. Let us assume that it was 260. The fourth step will consist of a scan of the fourth variable, VB2, using constant values for MA1 (5,) MA2 (29,) and VB1 (260). It will look like:

MA1:	5	5	5	5	5	...	5	5	5
MA2:	29	29	29	29	29	...	29	29	29
VB1:	260	260	260	260	260	...	260	260	260
VB2:	0	10	20	30	40	...	480	490	500

This scan will in turn produce an optimal value for VB2. Let us assume that it was 320. The fourth step will leave us with a value for each of the parameters MA1 = 5, MA2 = 29, VB1 = 260 and VB1 = 320.

If these results seem satisfactory, the process can be ended here. Satisfactory or not, however, it would be prudent to perform a few more iterations.

The second iteration would begin then with MA2 = 29, VB1 = 260, and VB1 = 320; MA1 would be scanned again. This would look as follows:

MA1:	1	2	3	4	5	...	13	14	15
MA2:	29	29	29	29	29	...	29	29	29
VB1:	260	260	260	260	260	...	260	260	260
VB2:	320	320	320	320	320	...	320	320	320

Assume then that a new best value for MA1 of 7 was found. A full second iteration would repeat the same process as mapped out in the first iteration example, but using the newly found best parameters.

It is best to repeat this process a few times or until there is no significant change in performance or parameters.

There are two main benefits to the prioritized step search: speed, and the assessment of the relative impact of each parameter on strategy performance. It is certainly easy to see that even if 20 iterations are required, this is still much quicker than a full grid search on a parameter space this large.

It also allows the strategist to get a more microscopic view of the significance or relative equality of each parameter in the optimization space. The most significant strategy parameter (if there is one) is that parameter the variance of which has the most dramatic impact on performance. Assume that a scan of MA1 produces the following results:

MA1	P&L
1	−$3,000
2	$2,500
3	$5,000
4	$10,000
5	$15,000
6	$12,000
7	$9,000
8	$7,000
...	.
15	−$3,000

In the same test, a scan of VB1 produces the following profits and losses:

MA1	P&L
0	$14,000
10	$14,000
20	$14,000
30	$14,000
40	$13,500
50	$14,500
60	$15,000
70	$13,000
...	.
500	$12,000

Different values of MA1 produced a more pronounced variability performance than did VB1. Different values of VB1 produced little change in profit and loss. The conclusion from these data is that variance in MA1 produces more significant performance change in this strategy than varying VB1.

This tells us two things. It suggests that the volatility bands do not provide a great deal of improvement to the performance of the trading strategy. There may consequently be a strong argument for their elimination. At minimum, it suggests that this parameter really need not be included in the optimization space. Given the small change in trading performance that different values of VB1 produce, there is little reason to perform a more in-depth search.

There are also two drawbacks to the prioritized step search. The lack of thoroughness due to the somewhat limited scope of the prioritized step search can prove to be a large drawback in some cases. This is particularly acute if the step search reveals that each parameter contributes significantly to performance. The lack of exhaustiveness of this approach then can lead to results that fall short of peak performance.

The second drawback is of a more minor sort. Whereas the step search is certainly highly economical in processor time, it is far more demanding on the time and decision-making abilities of the strategist.

Recall, however, how the multimarket and multitime frame test presented in the previous chapter can often allow a strategist to make a quick and somewhat reliable decision about trading strategy performance. In an analogous manner, the direct step search method can produce quick and relatively reliable insight into a multiple dimension optimization space.

Hill Climbing Search Algorithms

This search method is just one of many very fast direct search methods. The main difference in the hill climbing search method compared to the grid search is that it employs what might be called an *enlightened* or *informed* selectivity. A hill climbing search follows a path of increasing performance in the optimization space. It moves through this space with a purpose. Along the way, it rejects performance that is less than the best that has been found so far and allows only better performance and moves in that direction within the optimization space.

The net effect of this enlightened selectivity is the ability of such methods to determine a sound top parameter set while examining only a small proportion of the optimization space.

The benefit, then, of this selectivity of the direct search methods is that they are usually considerably more economical of processor time than brute force methods. This stems from the fact that a direct search method may only examine 5 to 10 percent of the potential candidates compared to the maximum number of combinations calculated in a grid search method. Consider that 10 percent of the 1,911,735 candidate optimization space from our previous example is 191,174, which, while still large, is more attainable.

The hill climbing search can also suffer from a lack of thoroughness. By not examining every strategy candidate, this method runs the risk of misidentifying the best strategy parameters. Also, the enlightened selectivity of any direct search method is provided by its application of the objective function. In a very real sense, the direct search method is only as good as its objective function(s.)

The hill climbing search method also works best when there is continuity in the optimization space. These types of methods can be easily fooled into selecting a local maximum as the global maximum. That is, they can select a top strategy for a particular area of the variable space and stop looking. They may consequently miss the best parameter set in the entire optimization space.

Figure 9.2 is a representation of a hill climbing search in a two-dimensional space with the global maximum circled at the top of the hill.

Multipoint Hill Climbing Search

This is simply the result of doing multiple hill climbing searches, each starting at a different point in the optimization space. There is an added layer in that this type of search needs to select the best strategy parameters from each local hill climbing search. The number of starting points is set by the strategist. The larger the number of starting points, the more comprehensive and the more time consuming the search is.

The multipoint hill climbing search is faster than a grid search and slower than a pure hill climbing search. It is less thorough than a grid search and more thorough than a hill climbing search. It is also less prone to being fooled by local maxima than a hill climbing search.

The multipoint direct search must select a group of different starting points. They can be chosen in a number of ways. One way is to pick them at random in the optimization space.

Figure 9.3 illustrates the start of such an optimization with a selection of five randomly selected starting points represented by stars.

Another way is to divide the variable space into equal sections and then pick the center of each subsection as the entry point. See the illustration that follows. The search then enters the variable space at its first point of entry and finds the best strategy in that area. If the search does not produce a candidate that meets the minimum performance criteria

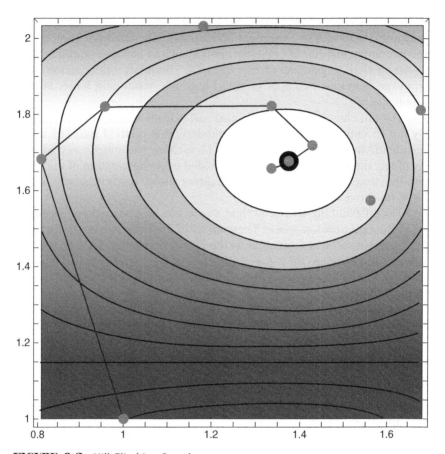

FIGURE 9.2 Hill Climbing Search

after a certain number of predefined steps have been executed, the search of the local region is ended and the search goes on to the next starting point. The top strategy is found and stored. The search then goes on to the next starting point and repeats the local area hill climbing process. If a candidate is found that meets performance criteria, this local top strategy is compared to the top strategy found in previous local area searches. If it is better, it becomes the new top model. If it is not as good, it is rejected. The multipoint direct search continues in this way until all the parameter spaces surrounding each of the predetermined entry points have been explored.

Figure 9.4 illustrates the start of such an optimization with a selection of four evenly spaced starting points, represented by stars, at the center of each quadrant of the optimization space.

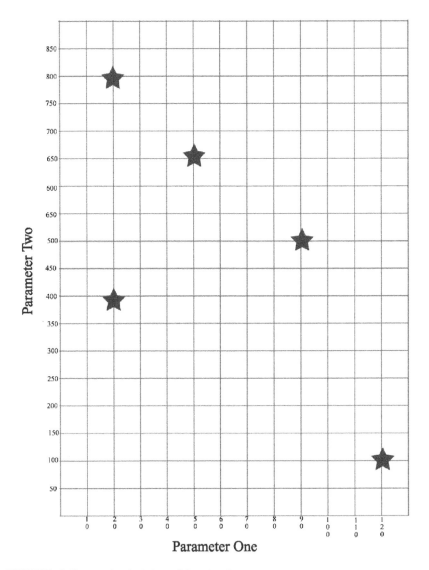

FIGURE 9.3   Randomly Selected Starting Points

ADVANCED SEARCH METHODS

As previously mentioned, there is an extensive literature on advanced search methods. There are many different methods and each have their advantages and disadvantages.

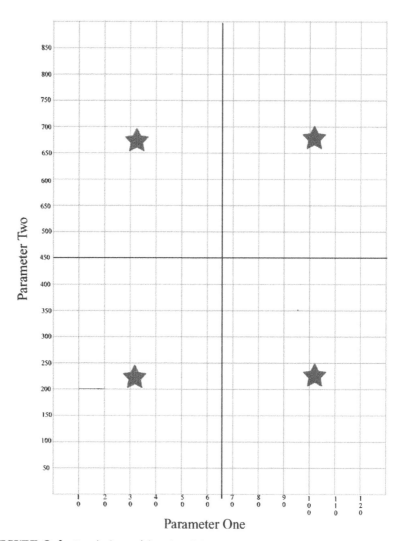

FIGURE 9.4   Evenly Spaced Starting Points

Any strategist, however, who wishes to explore multiple trading strategies of a complex nature with multiple parameters requiring optimization will need to avail himself of these search methods. Without them, the processing time required to research many strategies over a basket of markets and potentially a variety of time frames becomes prohibitive.

It is also important to note, however, that all advanced search methods move through the variable space guided by their objective function.

The use of advanced search methods consequently places a much greater reliance on the quality of the objective function itself.

Simulated Annealing[2]

Simulated annealing is an advanced, directed search method modeled after the cooling of molten metals, which, as their heat slowly escapes, tend to crystallize into patterns that minimize their own internal energy states. In simulated annealing, the search process takes the perspective of an individual parameter set (an *atom*) as it gradually becomes aligned with its ideal position and orientation in the crystal formation.

The simulated annealing (SA) optimization method was first published in the mid 1980s and retains a following for certain applications, although its use has been somewhat eclipsed in some areas by other advanced search methods that are described in the following sections. Because its operation is highly technical, this will be only a general overview. The strategist is recommended to review the literature for more detail.[3] There are strong similarities, however, between the mechanics of simulated annealing works and the hill-climbing search methods just described.

The following, in broad strokes, is how a simulated annealing optimization process works.

First, a parameter set is chosen at random somewhere in the possible optimization space. The objective function specified by the strategist is used to determine how good a solution this parameter set is. The goal of simulated annealing is to minimize the energy state or cost of the strategy. This can be thought of as simply the opposite, or negative, of the objective function as illustrated with the following formula:

Energy State of Parameter Set = −Objective Function of Parameter Set

An initial temperature with a large value is also assigned to the initial parameter set. This represents the concept that the optimization space starts off hot. This initial hot condition will encourage a lot of movement in the optimization space as is seen in the following.

As the annealing process moves the parameter set about in the optimization space, the energy level of the strategy's best spot seen so far is recorded, so that the search process always knows the location and lowest energy level of the best parameter set—the one with the highest objective function value—found up to this point.

Second, a neighbor of the parameter set in the optimization space is again chosen at random. What does it mean for a parameter set to be a neighbor? Remember that each parameter under optimization can be thought of as a dimension of the optimization space, so a neighbor is simply a parameter set where one or more of the values have been adjusted by a small amount, thereby placing the new parameter set nearby to the initial one in the optimization space. The energy state—the opposite of the value of the objective function—of this neighbor is also determined for the purposes of comparison.

Third, if the energy state of the neighbor is lower, that is, if the objective function's value is higher, the search moves to this new, better position in the optimization space. There is a tendency that the higher the temperature of the optimization space is, the greater the chance the parameter set will jump to a worse location. If the energy state of the neighbor is consequently higher, that is, the objective function's value is lower or worse, a random determination is then made as to whether it should move in that direction. In other words, if it's a better spot, the SA moves there, and if it's a worse spot and the space is still relatively hot, based on chance, it may or may not go there.

Fourth, if the current energy of the parameter set ever becomes too much higher as a result of its movement than the best and lowest energy level it has seen, it can always fall back to that location and resume the search once again from there.

Last, as the SA proceeds, the temperature of the optimization space slowly cools, approaching zero. The processes of cooling, moving, and readjusting repeat again and again until either a good enough parameter set is found or until the optimization process runs out of time.

To summarize, at the start of the simulated annealing process, a high temperature both encourages movement widely throughout the optimization space and discourages the search from getting stuck on local optima. With a hot space, however, there is a tendency that even if an area of the optimization space has no better neighbors, the strategy may leave the area anyway and not get stuck. Because the SA remembers the best area it has seen, if it never finds anything better, the maximum is not lost and it can return there again to explore that area further.

Also, as the temperature of the optimization space lowers, it becomes less and less likely for the SA to wander in a direction that is not superior. The optimization space has at this stage of the process been increasingly widely explored. If the SA has wandered in earlier stages of the process to a less desirable area, it will also have returned to the best spot to start over.

In an optimization space with dropping temperature, the SA increasingly settles in to more thoroughly explore the parameter sets around the best, lowest energy region it has seen. This increases the odds that as the search continues, it will continue to refine a good solution rather than look for another, better one that may be far away.

Because the best parameter set is always recorded by the SA, it is highly probable that given enough time, the strategy will have found some of the most interesting areas of the optimization space. The SA also has a built-in correction for any missteps taken toward worse areas. The end result is that as the simulated annealing optimization progresses, it will become increasingly probable that the best spot discovered for the strategy will be close to the true global optimum.

Genetic Algorithms

Genetic optimization algorithms (GAs) are a class of advanced search methods that emulate the biological process of evolution. They are widely used, robust, and fast. GAs were first introduced in the early 1970s but did not begin to achieve more widespread application until the early 1990s.[4]

Genetic algorithms:

1. Use chance to their advantage
2. Benefit from the combination of two good strategies to make a new, better strategy, incorporating the best aspects of each
3. Use the process of mutation to reduce the likelihood of getting stuck on a local optimum

Because the optimization spaces of many trading strategies tend to be spiky and complex, the efficiency of GAs in such spaces recommends them for trading strategy development.

The following is a simplified overview of the operation of genetic optimization algorithms. It is intended to provide an understanding of their operation and benefits. It is not intended as a step-by-step guide to their construction and application. For this, the strategist should consult the extensive literature for a detailed methodology.[5]

The first step is to choose at random an initial population or group of different candidate parameter sets. Each combination of parameters represents one possible implementation of the strategy. Each specific parameter set is called an *individual;* the *population* is the group of all of the candidate individuals. The initial batch of individuals are scattered throughout the optimization space.

The second step is to copy nonexclusive pairs of parameter sets from the current population into the next one, that is, the next generation. The chance that each parameter set selection will be copied is in proportion to its own fitness, which is measured by the objective function. The effect of this is that parameter sets with higher fitness will naturally dominate successive populations. Conversely, lower fitness parameter sets will have a greater chance of being left behind. This process is called *selection.*

The third step is to randomly select pairs of parameter sets and then exchange some of the parameters from one part of the parameter set pair to that of the other. This is called *crossover*. During this process, good values for one parameter set can be combined with good values for another parameter set to make a better parameter set. This is so even if the good values originally came from two different parameter sets.

The fourth step is to once again choose at random a new group of parameter sets. In these parameter sets, some parameters are replaced with new and different values. This is called *mutation*, and emulates the way that genetic information in organic life is not always faithfully reproduced with total accuracy from one generation to the next.

Although the word *mutation* carries with it negative cultural connotations, it can prove to be quite helpful in the long run if it is not excessive. In other words, not every mutation is a bad one—in life or in genetic optimization. Sometimes a mutation results in an individual—or parameter set—becoming better adapted to its environment—or market—than those that preceded it. If, in turn, a parameter set mutation performs poorly, that resulting set is not as likely to be passed on to the next generation. Consequently, the use of mutation to occasionally shake up the optimization process so as to minimize convergence on a local maximum does more good than harm. And, since the highest fitness parameter sets are likely to be copied into the next generation more than once, the best solution is also less likely to be lost to a chance mutation.

The GA proceeds by repeating the earlier-mentioned steps two to four for successive generations. In each generation, new populations of parameter sets are produced. This continues until:

1. A predetermined number of generations have been evaluated
2. A sufficiently good solution has been found
3. Significant progress, measured by improvement in the fitness of the population as a whole, is no longer made.

Convergence has been achieved when the current population under evaluation reaches a point where new generations no longer produce significant overall improvement. At this point, the population consists primarily of strategies with parameter sets among the best fitness values in the optimization space.

Genetic search methods have been shown to be some of the most helpful general purpose search methods available. While they are not guaranteed to find the very best solution possible, that is, the *global optimum*, they do tend to find very good solutions and those typically near the best possible solutions. And—and this is a big *and*—GAs accomplish this with far fewer evaluations than do simple search methods. A GA can typically identify the top parameter set by evaluating as little as 5 to 10 percent of the total candidate population.

Like all directed search methods, that is, those guided by their objective function, the choice of objective function is an integral part of a genetic optimization algorithm. This is because the individual parameter sets are compared to one another to determine their relative worth in light of the objective function. This is done without the advantage of evaluating every possible parameter set candidates. If an inappropriate fitness function is consequently used, the result can be an optimization that selects a poor parameter set for the strategy.

Particle Swarm Optimization

Like genetic optimization algorithms, particle swarm optimization (PSO) methods are modeled after biological organisms. Their search methodology is based on the observed behavior of flocks of birds and schools of fish. Like genetic algorithms, PSO is in the family of *stochastic* search methods, that is, those incorporating chance in their operation.

PSOs first emerged in 1995. They have demonstrated their utility as a powerful and effective directed search method. This is an overview to describe in general how particle swarm optimizers operate and their benefits. For more detailed information regarding their deployment, the strategist is advised to consult the PSO source materials.[6]

The first step in a particle swarm optimization process is to select a group of potential strategy parameter sets located randomly throughout the optimization space. A positive or negative velocity is also assigned by chance to each parameter set. This represents the speed at which the parameter set is adjusted and in what direction. In a sense, the parameter set can be visualized as a particle flying through the optimization space in all of its dimensions. Throughout the optimization process, the same particles, or parameter sets, persist, although their positions in the optimization space change continually.

Second, during each iteration of the PSO, each parameter set is updated or adjusted in its position by its respective velocity. This keeps the particles—parameter sets—moving in the same direction in each dimension of the optimization space. Their speed decays slightly with time in proportion to an inertial constant.

Third, each particle remembers its personal best location in the optimization space it has seen so far. Based on its current location in the optimization space, its velocity is accelerated to a small, chance-adjusted extent, back in the direction of its personal best location.

Fourth, each particle also updates the other particles when it finds a new global best spot, that is, a parameter set better than any of the other particles have found up to this point. As a consequence, each particle's velocity is accelerated by a randomly attenuated amount in the direction of this new global best location.

Stages two through four are repeated again and again for each particle. The resulting effect is to direct the PSO so that it lingers and thoroughly explores the area surrounding the best spot it has seen so far, while at the same time it is also gradually pulled toward the best spot that any particles have seen. This enables the PSO to potentially find new personal best spots in the most interesting areas of the optimization space uncovered by all of the particles to this point. This process continues until convergence.

Some types of particle swarms also feature communication among subsets of particles in the optimization space, such that they communicate and influence one another toward their own local best area as well. This feature encourages the PSO to more thoroughly explore different subareas of the optimization space, even if a somewhat better solution is also known to exist far away from where they currently are now.

Remember, that at any given time, the true—that is, as yet undiscovered—best solution may be nearby but has yet to be seen! The PSO encourages subgroups of particles to simultaneously further explore the best *nearby* solutions as well as to move in the direction of the yet undiscovered and possibly distant best known solution. This behavior of the PSO tends to minimize the likelihood of focusing too closely on any one local maximum and missing the global maximum.

Particle swarm optimizations have been shown to be very competitive with genetic optimization algorithms in a variety of situations. Both of these advanced search methods excel at quickly finding good enough solutions without the need to explore every candidate in an optimization space.

The optimization spaces of some of the more complex trading strategies are so large that even the fastest supercomputers could not explore them completely with a brute force method in an affordable and realistic time frame. The use of some type of advanced search method consequently becomes a practical necessity, even if the resulting solution might be somewhat short of the best, and perhaps elusive, solution.

Like genetic algorithms and other directed search methods, the effective application of a particle swarm optimization method relies highly on the quality and appropriateness of the objective function.

GENERAL PROBLEMS WITH SEARCH METHODS

There are some drawbacks to the directed search methods in general. Since a direct search method does not evaluate every possible candidate, there is a potential for a certain lack of thoroughness. This can be

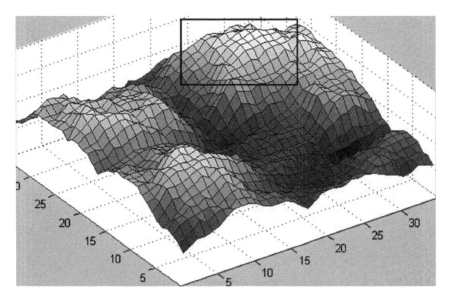

FIGURE 9.5 Optimization Space with Global Maximum

minimized by selection of the appropriate search method and its consequent quality, nature, and proper use. A hill climbing search is far more thorough than a step search. However, it is less thorough than a brute force grid search.

A second and perhaps more serious problem with direct search methods is that they will not always find the true performance peak, which is called the *global maxima*. As observed, directed search methods are a compromise between practical and theoretical necessity. A good directed search method, however, will find a satisfactory, if not the very best possible, solution.

What is a *global maximum?* It is the best performing parameter set for the trading strategy found with the entire optimization space. See Figure 9.5, which has a rectangle drawn around the global maximum.

A *local maximum*, then, is the best performing parameter set in a *local region* or subset of the entire optimization space. See Figure 9.6, which has a rectangle drawn around a local maximum.

The selection of a local maximum as the global maxima can occur for a wide variety of reasons. To a certain extent, it is one of the major considerations that guide the design of a search method. Consequently, the actual design of the search method is an important factor determining its efficiency in the proper identification of the global maxima. The *shape of the variable space* can also exert a significant influence on this process.many advanced search methods, for example, will encounter

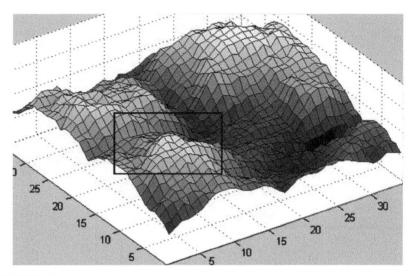

FIGURE 9.6 Optimization Space with a Local Maximum

problems when searching a very spiky or lumpy optimization space. A spiky optimization space is one with a large number of high performance *peaks* surrounded by steep and low *valleys*. See Figure 9.7 with four lower performance peaks in rectangles.

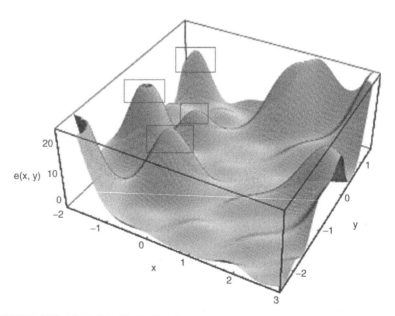

FIGURE 9.7 "Spiky" Optimization Space

THE OBJECTIVE FUNCTION

A search is only as good as its objective function. In fact, the objective function is the means by which the strategy evaluation application and the optimization process tells us whether a set of parameters are good or bad. The objective function evaluates a trading strategy. It is the *eyes* of the strategist into the optimization space.

Of course, the strategist is the ultimate arbiter of whether a parameter set is accepted or rejected. The larger the optimization space and the more sophisticated the search method, however, the greater the importance of the search function.

Any search method must be able to determine whether a trading strategy is good in order to accept or reject each model. The strategist might deem, for example, that the definition of a good trading strategy is that strategy with:

1. The highest net profit
2. The highest profit per trade
3. The highest percentage of winning trades, or one with the highest Sharpe Ratio

Hence, the *objective function* or *evaluation method* measures and ranks the quality of a trading strategy. By definition, any search method requires an objective function or a method of mathematically evaluating the performance of a trading strategy to operate.

Given the more widespread use of advanced search methods, the evaluation type takes on an even greater significance. Search methods are continually accepting or rejecting trading models in the process of seeking the best parameter set in the least time possible. It is therefore critical to use the best evaluation method possible.

Of course, the best evaluation method is that which will select the parameter set for a trading strategy that is most predictive of real-time trading success. The use of an inappropriate evaluation function may ignore a sound model; even worse, it may select a poor strategy.

Remember the proviso "Be careful of what you ask for because you just might get it"? This is an excellent rule of thumb to use as a guide for the strategist so as to select the most effective evaluation type. In the end, the best evaluation method will be that criterion or criteria that will select the most robust and profitable trading strategy. It is extremely prudent for the strategist to clearly identify which characteristics of a trading strategy she feels are most predictive of real-time trading success.

Let us see exactly how this works. For example, let us assume that *highest net profit* is the best evaluation method. (It is not, by the way.) If this highest net profit is used as our objective function while performing an optimization, however, the result will be the selection of those strategy parameters that produced the highest profit.

After all, profit is what trading is all about, is it not? Why then, is this bad procedure? Because research has shown that highest net profit alone is not an adequate measure of the overall trading performance and robustness of a trading model. For example, 60 percent of the highest net profit could be generated by a strategy with one large and likely unrepeatable trade, such as a short trade during the October 1987 stock market crash. Or, the bulk of this highest net profit could have been produced in the first half of the test period and could be masking a devastating loss in the second and most current half.

Furthermore, the search for the largest net profit in isolation completely ignores the question of risk. The strategy with the highest net profit could also have a very large and unacceptable drawdown. Or, the parameters selected may have too small a sample of trades, which brings into question the statistical validity of these parameters.

Net profit is simply one performance statistic. It falls far short, however, of the whole picture. The selection of those trading strategy parameters that are most likely to produce real-time profit is a more complex process. Additional performance statistics must be evaluated to arrive at this conclusion with some degree of confidence.

Net profit as a sole evaluation method ignores many of the characteristics important to this decision. Some of the key characteristics of a robust trading strategy are:

1. A relatively even distribution of trades
2. A relatively even distribution of trading profit
3. Relative balance between long and short profit
4. A large group of contiguous, profitable strategy parameters in the optimization
5. Acceptable trading performance in a wide range of markets
6. Acceptable risk
7. Relatively stable winning and losing runs
8. A large and statistically valid number of trades
9. A positive performance trajectory

The evaluation type should be designed to select the most robust and stable trading model. The most robust and stable trading strategy may or may not be the most profitable. The most stable trading strategy will be one that exhibits the characteristics listed earlier.

Furthermore, an unsound evaluation type can actually, and unwittingly, promote overfitting during the optimization process. An evaluation type that does not select models for their overall robustness places the credibility of the entire testing process in question. The robust trading strategy is that strategy most likely to produce sustainable real-time trading profit. The nonrobust trading strategy, conversely, is quite likely to produce real-time trading losses.

A REVIEW OF A VARIETY OF EVALUATION METHODS

Any trading strategy performance criterion can serve as an evaluation method. Any combination of different strategy performance criteria can serve as a more complex evaluation method. We will review the strengths and weaknesses of different evaluation types, both common and uncommon. This is by no means meant as an exhaustive list of evaluation measures.

Net profit or *gross profit* is the net gain or loss of the trading strategy. Although the trader is seeking the highest possible profit, net profit by itself is inadequate as an evaluation type.

Among the key reasons that net profit is inadequate as an overall measure of performance are that:

1. It can be excessively influenced by a single large win or loss or by a cluster of wins or losses
2. It ignores the distribution of trades and of returns
3. It is ignorant of the statistical validity or lack thereof of the trade sample size
4. It does not incorporate risk.

Net profit is an important measure of trading performance. It can be effective when used as a minimum criterion in a complex evaluation method.

Annualized rate of return is an alternate way of expressing net profit and loss. It is a useful measure of strategy performance because it makes it easy to meaningfully compare performance over different time periods and different markets. As a sole evaluation type, however, it is subject to the same criticism as net profit. It is useful as a minimum criterion.

Maximum drawdown is a measure of risk and an important measure of strategy performance. It is the largest drawdown or decline in the equity curve of a trading strategy from an equity peak. It is a defensive criterion, in that it is looking for the smallest dollar loss, not the largest dollar gain. It is also subject to the same distortions as net profit, but on the risk side.

Maximum drawdown as a sole evaluation method is subject to the same weaknesses as net profit, and together with the fact that it incorporates no measure of positive performance, it is unacceptable as a sole evaluation criterion. Maximum drawdown is useful, however, as a threshold in a complex evaluation method. Models exceeding a certain level of drawdown can be rejected outright.

Correlation between equity curve and perfect profit (CECPP) is an evaluation type that incorporates the distribution of trades and profit. More important, this unique measure measures the performance of the trading strategy performance to the actual profit potential provided by the market.

Perfect profit is a theoretical measure of market potential. It is the total profit produced by buying at every valley and selling at every peak that occurs during a historical period of market history. This is obviously impossible in practice, therefore the name *perfect profit*. Because of its method of calculation, perfect profit will constantly grow from the beginning of the historical test period to its end.

The *Equity Curve* of a trading strategy is the sum of the beginning account balance, closed trades and open trade profit tabulated bar by bar. A robust and profitable trading strategy will have an equity curve that steadily rises from the beginning of the historical test period to its end. An unprofitable trading strategy, conversely, will have negative—indicated as a steady deline—growth over this same interval.

Correlation between equity curve and perfect profit then is the *correlation coefficient* between the equity curve of the trading strategy and the perfect profit of the market on which the strategy is trading. The CECPP will range between −1 and +1. A value of +1 for CECPP suggests a good trading strategy. This tells us that as perfect profit is naturally increasing, the trading strategy equity is also exploiting this rise and is increasing. Conversely, a value of −1 would suggest a poor trading strategy. This tells us that as perfect profit is rising, trading equity is decreasing.

The formula for the correlation coefficient of perfect profit and the equity curve is

$$\text{Correlation Coefficient} = \text{Sum}[(x(i) - M'x)(y(i) - M'y)]/[(n-1) \times SD'x \times SD'y]$$

$$n = \text{Number of days in calculation}$$
$$x = \text{Perfect Profit}$$
$$y = \text{Equity Curve}$$

$$\text{M}'\text{x} = \text{Mean of Perfect Profit}$$
$$\text{M}'\text{y} = \text{Mean of Equity Curve}$$
$$\text{SD}'\text{x} = \text{Standard Deviation of Perfect Profit}$$
$$\text{SD}'\text{y} = \text{Standard Deviation of Equity Curve}$$

The higher the correlation, that is, the closer to $+1$, between a trading model's equity curve and the market's perfect profit, the more effectively the strategy is capturing market opportunity. Why? As we have seen, perfect profit is a cumulative measure and is therefore growing throughout the trading period. A good trading strategy will also show a steadily rising equity curve. If a market becomes quiet, growth in perfect profit will tend to increase at a slower rate. A good strategy will also share a similar flattening, or slow growth, instead of a dip of the equity curve during such a period. Similarly, when market volatility grows and the trend resumes, this will be reflected in growth in perfect profit. A good strategy will also share strong growth in profit during such times and this should be reflected as an increase in the slope of the equity curve.

CECPP, unlike net profit, will favor trading strategies that profit in conjunction with the growth of perfect profit and do not lose a great deal when the growth of perfect profit slows. As such, CECPP is an excellent candidate as a sole evaluation measure.

Pessimistic return on margin[7] (PROM) is an annualized yield on margin that is adjusted in a way that *pessimistically assumes* that a trading strategy will win less and lose more in real-time trading than it did in its historical simulation.

PROM adjusts the gross profit by calculating a new, mathematically adjusted pessimistic *lower* gross profit. The first step is to calculate the number of winning trades *reduced* by its square root or, in other words, *adjusted* by its standard error. This adjusted number of winning trades is then multiplied by the average winning trade to arrive at a new, adjusted lower gross profit.

PROM next adjusts the gross loss by calculating a new, mathematically adjusted pessimistic, *higher* gross loss. The first step is to calculate the number of losing trades *increased* by its square root or, in other words, *adjusted* by its standard error. This adjusted number of losing trades is then multiplied by the average losing trade to arrive at a new, adjusted larger gross loss.

A new adjusted gross profit or loss is then calculated using these adjusted pessimistic gross profit and gross loss values. This is then used to produce an annualized rate of return on margin.

The formula is:

PROM = {[AW × (#WT − Sq(#WT))] − [AL × (#LT − Sq(#LT))]}/Margin
    #WT = Number of Wins
    AW = Average Win
    #LT = Number of Losses
    AL = Average Loss
  A#WT = Adjusted Number of Wins
   A#LT = Adjusted Number of Losses
  AAGP = Adjusted Annualized Gross Profit
  AAGL = Adjusted Annualized Gross Loss
  A#WT = #WT − Sq(#WT)
   A#LT = #LT + Sq(#LT)
  AAGP = A#WT × AW
  AAGL = A#LT × AL

Let us consider an example. Assume:

1. A $25,000 annualized gross profit
2. 49 wins
3. A $10,000 annualized gross loss
4. 36 losses
5. A margin of $10,000

As a basis for comparison, let us first calculate an annualized rate of return on margin. This would be a 150 percent annualized return on margin ([$25,000 − $10,000)]/$10,000 = 1.5 × 100 = 150%).

In contrast, let us look at the PROM of this strategy.

Adjusted Number of Wins = 49 − Sq(49) = 42
Adjusted Number of Losses = 36 + Sq(36) = 42
Adjusted Annual Gross Profit = ($25,000/49) × 42 = $21,428
Adjusted Annual Gross Loss = ($10,000/36) × 42 = $11,667
PROM = ($21,428 − $11,667)/$10,000
PROM = 98 percent per year

This example clearly demonstrates why this measure is termed *pessimistic*. It assumes that a trading system will never win as frequently in real time as it did in testing and that the system will lose more frequently in real time as well. It reflects these pessimistic assumptions in a modification of net profit using standard error. As such, it is a more conservative measure.

PROM is a robust measure because it factors in a number of significant performance statistics such as gross profit, average win, gross loss, average loss, number of wins, and number of losses. Notice an added benefit of PROM resulting from its adjustment of gross profit and loss by the square root of their respective number. Taking advantage of the nature of the square root calculation, PROM penalizes small trade samples.

Consider the following:

$$Sq(100) = 10$$
$$Sq(100)/100 = 10/100 = 10\%$$
$$Sq(25) = 5$$
$$Sq(25)/25 = 5/25 = 20\%$$
$$Sq(9) = 3$$
$$Sq(9)/9 = 3/9 = 33\%$$

Notice how the smaller the number, the larger the square root is as a percentage of the number. The effect of this in PROM is that the smaller and statistically less reliable the number of wins and losses, the more pessimistically the profit and loss are adjusted.

Let us return to our initial example and vary only the number of wins and losses. Let us first look at the PROM of this strategy when the number of wins and losses are relatively large.

$$\text{Adjusted Number of Wins} = 144 - Sq(144) = 132$$
$$\text{Adjusted Number of Losses} = 121 + Sq(121) = 132$$
$$\text{Adjusted Annual Gross Profit} = (\$25,000/144) \times 132 = \$22,916$$
$$\text{Adjusted Annual Gross Loss} = (\$10,000/121) \times 132 = \$10,909$$
$$\text{PROM} = (\$22,916 - \$10,909)/\$10,000$$
$$\text{PROM} = 120 \text{ percent per year}$$

This PROM is 120 percent compared to the PROM of 98 percent of our first example with mid-range numbers.

Now let us look at the PROM of this strategy when the number of wins and losses are rather small.

$$\text{Adjusted Number of Wins} = 16 - Sq(16) = 12$$
$$\text{Adjusted Number of Losses} = 9 + Sq(9) = 12$$
$$\text{Adjusted Annual Gross Profit} = (\$25,000/16) \times 12 = \$18,750$$
$$\text{Adjusted Annual Gross Loss} = (\$10,000/9) \times 12 = \$13,333$$
$$\text{PROM} = (\$18,750 - \$13,333)/\$10,000$$
$$\text{PROM} = 54 \text{ percent per year}$$

This PROM is 54 percent compared to the PROM of 98 percent of our first example with mid-range numbers, and the PROM of 120 percent of our example with larger numbers.

Pessimistic return on margin is a good and robust measure of trading strategy performance. As an annualized return on margin, PROM is also a good way of comparing the performance of different trading models to one another as well as market to market.

There are two successively more stringent derivatives of PROM: PROM minus the biggest win and PROM minus the biggest winning run.

As their names imply, these measures downwardly adjust gross profit more aggressively than PROM.

PROM minus biggest win removes the largest single profitable trade from the gross profit and is then calculated according to the same formula as PROM. Its greatest benefit is the evaluation of a trading strategy without the impact of the biggest winning trade. This is generally a good practice, particularly when the sample size is small.

In the event there is no exceptionally large win, this measure is quite similar to PROM. Where a large win, however, such as a trade produced by a major price shock such as the stock market crash of 1987 or the first Gulf War, PROM minus the biggest win provides a measure of the strategy without this windfall profit.

PROM minus the biggest winning run removes the gross profit of the largest run of winning trades from the gross profit and is then calculated with the same formula as PROM. It provides a measure of the performance of a trading strategy performance minus an exceptional winning run, which, in turn, might have been caused by unusually opportune trading conditions.

In the search for the most stable and robust trading strategy, it is always best to prepare for the worst and hope for the best. It should be obvious that a trading strategy that produces a robust and attractive annualized return on margin while debited for its biggest winning run, is the trading strategy most likely to produce robust real-time trading profits.

MULTIPLE EVALUATION TYPES

Generally, a combination of different evaluation criteria will produce results that are superior to those produced by a single criterion. It should be clear that the robustness and performance of a trading strategy have multiple dimensions. The best single evaluation method or objective function would be one of the PROMs, and preferably the most stringent.

However, by using multiple performance criteria, it is possible to evaluate the various dimensions of performance and robustness. One of the easiest ways to do this is to set performance thresholds: performance floors and ceilings.

In this way, particular performance thresholds that contribute to robustness can be easily applied. For example, rank the top models using PROM, and set the following criteria:

1. Floor—Net return greater than $5,000
2. Ceiling—Maximum drawdown less than $5,000
3. Floor—A minimum of 10 trades per year

Ranking the top parameters by a robust measure such as PROM will eliminate many potential problems. Rejecting models that make less than $5,000 or have a drawdown more than $5,000 sets certain minimum performance criteria. Rejecting models that trade less than 10 times per year should ensure an adequate sample size. This will certainly identify a more robust class of trading strategies than will net profit.

CHAPTER 10

Optimization

N ow that the trading strategy has passed the multimarket and multi-period test, we know that the strategy is worthy of further development. The next stage in this development is the optimization of the trading strategy. The overall structure of the optimization process closely parallels that of the previous round of testing. There is one very important difference, however, in that the trading strategy is now taken through the actual optimization process.

The *New Oxford American Dictionary* provides the following definition of *optimize:* "To make the best or most effective use of."

According to this definition, then, to *optimize* a trading strategy is to make the most effective use of it. How does optimization accomplish this? The optimization process does so by the empirical examination and evaluation of all potential strategy parameter candidates. During the optimization process, a historical simulation will be calculated for a sufficient number of different values for the key strategy parameters that will have the most impact.

There are a number of different and valid terms that are used to describe the optimization process: the *test batch, test run, variable scan,* the *estimation process,* and so on.

The word *optimization* will mean the selection of the most robust set of *parameters* for a trading strategy. Furthermore, optimization is the identification and validation of those strategy parameters that are best capable of generating peak trading performance in real time.

Notice that the emphasis is on peak performance in real-time trading. This may seem to be the obvious goal of optimization. It is the goal and result of optimization done correctly. Unfortunately, many practitioners of optimization are not performing optimization correctly and they are consequently not able to achieve this goal. Sadly, many users of trading strategy development software still operate under the delusion that the trading strategy that shows the biggest profit under optimization is one and the same with the trading model that will generate peak real-time trading performance.

Before we proceed, consider the following mathematical definition of *parameter* from the *New Oxford American Dictionary:* "A quantity whose value is selected for the particular circumstances and in relation to which other variable quantities may be expressed."

A trading strategy comprises rules, formulae, indicators, and so on. Many of these different strategy components will have variables or parameters. For example, a period of three for a moving average is an instance of a parameter for an indicator. The rules, formulae, and other components provide the structure of the strategy. It might be said that the correct parameters for these components breathes life into the strategy.

In a practical sense, the optimization process is the calculation of the historical performance of a number of different instances of the trading strategy on a fixed historical price sample. For example, referring back to the MA trading strategy, an optimization of this strategy will entail the calculation of the historical performance of all of the different combinations of moving average lengths under examination on a historical sample of yen price data ranging from 1/1/1990 to 12/31/2005.

The results of each of these historical simulations will vary from one another because each simulation uses a different set of the model parameter values that are under optimization, that is, the subject of the test. For example, the MA strategy will examine the trading results of all possible combinations of MA1 from 2 to 12 at steps of 1 and for all possible combinations of MA2 from 20 to 40 at steps of 2. This will consist of 121 individual simulations, each with a unique pair of parameters for each of the moving averages.

A top parameter set is then selected from this batch of 121 historical simulation results, based on a set of evaluation criteria. Assume that the objective function is the Sharpe Ratio. Then, the parameter pair of moving average periods that produced the historical simulation with the highest Sharpe Ratio is selected as the best parameter set.

If this optimization process and selection are both done with the proper attention to all of the appropriate details and rules, the resulting top models will be those that offer the greatest potential for real-time trading profit.

OPTIMIZATION CONTRA OVERFITTING

Optimization has many pitfalls. There are many ways that it can be done incorrectly. These are explored in detail in this chapter. When done incorrectly, the strategist is deceived by the belief that the strategy is able to produce profits in real time in the same manner that it has done so in historical simulation.

One of the major premises of this book is that optimization is a valid, reliable, and essential part of the trading strategy development process. It is optimization that is done incorrectly that is the villain, not optimization itself, as some have been inclined to state.

Another major premise of this book is that optimization done *in*correctly is *overfitting*. This is explored in detail in Chapter 13: The Many Faces of Overfitting.

The principles and procedures presented in this book are designed to guide the strategist in the use and application of correct optimization methods. Part of this education is to point out the pitfalls of optimization so as to be aware of them and to avoid them.

Correct research and strategy development procedures will extract both maximum understanding and profit from trading strategies. Optimization is simple to understand. But it is very difficult to perform correctly without a full understanding of the proper methods and principles.

Different parameters for a trading strategy can lead to dramatically different profits and risks. Ideally, the performance of a highly robust trading strategy will have a great deal less variance among its different parameter sets. In practice, however, with many optimizable trading strategies, dramatically different parameter sets can lead to dramatically different trading performances. They can be the difference between winning and losing. This is why proper optimization is so important. It can be the arbiter between trading success and failure.

If optimization is done correctly, it will result in a robust trading model that reliably produces real-time trading profit in some proportion to that of its historical simulation. If the optimization is done incorrectly, however, it will most likely degenerate into overfitting and subsequent delusion as to the merit of the trading strategy. If such optimization errors remain undetected or are ignored, the result will be a trading strategy that shows very good results in historical simulation and very poor real-time trading performance.

How does the best intentioned effort at optimization go wrong and degenerate into what is commonly referred to as overfitting? It goes wrong when done with little regard for, or adherence to, proper statistical guidelines and procedures.

For insight into this, let us examine an example provided by the statistical modeling of time series. It is common knowledge among these practitioners that given enough variables and the proper equation, a curve can be made to fit any number of data points.

However, just because a beautifully fit curve produced by modeling software fits a time series closely, this is no guarantee that it will be the best predictor of future values in the curve. Closeness of fit alone does not imply sound predictive capacity.

Rather, it is the time-series model that best fits a large and representative data sample with sufficient degrees of freedom, robust parameters, and was developed following the correct statistical procedures that will be the best the predictor of the future.

Just as with time-series modeling, it is the trading strategy that has been developed on a representative sample of price history, has produced a statistically valid trade sample, exhibits robustness, and has performed well in a Walk-Forward Analysis that is most likely to produce real-time profits in proportion to its historical simulation.

A SIMPLE OPTIMIZATION

It will be useful to look at a concrete example of a simple optimization before exploring the detailed mechanics of designing and performing an optimization process.

Let us refer back to the two moving average crossover system (MA2). This will provide us with a good example of a simple optimization process. This optimization will be performed on yen for the 11-year historical period from 1/1/1995 through 12/31/2005.

Recall that MA2 generates trading signals when the two moving averages cross. The two candidates for optimization are the period or lengths of each moving average. Since the two moving averages are intended to measure two different rates of trend, their respective lengths should be relatively dissimilar.

Keeping this in mind then, the variables will be optimized—or scanned—over the following ranges:

MA1 from 1 to 10 in steps of 1, or:

11   22   33   44   55   66   77   88   99   110

MA2 from 15 to 60 in steps of 5, or:

115   220   225   330   335   440   445   550   555   660

These scan ranges examines shorter values for the first moving average to focus on faster trends and longer values for the second moving average to focus on slower trends. Now what will actually happen during this optimization process?

The computer will sequence through each possible value of the first moving average, beginning with the first candidate for the second moving average, and calculate a historical simulation of MA2's trading performance on yen for the 11-year period specified for each of the following parameter pairs. This process is also referred to as *evaluating* this parameter pair.

For example, the first 10 tests will use the following combinations of moving averages:

```
MA1:    1    2    3    4    5    6    7    8    9   10
MA2:   15   15   15   15   15   15   15   15   15   15
```

After all candidates for MA1 have been evaluated for the first candidate for MA2, this process will then be repeated with the second candidate for MA2. In other words, values from 1 through 10 for the short moving average are tested with the second candidate (20) for the long moving average. For example:

```
MA1:    1    2    3    4    5    6    7    8    9   10
MA2:   20   20   20   20   20   20   20   20   20   20
```

This process is then repeated until all possible combinations for these parameter candidates for both moving averages are evaluated. In this particular optimization, there are 100 (10 for MA1 × 10 for MA2) parameter combinations.

The trading performance for this batch of 100 different historical simulations are sorted and ranked, and a top parameter set is selected according to the objective functions employed by this process.

This is a typical, simple, brute force optimization of a simple two parameter trading strategy. Of course, the optimization process can be complicated by a more:

1. Complex trading strategy with many optimizable parameters
2. Sophisticated search method
3. Complex set of objective functions

No matter the complexity of any of these three components of the optimization process, however, it still follows the same course. That is the evaluation of a sufficient number of parameter sets to reliably select that parameter set that satisfies the objective function.

Now that we have a basic idea of the scope of the optimization process, we will explore these different aspects in detail so as to fully understand all of the implications.

THE OPTIMIZATION FRAMEWORK

Setting up the optimization framework is straightforward (see Figure 10.1). It does require thoroughness and attention to detail, however. There are four key decisions that must be made to set up the optimization framework:

1. The strategy *parameters* that are to be used in the optimization must be selected and the scan *ranges* to be used must be determined
2. An appropriate *data sample* must be selected
3. The *objective function* or functions that identify the best parameters for the trading strategy must be selected
4. Guidelines for the evaluation of the *optimization process* must be determined

The first two decisions will vary with each trading strategy to be optimized. The last two decisions are more structural and will most likely be very similar, if not identical, for each optimization.

The Parameters

Trading strategies can have quite a range in number of rules and formulae that can accept parameters that might benefit from optimization. It is always best to have the smallest number of optimizable parameters possible, and yet still provide the required flexibility. The greater the number of parameters to be optimized, the more likely it is that the results will be overfitted or optimized incorrectly.

Consequently, it is best to make every effort at the outset to identify the key strategy parameters to be incorporated into the optimization framework. Of course, the key parameters are those that have the most significant impact on performance. If a parameter has little impact on performance, there is no reason to include it in the optimization. Instead, a fixed value or *constant* should be used for these less significant parameters.

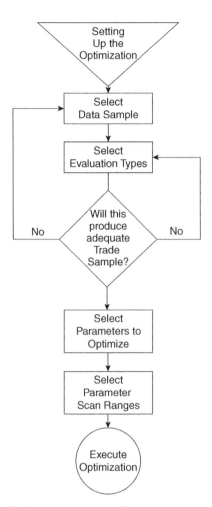

FIGURE 10.1 The Optimization Framework

If the relative significance of the model parameters is not known a priori, then an added empirical step must be performed to determine their significance. The easiest way to do this is to scan a relevant parameter range for each strategy variable, one at a time, holding the other strategy variables constant at a known reasonable value. A parameter is important if such a scan shows dramatic performance change. Conversely, a parameter is considered of less importance if such a scan shows little or no change in performance. Of course, such a test also raises the more important question as to whether this variable is needed at all in the strategy. It is always best to simplify a trading strategy to only those parameters, rules, and formulae that are necessary to produce peak performance. So, if the elimination of peripheral rules and parameters does not detract significantly from performance, reduce the strategy to just its necessary components.

Let us look back at our MA2 example to put this into context. Recall that it was the objective of this strategy to enter the market when the shorter trend (as tracked by MA1) crossed over the intermediate trend (tracked by MA2). From our intuitive understanding and empirical knowledge of moving averages, we know that the length of a shorter trend and that of an intermediate trend will vary from market to market and from time to time. Consequently, it is pretty clear that these two parameters should be included in the optimization framework.

We also note that MA2 uses moving averages calculated on the close. There are other prices fields such as the median, high, low, or open to use in this indicator. So to determine whether the choice of price field is significant to performance, we test MA2 with reasonable parameters for MA1 (5) and MA2 (20) for each of these fields. We find that these different fields make no appreciable difference in performance, so we can rule out a need to incorporate the price field as a parameter within our optimization framework.

The Scan Range

There are two main principles that affect the determination of the parameter range to be incorporated in the optimization framework. These are the theoretical and the practical.

First, let us consider the theoretical considerations. The parameter range should be one that is intuitively and reasonably appropriate for the indicator, rule or formula. In other words, scanning a range of 1 to 1,000 days for a short-term moving average contradicts the idea of short-term (often considered 3 to 10 days.) After all, how much logical sense does it make to evaluate a short-term average of 500 days crossing over a longer-term average of 1,000 days? Also, the outer limit of this range is well outside the typical range of values applied to moving averages (for example, 3 to 200 days). Consequently, a more appropriate (and reasonable) parameter range would be 2 to 14 days for a short-term moving average.

Next, let us consider the practical considerations. The computation time dictated by a scan range must be evaluated and weighted. Obviously, a small number of historical simulations take less computational time than an extremely large one. Even with today's computers, this is a very real consideration.

It becomes particularly relevant when doing multivariable scans over larger historical samples and over many markets. To scan a range of moving averages from 2 to 14 days in steps of 2 requires only seven tests

([(14 − 2)/2] + 1). This is insignificant no matter how slow the individual simulations. Conversely, to scan a range of moving averages from 1 to 200 in steps of one requires 200 tests. This requires more than 28 times the computing time. Again, this may not be all that significant a cost, but it would be pointless if the parameter has little or no impact on performance or if the values are outside the range of intuitive normalcy.

Recall that the number of historical simulations performed during an optimization is equal to the product of the number of candidates in each of the parameter ranges in the optimization framework. So, to scan a two-parameter strategy with 10 candidates each will require the calculation of 100 historical simulations (10 × 10). In contrast, to scan a five-parameter strategy with 10 candidates each will require the calculation of 100,000 historical simulations (10 × 10 × 10 × 10 × 10). As the development process progresses and the evaluation of additional strategies, time frame, and markets is required, the greater are the computational requirements.

Also, the size of the parameter step taken in a scan range is significant beyond its mere demands on computer time. Scanning a variable too closely (that is, at steps that are too small) can do more than just consume unnecessary processor time. It can inadvertently promote overfitting.

For example, to scan a short-term moving average from 1 to 14 days in steps of 1 is valid. To scan a long-term moving average from 20 to 200 days in steps of 1, however, will tend to increase the likelihood of overfitting.

It is difficult to set a hard and fast rule as to the determination of the step size that is appropriate. It is best, however, to keep the step sizes of each parameter to be scanned somewhat proportional to one another.

To better understand this concept of proportion, consider MA2 once again. Notice the difference in numeric value of a 5 percent shift the larger the base number. A 5 percent increase at a period of 20 produces 21 for the next candidate. Also notice, however, that a 5 percent increase at a length of 100 produces 105 for the next candidate. It is a good rule of thumb then, to make an effort to keep the numeric step size change in the different parameters in the optimization framework in approximately equal percentage proportion.

One way to do so is to look at the proportion of the starting values of the parameter ranges to each other. So, for example, if the first parameter range is 5 to 20 at steps of 1 and the second parameter range starts at 20 (i.e., 5 × 4) then to keep this all in proportion its range should end at 80 (20 × 4) and the step size should be 4 (1 × 4).

Another rule of thumb that is helpful is to keep the number of candidates in two relatively equal ranges equal in number. Consider that we chose to scan MA1 between 2 and 10 days at a step of 1. This yields nine candidates. We also chose to scan MA2 from 14 to 30. To keep this relatively equal in candidates, we can choose a step size that will achieve this goal. With rounding, we can see that a step size of 2 will also produce nine candidates.

It is not always an easy task, but it is important both from the theoretical and practical viewpoints to attempt to arrive at the appropriate number of candidates and to keep the different parameter scan ranges in relative proportion to one another. It is also very important to keep in mind that excessively fine scanning of a parameter range can be a significant contributing factor to overfitting and all of the attendant deception and danger associated with this grievous error.

The Historical Sample

It is important to point out at the outset of this section that the size of the historical sample is one of the most critical and perhaps least understood elements in the optimization of a trading strategy.

There has long been a belief among statisticians and trading strategy developers that the more price history, the better. I have never fully agreed with this assumption and my reasons for this are presented in *The Theory of Relevant Data* section of Chapter 11. In fact, what Walk-Forward Analysis teaches us is that the size of the estimation or optimization window and the size of the out-of-sample or walk-forward window are simply two more variables in the trading strategy. This is explored in more detail in Chapter 11: Walk-Forward Analysis.

There are two main principles that define the selection of a proper data sample: A sufficiently large enough sample to produce a statistically valid trade sample size, and a broad enough data window to include a sufficient range of market conditions, which should ideally include at least one sample each of the four major market types.

These two factors also have an impact on each other. The size of the historical sample must be sufficient to generate a statistically significant sample of trades. Traditionally, this should be at least 30 trades. In practice, this is rather small, and in fact, the more trades the better. A large sample of trades is one of the best defenses against overfitting. Also, the ideal sample should also include a large number of both long and short trades.

In practice, and because of the somewhat limited availability of historical data, this can be difficult to achieve in all cases. This is particularly true of slower, longer-term trading strategies. It is a very good rule of thumb, however, to always keep in mind. In the case of trade sample size, there is safety in numbers.

The number of data points used in the calculations of the trading strategy and its number of rules are said to consume data points that in turn restricts its degrees of freedom. The size of the data sample, consequently, must be large enough to accommodate these restrictions and retain sufficient degrees of freedom. In practice and with the use of adequate historical sample sizes, this is not typically a problem.

Consider the following example, however. A trading model that uses 2 moving averages is optimized on a sample of 200 days. The longest moving average in the range is 50 days. This will use 50 data points, thereby consuming 50 degrees of freedom. This length of moving average also reduces the data sample size. Trading cannot begin in the simulation until this moving average has been calculated. This in practice reduces the historical sample by 25 percent. This is too much. This test must therefore either be rejected or modified. It can be modified by expanding the size of the historical sample or by reducing the length of the longest moving average in the test.

Let us consider this example from the point of view of adequate trade sample size. Given a historical sample of 200 days of data, to create a trade sample of at least 30 trades, our strategy will need to make a trade approximately every six days. This is a relatively fast trading strategy. Given the scan ranges that we are employing with MA2, they are pretty unlikely to produce this number of trades for many of the combinations. Once again, there are the same two alternatives: The historical sample can be increased in size or the strategy can be made to trade more frequently by reducing the length of the moving averages to be evaluated.

The second principle can prove more difficult to meet. The historical sample should, as much as possible, be representative of the market as a whole. It should contain as many types of trends, patterns, and situations as possible. It should also contain at least one each of the four market types:

1. Bullish
2. Bearish
3. Congested
4. Cyclic

It should also contain a range of volatility levels, particularly high and low.

There are two guidelines to follow. Include as much variation in price data as possible in the historical sample relevant to the trading style of the strategy. This follows the rule of the largest and most general possible sample. If this proves impractical, include as much data as possible that is most similar to current market conditions. This follows the rule of the most relevant possible data.

No matter what the size of this historical sample, however, and no matter what the range of market types included, it is important that the strategist understand its composition. It is also essential that the strategist have some understanding of the relationship between the trading performance produced and its underlying historical sample.

Let us consider two examples in the abstract. In our first example, the trading strategy produced an exceptional return in historical simulation. Upon review of the data, it is observed that the historical sample is absolutely optimal for the strategy with no difficult periods. In other words, the strategy performed well under ideal conditions. This would be expected if it was implemented correctly and is based on a sound principle. We have no knowledge, however, of how it will perform under difficult conditions.

In our second example, the trading strategy produced a marginal-to-respectable return in historical simulation. Upon review of the data, however, it is observed that the historical sample ranged widely over a lot of very difficult market conditions. In other words, the trading strategy endured difficult circumstances and still produced a profit, marginal though it may be. Imagine how it might perform under ideal conditions.

Which strategy would you prefer to take into real-time trading?

The Objective Function

The guidelines for the selection of the objective function, evaluation type, or test criteria have been presented in detail in Chapter 9: Search and Judgment. At this stage in the design of the optimization framework, an objective function or functions must be selected. The only purpose of the objective function is to select the most robust strategy parameters from the optimization process. The most robust strategy parameters, of course, are not always the most profitable. By definition, however, the most robust strategy parameters are those that are most likely to produce reliable and sustainable profits in real-time trading.

In practice, the strategist will select a set of objective functions and work with those from strategy to strategy and optimization to optimization. After all, once the strategist determines an appropriate method of selecting a robust parameter set, this is unlikely to change all that often. It certainly may evolve with knowledge, experience, and expertise. But it is not likely to change dramatically each time a new strategy is to be evaluated.

The details of the objective functions may vary a bit for different strategies. It is even possible that somewhat different objective functions may be employed for the evaluation of different styles and paces of trading strategies. But, for the most part, a sound set of objective functions is more likely to remain a constant than a variable.

The Optimization Evaluation

There are two applications of the information that the strategist will derive from an evaluation of the results of the full optimization. The first application is the evaluation and judgment of the *quality* of the trading strategy and its top parameter set based upon an examination of all of the historical simulation results as a batch of information. It is not really possible to satisfactorily evaluate the quality and robustness of the top parameters selected during the optimization process without evaluating them in the context of the performance of all of the other parameter sets as a totality.

The second application is a more sophisticated application and extension of the first type of optimization evaluation. In other words, an evaluation of the robustness of the top parameter set is actually used in the Walk-Forward Analysis. This information can also be applied to make a go or no-go determination regarding the periodic parameter reoptimization that is part of the application of a trading strategy that has been evaluated with Walk-Forward Analysis and has been used in real-time trading.

A MULTIMARKET AND MULTIPERIOD OPTIMIZATION

We now know what we need to do to structure an individual optimization. Let us extend that to the design of a multimarket, multiperiod optimization (see Figure 10.2). This parallels by design the structure of the multimarket and multiperiod test described in the previous chapter. The purpose of this round of testing is to obtain a more precise evaluation of the profit and risk produced by optimal strategy parameter sets.

Optimization of the model is done on a diversified basket of markets to obtain a measure of the trading model's versatility and robustness. The more markets that a model can trade, the more useful it is. Also, the more diverse the markets that the strategy can trade, the more robust the strategy. Furthermore, this broader-based evaluation provides an additional measure of statistical validity. The fact that a model performs well on only one market, unless that was its specific intention by design, may well be a red flag.

The optimization of the strategy is also done on a selection of different time periods. This is to arrive at an evaluation of how the strategy behaves as market trends, volatility, and liquidity change. A strategy that trades well in a few time historical time samples and poorly in many others may require further study. Was the price action hostile in the periods in which the strategy performed poorly? This is an understandable weakness. If the price action was reasonable but just different, however, there may be a problem with the strategy. For instance, it may be overfit, or the underlying principle may be unsound. From a contrasting perspective, how was performance during extremely friendly price action? Performance is expected

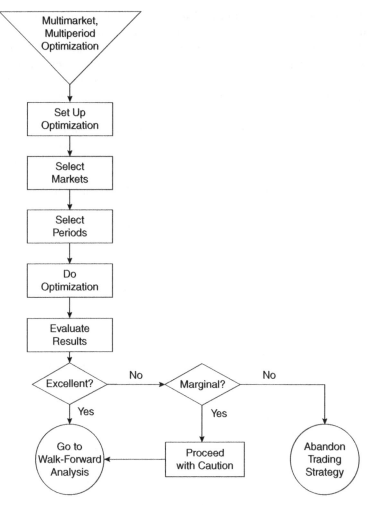

FIGURE 10.2 A Multi-Market and Multi-Period Optimization

to be good under these ideal conditions. If it is not, then there is a serious problem.

What will such an optimization process look like? For T-bonds, it will look as follows:

Optimize T-bond futures

Scan Moving Average   1 day to **31** days at steps of **2** days
Scan Stop Loss   1 points to **6** pts at steps of **1** points
Total number of parameter sets in this optimization is **96**

Do this optimization process on the following historical samples:

1/1/1997	to	12/31/1998
1/1/1999	to	12/31/2000
1/1/2001	to	12/31/2002
1/1/2003	to	12/31/2004
1/1/2005	to	12/31/2006

Total number of scans for five two year historical samples: **480**

Apply this same 96 candidate optimization, 5 historical sample process to the remaining 9 markets in the basket: coffee, cotton, crude oil, gold, pork bellies, soybeans, S&P 500, sugar, and Swiss francs.

Total number of scans for 10 markets, 5-period optimization: **4,800**

After this processing is complete, we will have a full multimarket, multiperiod optimization to evaluate. Let us see what we can find.

THE EVALUATION OF THE OPTIMIZATION

The evaluation of this overall optimization process begins with an individual assessment of the optimizations for each market and time period. It concludes with an analysis of the overall process in its totality.

As we saw in Chapter 8, the first level of robustness is revealed by the multimarket and multiperiod test. We can see how the second stage of robustness is revealed by its multimarket optimization later in this chapter. We will finally see how the last and most important stage of robustness is uncovered by the multimarket Walk-Forward Analysis in Chapter 11: Walk-Forward Analysis.

To determine the robustness and quality of the trading strategy itself, the robustness and quality of the optimization process must be evaluated.

One very important aspect of the robustness of a trading strategy is that which is revealed by an exploration of the robustness of its optimization. As it will soon be seen as the latter part of this process unfolds, the true robustness and character of a trading strategy can be revealed only within the context of the full strategy development process.

The overall robustness of the trading strategy and its optimization profile are established by the evaluation of its statistical validity and its shape.

Let us look at these aspects of robustness in more detail.

THE ROBUST TRADING STRATEGY

Recall the definition from Chapter 8: Preliminary Testing of robust as "able to withstand or overcome adverse conditions." This is a particularly appropriate definition when applied to a trading strategy. It suggests that a robust trading strategy will be able to withstand or overcome adverse market conditions. Expanding on this, we define *withstand* to mean "not lose a great deal of capital," *overcome* to mean "make some profit," and *adverse market conditions* as markets that are *extremely choppy and trendless* or *tight and congested.*

The first component, then, of a robust trading strategy is its durability and ability to survive during the inevitable adverse market conditions. An extension of this durability is that it is likely to have a longer shelf life in real-time trading than its less robust peers.

There is a second and less obvious component to the robust trading strategy, however. And, it is not so much a component of robustness as much as it is a consequence of robustness. That consequence is that a robust trading strategy is a trading strategy with a high likelihood of making real-time trading profits that are in rough proportion to those it has earned in its historical simulations. Conversely, the nonrobust trading strategy is very likely to perform very poorly in real-time trading.

It can be stated categorically that the *most robust trading strategy* is that trading strategy that performs in a profitable and relatively consistent manner over:

1. The broadest possible range of parameter sets
2. All the major market types
3. A majority of different historical time periods
4. Many different types of markets

Let us add some dimension to this description of the robust trading strategy. To highlight further, albeit with a bit of drama, let us contrast it with its extreme opposite, even at the risk of looking a bit absurd. Consider, then, the diametrically opposite *anti-robust* or *nonrobust* trading strategy, which exhibits profitable performance in:

1. One parameter set
2. Only in bull markets
3. One historical time period
4. One market

Does this make the point clear? The robustness of a trading strategy can only be fully measured in the context of the information uncovered by its complete development cycle.

The Robust Optimization

An optimization process will produce a group of historical simulations, one for each parameter set and each with their own set of performance statistics. This is called the *optimization profile*. A statistical analysis of the optimization profile will provide important information about the overall robustness of the trading strategy.

There are three main components or measures that define the robustness, or lack thereof, of an optimization profile:

1. A statistically significant proportion of profitable parameter sets within the total optimization space population
2. The distribution of performance throughout the optimization space
3. The shape of the profitable parameter sets within the optimization space

The first measure of robust performance is to determine whether the optimization profile has some degree of statistical significance. In other words, are there enough profitable parameter sets in the optimization profile to be able to conclude that these results were not simply a product of chance?

The second component of robustness is the distribution of the performance of the parameter sets within the optimization space. In essence, the more evenly distributed and the smaller the variation of performance from parameter set to parameter set, the more robust the trading strategy is deemed to be.

The third key measure of the robustness of an optimization profile lies in the shape and contour of the optimization. In general, the smoother and more continuous the shape of the optimization profile, the more likely it is that the trading strategy is robust. Conversely, the more spiky or discontinuous the shape of the optimization profile, the less likely it is that it is a robust trading strategy.

THE STATISTICALLY SIGNIFICANT OPTIMIZATION PROFILE

We can apply the concept of *statistical significance* in the evaluation of the optimization profile. Statistical significance simply provides a measure as to whether the result of a process is likely to be a matter of random chance. We can use this idea to provide some guidelines and apply this idea in a somewhat different manner to arrive at some useful conclusions about the optimization set.

In general, the greater the number of parameter sets in the optimization profile that produce profitable historical simulations, the greater the likelihood that these results are statistically significant and not simply the product of chance, and consequently the greater the robustness of the trading strategy and the selected parameter set.

For example, if only 5 percent of the parameter sets in the optimization profile are profitable, the top parameter set of this optimization and the entire optimization profile are statistically suspect; this presents a strong argument that they should be rejected. This is most likely not a robust trading strategy—at least not for the historical period and market for which it was optimized.

Conversely, the larger the percentage of profitable parameter sets found in the optimization set, the greater the likelihood that this is a sound and robust trading strategy. A sound strategy has many profitable parameter sets.

A good performing parameter set—a profit spike—surrounded by poor ones is unlikely to be a robust strategy capable of producing real-time profit. Such a strategy is more likely to be a statistical, albeit a seductive one, outlier. As a general guideline, a profitable parameter set surrounded by similar neighbors is more likely to be robust. In an analogous manner, the performance of all the parameter sets in the optimization space should be judged in a similar manner.

The law of large numbers tells us that if enough monkeys were to pound on enough keyboards for a long enough time, they could eventually produce this very book! In an analogous manner, if a large number of parameter sets are evaluated for a trading strategy, a small number of profitable results could occur simply due to chance.

Just as random chance can produce a few profitable parameter sets, it can also produce parameter sets with more marginal performance. We can use this somewhat subtle point to our advantage. For not only do we want to see an optimization profile with a large proportion of profitable parameter sets, we also want to see an average profit that is significantly larger than average.

Of course, this is a difficult measure to quantify. Most experienced strategy developers tend to have an intuitive sense of what a typical rate of return is for trading a particular market—that sense can be a guide in this evaluation. One can also compare it to more standard measures such as how it compares to the returns of a risk-free investment such as T-bills. Last but not least, the strategist may find a way to arrive at a somewhat objective measure of the performance of a random strategy on the market under evaluation.

TABLE 10.1 A Failed Optimization Profile

	Number	Percentage	Average
Number of Tests	1000	100.0%	$2,458
Profitable Tests	37	3.7%	$7,598
Losing Test	963	96.3%	($2,457)

Consequently, an optimization profile with only a few sound parameter sets is more likely to be a product of chance than is statistically significant. Consider Table 10.1, which shows the results of an optimization profile with less than 5 percent profitable parameter sets.

As indicated, a robust trading strategy will have an optimization profile with a large proportion of profitable parameter sets. In this example, only 3.7 percent of the parameter sets are profitable. This is suspect and should be rejected.

As a general guideline, at least 20 percent of the parameter sets should produce significant profit. See Table 10.2 for such a marginal optimization profile.

Of course, the greater the percentage of highly profitable parameter sets, the more robust the trading strategy is likely to be. Review Table 10.3 to see a very robust optimization profile.

The key to this measure of optimization profile robustness is, the more the better. Also, the greater the average profit for each parameter set, the better as well. This alone, however, is not sufficient. The shape and distribution of these profitable parameter sets is also very important.

TABLE 10.2 A Marginal Optimization Profile

	Number	Percentage	Average
Number of Tests	1000	100.0%	$5,447
Profitable Tests	224	22.4%	$9,767
Losing Test	776	77.6%	($1,983)

TABLE 10.3 A Robust Optimization Profile

	Number	Percentage	Average
Number of Tests	1000	100.0%	$9,671
Profitable Tests	671	67.1%	$12,671
Losing Test	329	32.9%	($1,324)

THE DISTRIBUTION OF THE OPTIMIZATION PROFILE

Once an optimization profile has passed the test of significance, it is next helpful to review the distribution within the total population of parameter sets. To achieve a quick and easy perspective on this, we calculate the average (mean), maximum, minimum, and standard deviation of the performance of all of the parameter sets. From these statistics, we can deduce the density, or lack thereof, of profitable performance. The more robust trading strategy will feature a large average profit with minimum variation. Variation is evaluated by the difference between maximum and minimum and the size of the standard deviation.

The more robust trading strategy will have an optimization profile with a:

1. Large average profit
2. Small maximum-minimum range
3. Small standard deviation

Additional valuable insights into the optimization set are provided by the count, average, total, and standard deviation of the net profit and loss of all of the trading simulations in the optimization space.

This information provides the following measures of the robustness of the optimization profile:

1. Top strategy parameter set performance is relatively close to the average of performance, preferably within one standard deviation
2. A profitable overall average simulation
3. Average simulation minus one standard deviation is profitable
4. Average simulation minus three standard deviations is profitable

Of course, this last qualification is a very demanding test. For this to be true, 95 percent of the parameter sets must be profitable. Consequently, if a strategy does not pass this hurdle, it is by no means reason for alarm. If it does, however, this suggests extreme robustness.

We can examine additional calculations, similar to these previous ones. They are a count, average, total and standard deviation of all *profitable* trading simulations.

From this information, we arrive at an evaluation of the robustness, or one lacking thereof, of the optimization profile by determining that:

1. The top strategy parameter sets are those that are relatively close to the average of all profitable simulations and preferably within one standard deviation

2. Profitable simulations comprise a significant if not majority percentage of the total

3. The ratio of the total profit of all profitable simulations divided by the total profit of all simulationsis significantly positive,

4. A smaller standard deviation of profitable simulations shows consistency and less variance

These relatively simple to calculate measures provide quick and reliable insight into the robustness of the optimization profile.

THE SHAPE OF THE OPTIMIZATION PROFILE

The shape of the optimization profile sounds like an abstruse concept. Difficult or not, this is an important aspect of the robustness of the trading strategy. The information we gather from this analysis is, in fact, actually relatively simple to understand.

A robust optimization profile has a relatively smooth space, and the smoother the better. The top parameter set has many profitable neighbors, and once again, the more the better.

This is easy to visualize, of course, with a two parameter optimization space. It becomes a far more difficult, if not practically impossible, task when dealing with a three parameter and more optimization space. The principles, however, are the same.

There are two polar extreme types of profiles that can be produced by optimization. The first, positive extreme is an extremely smooth and slow-changing space. This type of space is illustrated in Figure 10.3. The second, negative pole is that of a space filled with tall, narrow profit spikes surrounded by valleys of suboptimal or unprofitable performance. This type of space is illustrated in Figure 10.4.

Let us examine in more detail the optimization spaces of two different trading strategies. These are simple Pivot Charts created in Excel of the net profits of the optimization profile of these two strategies.

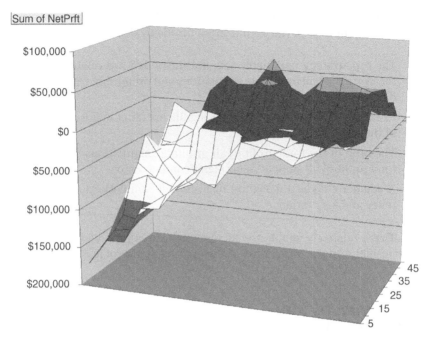

FIGURE 10.3   Pivot Chart of a Relatively Smooth Optimization Space

Let us first consider our positive case with a smooth parameter profile. Here we see the top parameter (TPS1 on the chart) set resting on top of a big, round, gradually declining hilltop of other profitable parameter sets. This case is good because such a strategy will prove very robust. Why? For two reasons: because the performance degrades at a gradual pace as more distant parameter sets come into play, and the top parameter set is surrounded by a large group of other profitable parameter sets. Any of these parameter sets are sufficiently profitable. In the case of a trading strategy, there is comfort in a wealth of interchangeably profitable parameter sets. Such a strategy derives its robustness from its relative insensitivity to parameter changes.

A robust one-variable optimization will produce a plot of profit performance with a top parameter set and performance that gradually declines on both sides of it. A robust two-variable optimization will produce a top parameter set on top of a smoothly declining hill. A robust three-variable optimization will produce a top parameter set in the center of a sphere with performance slowly declining as it moves away from the center. This geometric metaphor continues, of course, with higher-dimensioned parameter spaces. It just gets a lot harder to talk about and to visualize.

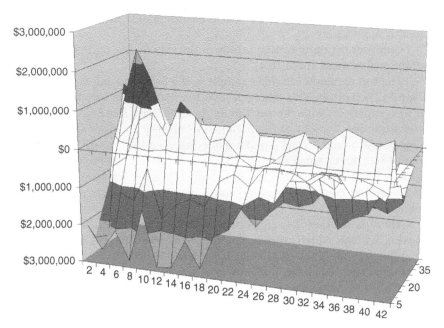

FIGURE 10.4 Pivot Chart of a Spiky Optimization Space

Let us now consider the negative case with a very spiky parameter profile (see Figure 10.4). Here we see the top parameter (TPS2 on the chart) set for this nonrobust trading strategy sitting at the top of a tall, steep profit spike with performance dropping like a rock for the next parameter set.

This is the optimization profile of a poor trading strategy. The optimization profile is comparable to a mountain range of extremely narrow and tall peaks springing straight up out of far lower valleys. Why is this bad? It is bad because such a strategy is lacking in robustness. Why? For two reasons: the performance falls and jumps erratically as near or more distant parameter sets come into play, and the top parameter set is surrounded by a small group of unprofitable parameter sets. Any small shift in a strategy parameter may well change a large profit to an equally large loss. Unlike our robust example, this strategy is not surrounded by friendly and profitable neighbors. Such is the character of an erratic strategy space.

The selected illustration of a spiky optimization profile is a bit extreme. They do exist, however. The selection of a parameter set that is a nonrobust profit spike instead of a robust parameter set is one of the most common causes of overfitting. It is important for the strategist to understand that a performance spike is typically a statistical anomaly and not the result of a viable trading strategy. A bit more discussion and illustration is consequently appropriate.

Consider the optimization profile of the simple, one parameter trading strategy illustrated Table 10.4.

The top parameter in this example is the 6-day moving average, yielding a $12,500 profit. This does not look too bad in isolation. When looked at in comparison with the surrounding parameters, however, it looks far less attractive. Looking at the parameter one step on either side—moving averages of 5 and 7 days—performance is seen to drop off steeply to a loss of $500 and a small profit of $3,000, respectively. And two parameters removed, the deterioration of performance is even worse with losses of $8,000 and $13,000. This is clearly an isolated performance peak, and not reliable.

There is another, lesser, performance peak, however, for the 13-day moving average, which produced a profit of $7,000. This is significantly less than the previous peak of $12,500. If we take the results of its surrounding parameters into consideration, however, it suddenly looks more appealing. The parameters one step higher and lower from this peak produce profits of $6,500 and $5,000, respectively. The parameters two steps away produce profits of $6,000 and $4,500, respectively. The performance of this lower parameter peak has comparable profits on either side. This secondary peak, consequently, features more robust performance than the first profit spike performance peak.

TABLE 10.4 Optimization Profile for One Parameter Strategy

MA1	P&L
1	−$14,000
2	−$16,000
3	−$12,000
4	−$8,000
5	−$500
6	$12,500
7	$3,000
8	−$13,000
9	−$8,000
10	$4,000
11	$6,000
12	$6,500
13	$7,000
14	$5,000
15	$4,500

If net profit alone were our objective function, the profit spike at the six-day period would be selected over that of the superior parameter of the 13-day period. We can gain some insight into the impact of more sophisticated objective functions by looking at this example a little further.

Let us see which parameter would be picked if we employed an objective function that averaged the performance of the top parameter with its two nearest neighbors and selected the best parameter together with its neighbors.

The first top parameter at a six-day period had a profit of $12,500 and its two nearest neighbors had profit and loss results of −$500 and $3,000. These three averaged together produce a profit of $5,000 as calculated here.

$$(\$12,500 - \$500 + \$3,000)/3 = \$5,000$$

The second top parameter at 13 days had a profit of $7,000 and its two nearest neighbors had profit and loss results of $6,500 and $5,000. These three averaged together produce a profit of $6,167 as calculated in the following.

The second peak of $7,000 had nearest neighbors of $6,500 and $5,000. Averaged, they produce a new candidate of $6,167, calculated here.

$$(\$7,000 + \$6,500 + \$5,000)/3 = \$6,167$$

When seen in this light, which parameter is superior: the profit spike or the parameter set with strong neighbors?

HOW DOES THE STRATEGY RESPOND TO OPTIMIZATION?

Now we understand how to evaluate the robustness of our trading strategy through its resulting optimization profile. We must now evaluate whether or not the trading strategy, in fact, has responded positively to the optimization process.

There is always an outside chance that the strategy parameters chosen a priori in the first test are in fact the optimal parameters for the trading strategy. This is highly unlikely to be the case for a 10-market, 5 historical optimization process.

A trading strategy is deemed to benefit from optimization if an overall significant improvement in trading performance in the majority of markets in our basket and the majority of historical samples is observed.

Synergies often exist between the multiple parameters of a trading strategy. It is one of the major purposes of optimization to uncover the full extent of these synergies. For these reasons, the multimarket, multiperiod optimization should be expected to produce near peak profit performance. This is the major purpose of optimization.

It is to be expected that overall trading performance as measured by risk-adjusted return will improve during optimization. Improvement must be large enough to be statistically significant. For example, if the average annualized rate of return produced for our basket during the multimarket, multiperiod test is 5 percent, an improvement to 7 percent is neither significant nor attractive. An improvement to a rate of 15 percent, in contrast, is both significant and more attractive.

DOES THE STRATEGY DESERVE FURTHER DEVELOPMENT?

If the average return of the trading strategy after optimization is negative or mediocre, then it can be concluded at this point that the trading strategy is without merit. Further testing is not recommended. Discard the strategy or return to the design stage.

One must also consider the possibility that this outcome was the result of an inappropriate optimization framework. If upon review, this proves to be a possibility, redesign the optimization framework and repeat the multiperiod, multimarket optimization.

If the risk-adjusted average performance of the trading strategy throughout the market basket and for a majority of the historical samples is profitable and the risk acceptable, however, this trading strategy should be taken to the next and final round of testing. The trading system must now be put to the final and decisive test: the Walk-Forward Analysis.

CHAPTER 11

Walk-Forward Analysis

When a trading strategy has demonstrated that it benefits from optimization, the next step then is to take the strategy through the last and definitive stage in the development process: the *Walk-Forward Analysis*. The Walk-Forward Analysis judges the performance of a trading system exclusively on the basis of postoptimization or out-of-sample trading.

The performance of a trading strategy on data which were never part of the optimization process is a far more reliable measure than performance based solely on in-sample simulation.

If a trading strategy performs well under a Walk-Forward Analysis, it has shown itself to be robust and capable of producing real-time trading profit. In addition, Walk-Forward Analysis is the closest possible simulation of the way in which an optimizable trading strategy is typically used in real time.

Walk-Forward Analysis provides answers to four essential questions that are necessary to begin and to continue trading a strategy with intelligence and confidence:

1. Is the trading strategy robust? Will it make money in real-time trading?

2. What rate of return will the trading strategy produce in real-time trading?

3. How will the typical changes in market behavior such as trend, volatility and liquidity affect trading performance?

4. What are the best parameters to use in real-time trading to produce maximum profit with minimum risk?

Of course, it is rather obvious that the most important question answered by WFA is the first: Does the strategy have life after optimization? Is it a real and robust trading strategy or a curve-fit delusion? Will it make money in real time?

After the strategist has obtained an affirmative answer to the first question, the information provided by the next two questions might really seem like bonuses. The identification of the optimal parameter set for current real-time trading, as important as it is, might almost seem like an afterthought!

The rates of return and risk information provided by WFA are superior to those provided by a typical optimization. Finally, because of the periodicity of WFA, it provides far more useful insight into the performance of the trading strategy during market changes than the typical optimization. And it does so more easily and readily.

IS THE TRADING STRATEGY ROBUST?

A robust trading strategy is, by definition, one that is durable under changing market conditions, and will produce trading profits in real time consistent with those produced in its historical simulation.

The primary goal of the walk-forward test is to determine whether the performance of a trading model under optimization is the result of a robust and repeatable process or the illusory result of overfitting. In other words, the primary purpose of a Walk-Forward Analysis is to determine whether a trading strategy's performance is real or not. We look at the issue of overfitting in more detail in the next section.

The performance of a trading strategy that is based upon a sound and robust process will have a predictive capability—the capacity to produce real-time profits—on unseen, that is, out-of-sample market activity.

Walk-forward analysis is also the most effective method to identify the optimal strategy parameter set that will perform profitably in real-time trading. A trading strategy that does not stand up to Walk-Forward Analysis is most likely a trading strategy that is not going to produce profits in real-time trading either.

ROBUSTNESS AND WALK-FORWARD EFFICIENCY

Another way that Walk-Forward Analysis measures the robustness of a trading strategy is through the calculation of a statistical measure unique to it called *Walk-Forward Efficiency* (WFE.) Walk-Forward Efficiency is a unique measurement of the quality of the actual optimization process. There is evidence that suggests that even a sound strategy can be over-fit through improper optimization procedure. This can be done in many ways and will be explored in more detail in Chapter 13: The Many Faces of Overfitting.

Walk-Forward Analysis is the only way to arrive at a statistically reliable measurement of this property of an optimization process. This measure compares the annualized rate of postoptimization profit with that of in-sample optimization profit. The section "What Rate of Profit Should We Expect?" later in this chapter shows how WFE is calculated.

A trading strategy is likely overfit if it has a low Walk-Forward Efficiency; in other words, if the rate of return of out-of-sample trading is decidedly lower than that of in-sample trading.

If a trading strategy is achieving a WFE of only 25 percent, there is probably something wrong. The trading strategy is either unsound or overfit.

A properly fit and robust trading strategy should achieve out-of-sample performance at levels similar to those achieved in-sample. If a sound strategy is producing a low WFE, there has probably been an error in the optimization framework and it is consequently overfit. After review and further testing, however, if the WFE does not rise, the trading strategy is just not good.

Research has clearly demonstrated that robust trading strategies have WFEs greater than 50 or 60 percent and in the case of extremely robust strategies, even higher. In fact, there is no reason why a trading strategy cannot exceed in-sample performance in out-of-sample testing as well as in real-time trading.

A sound trading strategy is likely to exceed in-sample performance if postoptimization market trends and conditions provide greater profit potential than those during optimization.

THE CURE FOR OVERFITTING

Overfitting is formally defined and analyzed, and methods for its prevention are discussed in detail in Chapter 13: The Many Faces of Overfitting. At this point, it is sufficient to point out that overfitting is a mistake in the strategy development process. Overfitting has many causes.

The reason that overfitting is harmful is that the trading performance of an overfit strategy is a *fiction.* It is not something that can be traded, at least without losing a lot of trading capital.

Whereas the causes and prevention of curve fitting are far from obvious, the symptoms of an overfit trading strategy are painfully obvious. The overfit trading strategy will produce very impressive results during simulation and often *devastatingly poor performance during real-time trading.*

Research has demonstrated two striking truths about overfitting. An overfit trading strategy has an extremely high likelihood of losing money in real-time trading. Even a poor trading strategy will produce attractive performance in some of its historical simulations. In the case of the overfit strategy, however, this performance is more likely to be a result of chance and an abuse of the development process.

It is probably far more disturbing, however, to know that a good trading strategy can lose money in real-time trading if it has been improperly developed and consequently overfit.

One of the greatest advantages of Walk-Forward Analysis is that it is very difficult to abuse and consequently, whereas it is possible, it is very difficult (even if not impossible) for the strategist using WFA—with his eyes open—to overfit a trading strategy.

I have always viewed Walk-Forward Analysis as an idiot-proof way of optimizing a trading strategy. Extensive experience has not proven this wrong.

Why is Walk-Forward Analysis such a robust testing method? It is because it adds a very important step to the traditional optimization procedure. It evaluates the performance of the trading strategy on price data that was not part of the optimization process. In other words, a Walk-Forward Analysis is an evaluation of a trading strategy exclusively on the basis of its performance on out-of-sample price data—data that have not been seen by the optimization process.

Experience has shown that an unsound strategy will not perform well in a Walk-Forward Analysis. In other words, a poor strategy will not pass a Walk-Forward Analysis. There is also a high probability that a sound strategy that has been overfit in some way will also not pass a Walk-Forward Analysis.

Research has also shown that an unsound or overfit strategy can make money in one or a few individual walk-forwards. Such a model, however, will not make money over a large number of walk-forwards, and will consequently fail the full Walk-Forward Analysis. To achieve the greatest statistical validity and confidence, therefore, a number of walk-forwards must be performed on a trading strategy. As in all things statistical, the more data, greater the confidence. A trading strategy that makes a significant overall profit with a large number of profitable individual walk-forwards is unlikely to be a product of chance or accident.

A MORE RELIABLE MEASURE OF RISK AND RETURN

The second major advantage of Walk-Forward Analysis is a more accurate and reliable measure of the profit and risk of the trading strategy. The result of a Walk-Forward Analysis is a statistical profile of trading performance with the same information as the typical optimization performance summary. The difference, however—and this is a *big* difference—is that the WFA statistical profile is the product of *postoptimization* trading. The only role that in-sample performance plays in a WFA is to provide a basis for comparison of out-of-sample and in-sample performance in the form of the WFE statistic. Of course, WFE is a precise comparison and measurement of the rates of walk-forward trading profit versus optimization trading profit.

If we find that out-of-sample and in-sample performance are very much in alignment, so much the better. For this tells us that we have a very robust trading strategy. In case it is significantly different, however, with the WFA out-of-sample analysis of risk and reward, we have statistics that are more likely to conform to real-time trading performance.

As a result of the Walk-Forward Analysis, the strategist has a more accurate and reliable measure of risk with which she can, with greater confidence, capitalize her trading account and balance her portfolio. The strategist also has a more reliable and realistic measure of trading profits on which she can base her expectations.

The bottom line here is that all of the typical statistical measures of performance provided by a Walk-Forward Analysis are more accurate and reliable than the same statistics produced by an in-sample optimization.

ASSESSING THE IMPACT OF MARKET CHANGES

The third benefit offered by the Walk-Forward Analysis is that it provides insight into the impact of trend, volatility, and liquidity changes on trading performance. Research has shown that trend changes, which by nature occur swiftly, and large shifts in both volatility and liquidity, can have a large and often negative impact on trading performance. Of course, a good, robust model will be more capable of toughing out and trading profitably during such changes.

The Walk-Forward Analysis as a whole rolls over an extensive period of time, yet it analyzes and views trading performance separately in smaller cross-sections of time. Studying this wealth of time-sliced trading performance can provide a great deal of useful information regarding the impact of market changes on trading performance. A study of performance on a time-period-by-time-period basis will easily isolate and show the positive or negative impacts of unusual, nonrecurring events such as the stock market crash of 1987 or the Persian Gulf War. It just as easily provides the same information on the impact of typical market changes such as from low volatility to high volatility or from bull market to bear market.

Of course, some of this information is produced by an optimization. The fact that a WFA calculates a full performance summary for each in-sample and walk-forward window, however, provides a wealth of additional information that is unique to this form of analysis.

THE BEST PARAMETER SET FOR TRADING

One of the main results of any optimization process—be it the standard or the more robust Walk-Forward Analysis—will be the optimal parameter set to be used for the trading strategy during real-time trading.

The WFA, being a more statistically robust procedure, is more likely to produce a parameter set that is more likely to be reliable and produce real-time trading profit. However, and this is once again a very *big* however, the parameter set provided by the WFA for real-time trading is more likely to be better suited to the current market environment. And—and this is a *big* "and"—the parameter set thereby provided comes with an expiration date.

Why? The most appropriate parameter set and its shelf life are both a unique product of the Walk-Forward Analysis. As is explained later in this chapter, the length of the optimization window and of the walk-forward window both become parameters of or part of the very structure of the trading strategy. In other words, part of the information provided by a Walk-Forward Analysis is the optimal length of price history to be used during the reoptimization process to identify the parameter set most likely to provide optimal real-time trading performance. The Walk-Forward Analysis will also provide the length of the optimal time period for which this parameter set is likely to produce consistent real-time trading profit before performance deterioration sets in.

The strategist will typically resort to a priori reasoning to determine the appropriate length for the optimization window. This reasoning often simply runs along the line of "The more price data, the more reliable the results" or "We are in a bull market now, so let's look back to just before its beginning." Both approaches have their rewards and risks, of course. The WFA, however, provides us with this information on the basis of an empirical analysis of the performance of the trading strategy on the targeted market.

There also are typical approaches to the determination of the shelf life of the parameter set. There is typically an arbitrary time period, such as annually, at which the strategist will reoptimize the trading strategy to arrive at a new parameter set. Or, the strategist waits until real-time trading performance deteriorates to such an extent as to be uncomfortable. Both approaches, once again, have their risks and rewards.

The strategist who employs Walk-Forward Analysis, however, has no such dilemma or need to resort to arbitrary reasoning. The WFA provides the shelf life of the parameter set in the form of the length of the walk-forward window. Again, this information is arrived at through empirical analysis and not speculation or whimsy.

We need to explore the theory of relevant data to more fully understand the reasoning behind Walk-Forward Analysis.

THE THEORY OF RELEVANT DATA

The theory of relevant data balances the two major, and often opposing, requirements of trading system development: peak performance and statistical rigor.

Peak Performance

Peak trading performance is maximal trading profit with minimal risk. It is best achieved by a trading strategy and a parameter set that is adapted to current market conditions. For example, let us assume current market action is a strong bull market with good volatility and an abundance of clear price swings. Is it not logical that a trading strategy will take advantage of these conditions and produce peak profit and minimum risk if its parameters are most suitable to these conditions? To bring further light to this conclusion, consider how well a strategy might do in these conditions if its parameters were most suitable to a nontrending market with low volatility? The strategy will most likely not fare nearly as well.

It is axiomatic in trading strategy development that there are conditions under which a trading strategy will excel and there are conditions under which a trading strategy will not.

From this point, it is not too much of a reach to conclude that our trading strategy will perform best if it can be tailored to current market conditions. The other axiom of trading strategy development demands, however, that we use sufficient price data to produce robust results.

The question becomes, consequently, what are enough data?

Statistical Rigor

We have discussed—and *stressed*—throughout this book the great need for statistical rigor in all stages of the development of a trading strategy. The same high standards of statistical rigor also must be adhered to for the Walk-Forward Analysis and its use of relevant data.

A Walk-Forward Analysis, just like a standard optimization, must be sufficiently extensive so as to produce enough trades, cover enough data, allow for sufficient degrees of freedom, and cover a comprehensive range of types of market. Of course, the WFA does this by extending over a long range of history. It just does it in a different way.

Recall that one of the main prerequisites of the theory of relevant data is that it uses only that price data that is most like current market conditions. Of course, given the nature of markets, a set of conditions can last for a very short time, in which case, it is more or less irrelevant. Alternatively, a set of market conditions can persist for many years as well, in which case, the most relevant data may also be large enough to provide statistical rigor.

The reality, however, is that the most relevant data is often typically neither irrelevantly small nor large enough to satisfy the most demanding statistician. It is typically somewhere in the middle.

The look back, consequently, to relevant data should be as large as possible as dictated by the restrictions imposed by:

1. Statistical requirements
2. Current market conditions
3. The nature of the trading strategy

It is very important to note that the statistical rigor of the Walk-Forward Analysis is not anywhere near as heavily affected by the size of the optimization window as would be that of a typical optimization. That is because the Walk-Forward Analysis concatenates the results of all of the walk-forward windows and derives its statistical rigor from the length of the overall Walk-Forward Analysis, not the size of its optimization window.

A WFA should be as long as possible, typically at least 10 to 20 years, whenever possible. A WFA of this length can produce 10, 20, or more walk-forwards. The combined performance of these multiple walk-forwards will often be sufficient to yield statistical rigor.

Consequently, a long Walk-Forward Analysis is able to use shorter length in-sample windows to achieve both optimal trading performance from its use of the most relevant data and statistical rigor at the same time.

To better understand why the rolling optimization window of the Walk-Forward Analysis is able to perform this delicate balancing act, we need to get a better idea of the many ways that market conditions can change.

SHIFTING MARKETS

This balancing act between relevant data and statistical rigor would, of course, never arise if markets did not change their behaviors from time to time. The strategist, however, can make the best of this by taking advantage of the opportunities this situation presents.

Some think that the markets never really change and that adapting a trading strategy to current conditions is the greatest of sophistries. Others think that markets change occasionally—or perhaps seismically shift at the most basic levels and consequently obliterate all trading strategies based upon pre-change data.

Yet others think that a market is a mix of infinitely different varieties and in this mix a market never really changes its fundamental nature. Others have suggested an even more radical departure in the view that there is no "one market" but rather "an endless succession of ever different minimarkets" with no relation from one to the next.

I discussed at some length in the Preface the intertwining evolutions of the contemporary markets on the one hand, and that of communication and computer technologies on the other. As technologies evolve and market participation grows, increasingly efficient markets are the result. Recall that it is one of the basic axioms of this book that it is the nature of a market to continually evolve and adapt to changing conditions. In other words, one of the fundamental characteristics of the nature of a market is for it to change. And in that continuous change there is continuity. For practical purposes, however, let us further state that market conditions do shift and change and they shift and change enough to make it advantageous for some trading strategies to periodically adjust to these shifting conditions.

J.P. Morgan, the legendary financier and market operator, was once asked by a newcomer to trading looking for a hot tip, "What will the market do today, J.P.?" Morgan shrewdly and accurately replied, "It will fluctuate." Let us review then the various ways that markets shift and fluctuate.

THE VARIETIES OF MARKET CONDITIONS

There are persistent seasonal tendencies in many markets, particularly agricultural markets, which are vigorously buffeted by weather conditions during the various seasons. All markets will have bull and bear cycles as they are affected by alternating patterns of contracting and expanding supply and demand. Financial markets are affected by the business cycle. All markets will have periods of low volatility and trendlessness caused by stable underlying economic patterns or by opposing market forces in equilibrium. There will always be periods of high volatility and soaring prices, that is, the classic bull market. Markets also experience vertical and devastating price drops caused by crises and calamity.

Then you have markets with a strong tendency to trend, in either direction, such as the currency markets. Such strongly trending markets are much less subject to tradable price swings within their larger trend swings.

On the other hand, there are markets that are highly mean reverting such as the S&P or NASDAQ futures. Such markets offer a preponderance of price swings, yet they will also have periods of strong trend.

Yet, there is support for the view that a market comprises a succession of small minimarkets. It is just a matter of the perspective one takes. The very short-term trader might well view a five-day run-up as a bull market. The long-term trader might simply view this as a minor bull correction in a long-term bear market.

Continuously changing volatility adds a high degree of complexity to the standard up, down, sideways, and congested market phases. Recent studies are highly suggestive of a strong cyclic component to changes in volatility. There has always been a school of thought that claims that markets are driven by the complex interplay of many cycles.

As markets reach higher price levels, volatility also increases. When a bull or bear market draws to its end, these are often punctuated by highly volatile market activity.

Bull or bear trends do not always end the same way. Sometimes a bull trend can be quickly and surgically ended with a one-day key reversal and turn into a plunging bear trend. The reverse, of course, is sometimes true of bear markets. Other times, a bull or bear market, especially if extended, can end in a long period of sideways, low volatility consolidation.

Volatility can contract sharply and trend can evaporate because of a lack of interest in a market. After T-bills made a classic, high volume, high volatility 1,000-point rally in 1979, the market consolidated for months in a narrow trading range with very low volatility.

Contracting or expanding liquidity can have a dramatic effect on market structure. Illiquid markets feature small trading ranges and lots of gaps in price action. Conversely, highly liquid markets feature far fewer gaps and a smoother price movement.

This discussion makes clear the many ways that markets can shift and turn. We also know how a strategy can benefit from optimization on those price data that are most relevant to current price action. What is the price to be paid, however?

One of the strong points of walk-forward testing is its ability to identify the best optimization and trading windows for a trading strategy. As such, it is the perfect method with which to achieve maximum trading performance by adapting to current conditions while maintaining statistical robustness.

THE WALK-FORWARD

What then, is a walk-forward test? It is a two-step process. The first step consists of a traditional optimization. A trading strategy parameter space is explored for the optimization sample data and a top parameter set is identified by the objective function.

It is the second step, however, that distinguishes the walk forward and is the source of its unusual strength. In this step, the performance of the top parameter set is evaluated on an additional, adjacent sample of price history that was not included in the optimization price sample. In other words, the top model is tested in a simulation of real-time trading. This second step is a measure of the postoptimization performance of the identified parameter set.

To recap then, a walk-forward is a two-step process. The trading strategy is first optimized on a historical sample. It is then traded on a new and unseen historical sample. This process is also known as *out-of-sample testing* or *double-blind testing.*

A walk forward is the only method that provides a measure of postoptimization trading performance. It is also one of the very best methods available to evaluate the robustness of a trading strategy.

THE ROLE OF THE WALK-FORWARD

If the strategist has recourse to tools that can perform automated Walk-Forward Analysis, of course, this is the recommended next step. The individual walk-forward then is simply an example of one of the major components in a full Walk-Forward Analysis.

If automated WFA is not available, however, then the use of the walk-forward for validation and confirmation is highly recommended. In fact, I would say that a strategist would be at a severe disadvantage deploying a trading strategy that was not tested to at least this level.

Of course, even a few individual walk-forwards do not provide the wealth of information and confidence of a complete Walk-Forward

Analyse comprised of a large sample of individual walk-forwards. However, it is decidedly better than proceeding on to trading from a totally unverified optimization.

It is consequently good procedure to do what amounts to a rather tough and general-purpose walk forward. The size of the in- and out-of-sample windows will depend on data availability and the pace and style of the strategy. Let us assume then, that we are evaluating a longer-term trading system and that we have 15 years of data available.

Let us set up an example. The strategy will be optimized on 10 years of price history and a walk forward will be done on 5 years. So, the strategy is optimized for the time from 1/1/1990 to 12/31/1999. The best parameter set is then tested on five years of out-of-sample data from 1/1/2000 to 12/31/2004. If more data are available, a walk forward can also be done with data adjacent to, but before, the in-sample. So, in this case, the best parameter set can also be walked backward to the five-year period from 1/1/1985 to 12/31/1989. Given that 20 years of data are available, it is also recommended that a test be done in the middle as well.

Running a set of parameters based on a 10-year optimization for 5 years out-of-sample is a fairly rigorous test because of typical shelf life issues. It is recommended, however, in the absence of a full Walk-Forward Analysis. It is also recommended that if this course of testing is followed, that it be done on at least 10 different diversified markets so as to add greater statistical validity to an already somewhat inadequate test.

At this point, there are three main conclusions:

1. If the strategist finds that his strategy loses money in the majority of these walk forwards, he knows that he does not have a tradable strategy.

2. If the strategy performs with some degree of moderate or limited profit in a majority of these tests, this may be an argument for a somewhat poor-to-overfit trading strategy.

3. If it performs with out-of-sample profit in proportion—factoring in differences in market conditions between the in and out of sample data windows—to its in-sample profit in the majority of tests, this is likely to be a rather robust trading strategy.

SETTING UP A WALK-FORWARD

As we have seen, a single walk forward is a two-step process. The first step is optimization. The second step is the evaluation of the performance of the selected parameter on out-of-sample price data.

A walk forward requires the following components:

1. Scan ranges for the variables to be optimized
2. An objective or search function
3. Size of the optimization window
4. Size of the walk-forward, trading or out-of-sample window

The length of the optimization window is determined by the:

1. Availability of data
2. Style of trading strategy
3. Pace of trading strategy
4. Relevancy of data
5. Shelf-life of the trading strategy's parameters.

In general, the faster-paced a trading strategy, the more likely it is to benefit from shorter optimization and walk-forward windows. Start with windows from one to two years in length. Conversely, the slower that strategy, the longer the window needed. Start with windows from three to six years in length. These values, of course, are highly variable because of a number of factors.

The size of the walk-forward window is typically a function of the size of optimization window. Typically, a walk-forward window should be somewhere in the area of 25 to 35 percent of the optimization window.

The size of these windows is best determined empirically. This will be explained more fully in the section on Walk-Forward Analysis. The why of it, however, is a much more complicated story. It lies in the very complex nature of market dynamics. This is a topic far too complex and in-depth for this book.

It starts with market cycles, proceeds through fractals and complexity theory and ends, for now, with strange attractors. The level, depth, and quality of scientific research into market dynamics is at an all-time high. And as billions and billions of dollars of profit continue to be extracted from markets by scientifically trained quants, this trend will progress to ever-higher levels.

Returning to our topic, if market conditions never varied from those evaluated in the optimization window, a trading strategy would never require reoptimization. In practice, however, a strategy optimized properly on two years of price history will likely remain usable for between three and six months of real-time trading. A model built on five years of price history will likely remain usable for between one and two years of real-time trading.

AN EXAMPLE OF A WALK-FORWARD TEST

To illustrate, consider the following example of a 2-variable parameter scan done with a trading strategy called *RSI_CT* on a 48-month optimization window of S&P 500 futures price data.

Price History:	S&P 500 Futures
Optimization Window Size:	48 Months
Historical Period:	1/1/2000–12/31/2003
Buy Variable:	Scan 0 to 300 in Steps of 20
Sell Variable:	Scan 0 to 300 in Steps of 20

This first step of the walk-forward test does a standard optimization scan of two key model variables on S&P price data from 1/1/2000 to 12/31/2003 on a parameter space encompassing 256 candidates. At the conclusion of this standard optimization, the objective function will have identified a top parameter set.

The second step in this walk-forward will determine the postoptimization performance of the top parameter set identified in the first step. In this step, new pieces of historical data, called the *trading window* or *walk-forward window* are then tested separately. In other words, the performance of the top parameter set is evaluated on this new, out-of-sample, historical data. The results of this walk-forward looks as follows:

Price History:	S&P 500 futures
Historical Period Tested:	1/1/2000–12/31/2003
Trading Window:	6 Months
Trading Window Tested:	1/1/2003–6/30/2003
Optimization P&L:	$47,390
Annualized Optimization P&L:	$11,847
Trading P&L:	$20,265
Annualized Trading P&L:	$40,530
Walk-Forward Efficiency:	341 percent

To paraphrase, a top parameter set is identified by way of optimization on a 48-month period of history and is then traded or walked forward on a 6-month period of history immediately after the optimization window. The top parameter set made $47,360 during its 48-month optimization test, which is an annualized profit of $11,847. The top parameter set, in turn, made $20,265 during its six-month postoptimization test, which is an annualized profit of $40,530.

This is impressive. Still, *one* successful or profitable—or unprofitable—walk-forward could still be a product of chance. To more effectively eliminate the likelihood of this being a result of chance, it is essential to conduct as many additional walk-forwards as possible.

This more comprehensive evaluation with multiple walk-forwards is called a *Walk-Forward Analysis*. A Walk-Forward Analysis is a series of individual walk-forward tests. In addition, a WFA provides additional statistical analysis of these results, which allow us to form conclusions about the overall robustness of the trading strategy as well as a number of other useful things. In addition, a WFA grows in statistical reliability with the number of individual walk-forward runs it includes.

THE WALK-FORWARD ANALYSIS

A Walk-Forward Analysis, then, is a set of individual, sequential walk-forwards performed on a comprehensive and representative sample of price history (see Figure 11.1). Typically, the longer the sample, the greater the number of walk-forwards, hence the greater the statistical reliability of the WFA. It is the most comprehensive form of testing to which a trading strategy can be submitted. It is also the most reliable—and easiest—method of evaluating the robustness of a trading strategy. Furthermore, a Walk-Forward Analysis is the closest approximation or simulation of the way in which an optimizable trading strategy is typically used in real-time trading.

A full Walk-Forward Analysis, in the parlance, *walks forward*, or rolls the optimization and trading windows through the entire historical sample. The size of the step window determines the interval at which the optimization window is walked forward or advanced through the full historical sample. A Walk-Forward Analysis then is a sequence of individual walk-forwards structured so as to trade every day in the historical sample on an out-of-sample basis.

This results in a set of performance statistics for each in-sample optimization run and for each walk-forward or out-of-sample run. A full Walk-Forward Analysis, of course, first records all of these reports and next performs some statistical analysis of this information.

The ability to evaluate a trading strategy exclusively and solely on the basis of postoptimization performance is one of the most dramatic and valuable departures of Walk-Forward Analysis from other forms of evaluation.

Without recourse to Walk-Forward Analysis, the strategist is left with optimization, an analysis thereof, and perhaps a few individual walk-forwards. The strategist is left to whatever statistical measures he can

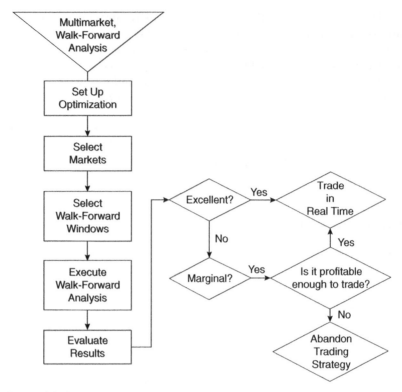

FIGURE 11.1 The Walk-Forward Analysis

derive to form some satisfactory conclusion with regard to the robustness of a trading strategy and its real-time potential. There are occasions when this evaluation seems relatively simple. There are also occasions when it is very difficult.

In contrast, with recourse to Walk-Forward Analysis, the strategist, with little effort or risk of error, can form a solid opinion as to the robustness of a trading strategy. A trading strategy which performs extremely well under a Walk-Forward Analysis offers very solid prospects of real-time profit.

The Purpose of the Walk-Forward Analysis

The primary purpose of the Walk-Forward Analysis is to prove the validity and robustness of a trading strategy and of its optimization process to the fullest extent possible. It extends the benefits of the walk-forward test over a large enough sample of price data and a large number of walk-forwards to supply a high degree of statistical rigor. A Walk-Forward Analysis that includes a large number of walk-forwards will greatly diminish the likelihood that the resulting performance is a product of random chance.

The second purpose of a Walk-Forward Analysis is to arrive at a more accurate picture of the profit and risk profile of the trading strategy. The statistical analysis of the performance of a trading strategy trading out-of-sample certainly provides a higher degree of confidence than the same analysis on in-sample trading, which provides no confidence in and of itself.

A comparison of the postoptimization performance with that of optimization performance also provides us with a more realistic and reliable estimation of future profit. It is time to begin to trade the strategy. It is known from its Walk-Forward Analysis and its WFE statistic that the trading strategy has walked forward at a pace equal to 75 percent of that of optimization. The optimization for the most current data has produced a profit of $20,000 per year. The WFE of 75 percent indicates that the model should profit somewhere in the area of 75 percent of $20,000 per year, or $15,000 a year. This is a helpful measure when then assessing the real-time performance of the strategy.

The Walk-Forward Analysis also provides a more accurate insight into maximum drawdown. There are limits to the accuracy of the maximum drawdown found in optimization when used as an anticipatory measure of real-time trading drawdowns. This stems from a drawback of the optimization process. Most models with large drawdowns will be rejected during optimization. In contrast, the drawdowns measured during the walk-forwards are much closer to those found during real-time trading. In addition, a Walk-Forward Analysis will provide a maximum drawdown for each in-sample and each walk-forward window. These can be evaluated and an average, minimum, maximum, and standard deviation calculated providing a more in-depth view of drawdown than that provided by one in-sample optimization.

The third purpose of the Walk-Forward Analysis test is to verify the validity of the optimization process itself. As has been observed, an unsound strategy will simply fail a Walk-Forward Analysis. This is unambiguous and final.

It not so well known or understood, however, that a sound strategy can be overfit and because of *that* can perform poorly on a walk-forward. The same things that can cause a standard optimization to cause overfitting and thereby produce unreliable results can also come into play and cause a Walk-Forward Analysis to perform at a level lower than would be expected from the true robustness of the trading strategy. Considerations such as too few degrees of freedom, incorrect optimization and test window sizes, too wide scan ranges or too fine scan increments, too many optimizable parameters, and so on can all confound the search for robust walk-forward performance.

If the strategist consequently has reason to believe that the trading strategy is truly robust, yet it produces a low WFE during its Walk-Forward Analysis, this is cause for reevaluation. The Walk-Forward Analysis framework should be reviewed for error. If this can be detected, then the errors should be corrected and a new Walk-Forward Analysis performed.

If this new analysis produces results that are more in line with expectations, then the original opinion of the strategist has been confirmed. If it still performs at a level below expectation after these corrections have been put in place, however, the strategist must consider the likelihood that she was wrong about the trading strategy from the start and move on to new ideas.

The Walk-Forward Analysis is a rigorous simulation of the way in which an optimizable trading strategy is most often used in real-time trading. An important question among users of optimization software is how often the trading system should be reoptimized. The fourth goal of the Walk-Forward Analysis then is to answer this question. The Walk-Forward Analysis answers this question empirically, which, of course, is the best way.

The use of a trading strategy developed with Walk-Forward Analysis should mirror in real-time use the optimization and walk-forward windows identified thereby. If the walk-forward window is three months, then the model must be reoptimized at the end of every three months of trading and so on for different window sizes.

An important part of this practice is to perform this periodic reoptimization with discipline and on schedule whether or not the strategist thinks it needs it or not. The periodic reoptimization that flows from the application of Walk-Forward Analysis to real-time trading is *pre-emptive.* WFA takes the high ground in regard to this truly thorny issue as to when to reoptimize. It does so by systematically refreshing the parameter set of the trading strategy by keeping with a reoptimization schedule and process that has been empirically proven to be effective.

Finally, the unique time-sliced perspective provided by the various Walk-Forward Analysis reports provides a useful and penetrating insight into the impact of changing market conditions on the performance of the trading strategy.

Trading strategies typically have their worst drawdowns when trends or market conditions change. The rolling windows of the Walk-Forward Analysis provide a unique perspective showing exactly what has happened historically when the strategy encounters changing market conditions. The robust trading strategy is more capable of weathering changing conditions without catastrophic losses. The impact of such changes, however, can be masked by standard optimization. They are both revealed by the Walk-Forward Analysis and accommodated by its built-in adaptation to changing conditions through periodic reoptimization.

An Example of a Walk-Forward Analysis

To illustrate, let us consider the example of a Walk-Forward Analysis that consists of 30 individual walk-forward tests of the RSI_CT trading strategy. This analysis will report the optimization performance of the RSI_CT for 30 different periods of contiguous price history. The reward, risk, and robustness of optimization are evaluated by the objective functions and a top parameter set is selected for each.

The Walk-Forward Analysis of RSI_CT will also calculate the postoptimization, or walk-forward, performance for each of the 30 individual walk-forwards. In other words, this WFA will perform 30 out-of-sample tests, including a calculation of performance measures of postoptimization trading. It will also provide performance measures of this postoptimization trading.

Let us summarize to this point: this WFA of RSI_CT will provide information regarding the performance of 30 different optimizations, 30 individual walk-forwards or out-of-sample tests, a statistical analysis of all of this, and performance statistics comparing in and out-of-sample performance.

Furthermore, this particular Walk-Forward Analysis covers a broad historical sample that includes a spectrum of different trend and volatility conditions. This will provide both statistical reliability and a de facto analysis of RSI_CT's ability to weather a variety of changing market conditions.

It is one of the great strengths of Walk-Forward Analysis that a successful set of multiple walk-forward tests on a substantial and sufficiently diverse historical sample *is* a demonstration of the robustness of the trading strategy in the face of many different types of market conditions.

The Walk-Forward Analysis on RSI_CT[1] specifications are as follows:

Price History:	S&P Futures
Historical Period:	1/1/1990–12/31/2005
Estimation Window Size:	36 Months
Test Window Size:	6 Months
Step Window Size:	6 Months
RSI Period:	Scan 2 to 50 in Steps of 2
OB_Level:	Scan 0 to 80 in Steps of 20
OS_Level:	Scan 0 to 80 in Steps of 20
Objective Function:	Pessimistic Return on Margin

The Walk-Forward Analysis proceeds as follows. S&P 500 futures price data for the first optimization window from 1/1/1990 to 12/31/1992 is first loaded. An optimization using the two chosen variables is performed. The parameter set for RSI_CT having the best PROM is recorded. This parameter set is then walked forward on the walk-forward window from 1/1/1993 to 06/30/1993. These results are documented before proceeding to the next optimization window.

The Walk-Forward Analysis proceeds in this manner one optimization and one walk-forward at a time through all of the specified historical data. The Walk-Forward Report details the results of the Walk-Forward Analysis on a walk-forward by walk-forward basis. Table 11.1 presents these results.

The numbers in the Net Profit & Loss column present profits for the different 6-month walk-forward or postoptimization trading periods. The numbers in the Walk-Forward Efficiency column are ratios of annualized walk-forward and optimization Net Profit & Loss.

The Walk-Forward Summary Report presents performance statistics for the total of all of the walk-forward windows. This is a report of the performance of RSI_CT for 13 years of out-of-sample trading (see Table 11.2).

IS THE STRATEGY ROBUST?

An examination of the results of this WFA of RSI_CT will provide an estimation of its robustness and thereby of its real-time trading prospects.

From Table 11.1, we see in the first row 1 that the top parameter set identified in the first optimization window (01/01/1990 to 12/31/1992) produced a walk-forward profit and loss of $3,763. This is the profit made by the top parameter set in the first six months of postoptimization trading (1/1/1993 to 6/30/1993) following the 36-month optimization window. Once again, this is a good result. It is but one walk-forward, however, and this could be the result of chance.

Each line in Table 11.1 reports the same information for 29 additional walk-forwards. We can see that all 19 out of 30 of these in-sample and walk-forward performance results were profitable. We can see from an examination of Table 11.2 that the total net profit is $154,350 for all 30 walk-forwards. This trading strategy made money in 63 percent of the postoptimization test windows. This is a convincing result.

The most important conclusion we can draw from this Walk-Forward Analysis, however, is that this trading strategy *worked*. What does this mean? This means that this trading strategy made money on price history which it had never seen. It also means that the trading strategy made money over 30 consecutive 6-month periods of unprecedented volatility and trend change. This model can be considered robust. This trading strategy is also ready to trade in real time.

TABLE 11.1 Walk-Forward Analysis in Detail

Walk-Forward Analyst
Walk-Forward Report
S&P
From: 01-01-1990 To: 12-31-2007
System: RSI.CT

Start	End	Net Profit & Loss	Maximum Drawdown	Annualized RRR	Winning Percentage	Walk-Forward Efficiency
1/1/1993	6/30/1993	$3,763	–$6,013	125.2%	0.0%	36.2%
7/1/1993	12/30/1993	–$4,088	–$6,100	–134.0%	0.0%	–68.0%
1/1/1994	6/30/1994	–$6,962	–$8,725	–159.6%	0.0%	–85.0%
7/1/1994	12/30/1994	$1,688	–$7,563	44.6%	0.0%	30.8%
1/1/1995	6/30/1995	–$6,575	–$9,875	–133.2%	63.6%	–131.7%
7/1/1995	12/30/1995	–$16,438	–$16,638	–197.6%	0.0%	–409.7%
1/1/1996	6/30/1996	–$14,563	–$18,500	–157.4%	0.0%	–275.8%
7/1/1996	12/30/1996	$10,425	–$14,588	142.9%	0.0%	132.2%
1/1/1997	6/30/1997	$22,400	–$21,850	205.0%	0.0%	336.4%
7/1/1997	12/30/1997	$18,988	–$28,900	131.4%	0.0%	147.0%
1/1/1998	6/30/1998	$46,825	–$17,000	550.9%	0.0%	249.8%
7/1/1998	12/30/1998	–$27,150	–$59,950	–90.6%	0.0%	–156.4%
1/1/1999	6/30/1999	$78,450	–$17,000	922.9%	0.0%	501.7%
7/1/1999	12/30/1999	$3,775	–$34,175	22.1%	0.0%	22.1%
1/1/2000	6/30/2000	$81,000	–$46,675	347.1%	53.8%	320.8%
7/1/2000	12/30/2000	$35,850	–$25,800	277.9%	58.1%	109.0%
1/1/2001	6/30/2001	–$33,825	–$55,500	–121.9%	44.8%	–74.7%
7/1/2001	12/30/2001	$5,375	–$56,625	19.0%	41.7%	16.4%

(Continues)

TABLE 11.1 Walk-Forward Analysis in Detail (*Continued*)

1/1/2002	6/30/2002	$25,850	-$19,600	263.8%	58.3%	86.6%

Walk-Forward Analyst
Walk-Forward Report
S&P
From: 01-01-1990 To: 12-31-2007
System: RSI.CT

Start	End	Net Profit & Loss	Maximum Drawdown	Annualized RRR	Winning Percentage	Walk-Forward Efficiency
7/1/2002	12/30/2002	$14,425	-$27,825	103.7%	51.7%	49.2%
1/1/2003	6/30/2003	$23,775	-$40,050	118.7%	0.0%	50.8%
7/1/2003	12/30/2003	-$34,200	-$52,925	-129.2%	0.0%	-70.0%
1/1/2004	6/30/2004	-$36,475	-$43,125	-169.2%	0.0%	-87.8%
7/1/2004	12/30/2004	$6,750	-$15,250	88.5%	0.0%	18.8%
1/1/2005	6/30/2005	-$20,125	-$37,650	-106.9%	0.0%	-100.1%
7/1/2005	12/30/2005	$3,250	-$20,900	31.1%	53.3%	16.2%
1/1/2006	6/30/2006	$475	-$19,750	4.8%	66.7%	2.9%
7/1/2006	12/30/2006	-$5,875	-$26,900	-43.7%	66.7%	-32.9%
1/1/2007	6/30/2007	-$10,400	-$24,350	-85.4%	0.0%	-47.9%
7/1/2007	12/30/2007	$1,725	-$4,200	82.1%	0.0%	9.0%
Total		$168,113				
Maximum		$81,000	-$59,950	922.9%	66.7%	501.7%
Minimum		-$36,475	-$4,200	-197.6%	0.0%	-409.7%
Average		$5,604	-$26,133	65.1%	18.6%	19.9%
Standard Deviation		$28,347	$16,258	238.4%	27.2%	177.6%

TABLE 11.2 Walk-Forward Analysis is Performance Summary

Summary Report for Session
RSI_CT_WF_sp SP-9967.TXT 1/1/1990 to 12/31/2007. System is RSI_CT()

Performance Summary: All Trades

Total net profit	$154,350.00	Open position P/L	($19,625.00)
Gross profit	$756,050.00	Gross loss	($601,700.00)
Total number of trades	218	Percent profitable	51.38%
Number winning trades	112	Number losing trades	106
Largest winning trade	$90,150.00	Largest losing trade	($57,875.00)
Average winning trade	$6,750.45	Average losing trade	($5,676.42)
Ratio average win/average loss	1.19	Average trade (win & loss)	$708.03
Maximum consecutive winners	8	Maximum consecutive losers	8
Average number bars in winners	15	Average number bars in losers	18
Maximum intraday drawdown	($112,875.00)	Maximum number contracts held	1
Profit factor	1.26	Yearly return on account	8.05%
Account size required	$112,875.00		

Performance Summary: Long Trades

Total net profit	$143,850.00	Open position P/L	$0.00
Gross profit	$386,175.00	Gross loss	($242,325.00)
Total number of trades	109	Percent profitable	51.38%
Number winning trades	56	Number losing trades	53
Largest winning trade	$90,150.00	Largest Losing Trade	($15,825.00)
Average winning trade	$6,895.98	Average Losing Trade	($4,572.17)
Ratio average win/average loss	1.51	Average Trade (win & loss)	$1,319.72
Maximum consecutive winners	8	Maximum consecutive losers	5
Average number bars in winners	22	Average number bars in losers	7
Maximum intraday drawdown	($95,200.00)	Maximum number contracts held	1
Profit factor	1.59	Yearly return on account	8.89%
Account size required	$95,200.00		

(Continues)

TABLE 11.2   Walk-Forward Analysis Performance Summary (*Continued*)

Summary Report for Session
RSI_CT_WF_sp SP-9967.TXT 1/1/1990 to 12/31/2007. System is RSI_CT()
Performance Summary: All Trades

Performance Summary: Short Trades

Total net profit	$10,500.00	Open position P/L	($19,625.00)
Gross profit	$369,875.00	Gross loss	($359,375.00)
Total number of trades	109	Percent profitable	51.38%
Number winning trades	56	Number losing trades	53
Largest winning trade	$35,875.00	Largest losing trade	($57,875.00)
Average winning trade	$6,604.91	Average losing trade	($6,780.66)
Ratio average win/ average loss	0.97	Average trade (win & loss)	$96.33
Maximum consecutive winners	8	Maximum consecutive losers	8
Average number bars in winners	8	Average number bars in losers	29
Maximum intraday drawdown	($84,200.00)	Maximum number contracts held	1
Profit factor	1.03	Yearly return on account	0.73%

WHAT RATE OF PROFIT SHOULD WE EXPECT?

Walk-Forward Efficiency (WFE) is a measure that allows us to compare walk-forward or postoptimization to in-sample or optimization performance. Recall that WFE is the ratio of an annualized walk-forward profit and loss to an annualized optimization profit and loss.

The average WFE for the entire WFA is calculated as follows. The annualized profit and loss for the 30 36-month optimization periods is $8,278 ($745,040/90 years = $8,278). RSI_CT produced an annualized profit of $8,278 during optimization.

The annualized profit for the 36-month walk-forward periods is $11,208 ($168,113/15 years = $11,208). RSI_CT earned walk-forward or out-of-sample profits equal to 135 percent ($11,208/$8,278 = 135%) of those profits earned in-sample.

WFE can be used to provide some estimation of the rate of profit to be earned during real-time trading. Extrapolating, in other words, if RSL_CT produces $10,000 a year in profits during optimization, it can be expected to make approximately $13,500 (10,000 × 1.35 = 13,500) plus or minus in real-time annualized profits over time.

WHAT IS THE RISK?

The average maximum drawdown during optimization was $26,133, with a high of $59,950 and a low of $4,200. As a general rule, a trading strategy that produces a real-time drawdown that exceeds optimization drawdown by a wide margin—all things being equal—may be showing signs of trouble. Therefore, a walk-forward maximum drawdown is an important measure of risk and must be closely watched.

WALK-FORWARD ANALYSIS AND THE PORTFOLIO

We have clearly seen how to set up a Walk-Forward Analysis for one market. We should also have an appreciation for the unique benefits that accrue from this very demanding and final method of trading strategy evaluation.

To draw the final, most general conclusions regarding our trading strategy, we must perform walk-forward analyses for each of the markets on which it will be traded. All of the same measures of evaluation for a Walk-Forward Analysis apply to each of the subsequent WFAs that must be done.

Doing this performs two functions. The first is to determine whether the trading strategy can be successfully traded over the full basket of markets in our portfolio. Of course, it would not be surprising if the strategy is not profitable in every market; if it is though, all the better.

This brings us to the second function of our basket of walk-forward analyses. The more robust the results of each WFA on each market in our basket and the more markets for which it is successful, then the more robust our trading strategy can be judged.

A Walk-Forward Analysis that is clearly profitable over the full basket of markets is a very sound and robust trading strategy. Not only has our trading strategy passed the most rigorous and demanding evaluation process known, but it has also done so over a diversified range of markets.

This trading strategy can now be traded with confidence, yet our eyes must remain wide open.

CHAPTER 12

The Evaluation of Performance

A t this point in the trading strategy development process, it is known that a trading strategy:

1. Is built and operates according to specification
2. Performs consistently with theoretical expectation
3. Is sufficiently robust to pass the multimarket, multiperiod test
4. Benefits from and improves with optimization
5. Has performed successfully on Walk-Forward Analyses for a diversified basket of markets
6. Is sufficiently robust and ready to trade in real time

It is now time to evaluate this robust and promising trading model as an investment by reviewing its internal structure.

THE TRADING STRATEGY AS AN INVESTMENT

Given the arduous creative and design process and the resources and time investment required to test, evaluate, and develop an automated trading strategy, it is easy—perhaps all too convenient—to forget that it still must compare favorably with the full universe of other potential investments. Once the development of a trading strategy has come to this point, it may be difficult to abandon even if it is just not as good as the competition. The purpose of this chapter is to provide a context for the evaluation of the trading strategy with reference to the competition.

THE DIMENSION OF RISK

The risk of trading futures, which are naturally highly leveraged, is on the extreme end of the risk spectrum and even when done well can be almost unlimited. The holder of a futures position is liable for any deficits that occur in her account beyond the money on deposit. Overnight risk, for example, can be devastating. Recall the 20-point close to open drop in S&P 500 futures on October 19, 1987. For starters, overnight longs sustained a $10,000 loss per contract on the open of this unusual day. In retrospect, the nineteenth and twentieth were statistical outliers and are not common. However, these black swan events can and do occur and they must be factored into the risk profile of anyone trading futures.

Even in markets with daily limits, overnight risk is still not completely eliminated. Markets with daily limits faced with market-wrenching news can produce a run of locked-limit days. The effect of this scenario can be severe financially, not to mention psychologically. This too must enter into the risk equation.

The yield of futures trading strategy, consequently, must be evaluated in light of the greater risk associated with it. Returns must accordingly be substantial enough to justify this higher level of risk because of the outside potential of risk of ruin. Risk must be well-defined, thoroughly understood, and acceptable. Strict money management principles must be applied to defend against catastrophic loss. A futures—for that matter, any type of—trader can never be too careful.

COMPARE THE STRATEGY TO THE ALTERNATIVES

A trading model ultimately competes with virtually risk-free, low-yielding investments such as T-bills, certificates of deposit, money market accounts, and savings accounts.

For example, $10,000 invested in a T-bill may generate a 3 percent yield with no risk of capital loss. An investment in U.S. government securities has long been considered a risk-free investment. Hence, whereas this is not a high return, it is a risk-free return. In contrast, $10,000 traded in futures runs a risk of the loss of all of the invested capital and more. Consequently, the return must be greater to compensate for this higher risk.

It might seem absurd to think that a futures trading strategy might offer such a low return. An inspection of the performance of a number of commodity trading advisers, however, will show that some don't even do that well.

A trading strategy must also be compared to other investment alternatives such as stocks, bonds, real estate, and art. Successful investment in these areas requires different expertise. Yet a trading strategy must perform in a way that is competitive with them.

Its performance must also be compared to that of professional commodity trading advisers and hedge fund managers. Furthermore, the trading strategy must be compared to commercially available trading strategies.

The expenses of maintenance and operation—computers, price data, software, employees, and time—needed to execute the trading strategy must also be considered as a cost of doing business. If a trading strategy is expensive to operate and maintain, then its returns must be sufficient to overcome these additional costs.

In short, the profit and risk profile of a trading model must be superior, or at least sufficiently attractive in some other way, to other forms of competing investments to justify its existence.

MAXIMUM DRAWDOWN AND TRADING RISK

All business is done at a cost. The cost of trading profit is determined by two things: risk and margin.

The single most important measure of risk for a trading strategy is its maximum drawdown. *Maximum drawdown* (MDD) is the dollar value of the largest decline from equity high to a subsequent equity low.

The other two major forms of identifiable risk of a trading strategy are the risk per trade and the overnight risk.

Risk per trade is simply the amount of trading capital at risk on a trade-by-trade basis. As such, it is more correctly a concern of trading strategy design.

Overnight risk or market risk is that which is incurred by a trading position that remains open overnight. As discussed in Chapter 6: The Historical Simulation, overnight risk is subject to the somewhat unpredictable close to open change. At times, this can be quite substantial. This form of risk, however, is also best dealt with at the design level.

Why is maximum drawdown the most important measure of risk? It is because it is the *largest* measure of the risk of a trading strategy. Because of its size and duration, maximum drawdown holds the potential to completely erase all of the capital in a trading account. If it is not properly addressed through a correct trading capitalization, it can be a risk to the continuation of trading. Maximum drawdown, then, represents *catastrophic* risk for an *undercapitalized* trading account.

Maximum drawdown, or some multiple thereof, is widely used as one of the primary measures of the maximum potential risk of a trading strategy. The operating assumption behind this assessment is that if a trading strategy has endured a drawdown to this extent in historical simulation, even in the form of a Walk-Forward Analysis, then an equity drawdown of similar extent is likely to be seen again in real-time trading.

We see in later sections how maximum drawdown is used to calculate the needed capitalization for a trading account. If maximum drawdown is accurate, the account will be properly capitalized. If MDD is in fact too large, however, the result will be an underperforming trading capital. Conversely, if MDD turns out to be too small, it places the trading capital at excessive risk. If MDD is very small with regard to subsequent real-time drawdowns, the trading capital may be at risk of catastrophic loss.

How can our measure of maximum drawdown be too small or too large? The answer to this is rather complex and somewhat beyond the scope of this book.

There are two main points, however, that can be observed in this regard. The first is more straightforward and more readily addressable. The size of maximum drawdown is usually a function of one of two things. Typically, all things being equal, maximum drawdown will tend to expand and contract in proportion to the expansion and contraction of volatility.

This can lead to a MDD measurement that is too small if it was produced during an historical simulation with low volatility. If volatility increases during real-time trading—especially if it is far in excess of that in its historical simulation—the trading strategy is then likely to produce larger real-time drawdowns. If the trading account has been capitalized with this now too small MDD, it is at undue risk.

Conversely, a MDD measurement can be too large if it was produced during a historical simulation with high volatility. If volatility decreases during real-time trading, the trading strategy is likely to produce smaller real-time drawdowns. If the trading account has been capitalized with this now too large MDD, it will be insufficiently leveraged and consequently underperforming.

Overcapitalization and underperformance, of course, is a better situation than undercapitalization and the consequent risk of ruin. It is best to avoid both conditions, however.

The second cause of an inaccurate measure of maximum drawdown is more complex. Advances in math and statistics have uncovered weaknesses in standard statistical measures applied to financial time series. The first weakness is of a more mundane nature; the second is more arcane.

There is a newer area of statistics called robust statistics. This area has to do with the use of statistical measures that have been produced by samples of a size, among other reasons, that produce measures lacking in robustness. All of the statistics produced by the historical simulation of a trading strategy fall into this category. They will consequently be a bit fuzzier than the more robust statistics produced by larger samples. *Fuzzy* means that they will have larger standard deviations and will consequently vary quite a bit more than might be desired.

Furthermore, and this more arcane reason is *highly* significant, Benoit Mandelbrot, the creator of fractal geometry, has demonstrated to my satisfaction, and to that of many others, that financial time series do not have a normal distribution. Rather, they conform to a fractal distribution.

To exploit this to its fullest, requires the use of some very sophisticated math. In the absence of this math, however, one thing that we can conclude from this, and with some utility, is that we have yet another very credible source that is telling us that any statistics we calculate on a financial time series will be in error to some degree or another.

This is a potentially far more serious degree of error than that produced by the lack of robustness discerned in these statistics from the discoveries of robust statistics. For those who wish to explore this very difficult area further, the writings of Mandelbrot should be consulted.[1]

As a consequence of all these different factors, however, it is a very reasonable assumption that the most accurate measure of maximum drawdown that we can derive with current statistical measures is likely to remain to some extent inaccurate.

Maximum Drawdown in Context

Because maximum drawdown plays such a definitive role in the assessment of the trading model from the viewpoint of risk, there are a few other factors worthy of consideration as well.

Maximum drawdown is, of course, the biggest drawdown in equity. There are many other equity drawdowns, however, and it is helpful to look at the maximum drawdown in relationship to these other drawdowns. It is helpful to know the average and the minimum drawdowns as well. A more robust model is likely to have a tighter clustering of drawdowns.

If MDD is dramatically larger, three times the size, for example, than average drawdown it is not cause to abandon the strategy. It is important, however, to have some idea of why this is the case. In general, it is important to understand the market conditions under which the maximum drawdown has occurred.

Sometimes a MDD is the result of a price shock. A *price shock* is an unusually large price change. By definition, price shocks are outliers or statistical anomalies that occur infrequently. The crash of 1987 was just such a price shock. Price shocks are often caused by significant business, economic, or political events such as the outbreak of war, the unexpected collapse of a major company, a major oil find a devastating terrorist attack, or the assassination of a major political leader. A price shock can result in a windfall if you are positioned in its direction or an extremely large loss if you are not. Price shocks by their nature are unexpected and cannot normally be predicted. A trading strategy needs to be able to accommodate them by design or by risk management—in other words, to expect the unexpected.

At other times, MDD is a result of an extended period of market conditions hostile to the trading strategy. Maximum drawdowns typically occur either in congested markets or in highly volatile, choppy markets of extended duration. Both conditions are antithetical to many trading strategies. It is therefore a positive sign if the maximum drawdown of the trading model occurred during a period featuring such adverse market conditions, for this would be expected.

It would be quite troubling, however, to find that the maximum drawdown occurred during market conditions that are indistinguishable from those which produced, for example, one of the largest profitable equity swings.

Most trading strategies prosper during periods of strong and sustained trends or of high volatility and strong, clear price swings. A maximum drawdown during such a period would definitely be a matter of concern. If it cannot be satisfactorily explained, it may present a strong argument to either abandon or redesign the trading strategy.

Maximum Drawdown and the Trader

Maximum drawdown, one may hope, is the largest decline in equity that a trader must live through. MDD can often be of long duration as well.

Consequently, the experience of a maximum drawdown in real-time trading is usually a stressful experience for the trader. As such, while it is depleting trading equity, it may also put the trader's discipline to the utmost test.

The psychological make-up of most traders is resistant to extended periods of loss even if the total loss is not particularly large. Trading is about making money. To many traders, however, trading is also about being right. Whereas this is not a good quality for a trader to have, it is oftentimes all too accurate. Losing streaks can damage the ego and the confidence of the trader. Whereas the ego will survive, the potential loss of confidence can be dangerous to trading success.

Drawdowns are an inevitable part of trading. It is therefore best for the trader to do all that is possible to prepare for the inevitable. One of the most effective forms of preparation is to develop a full understanding and knowledge of drawdowns and, in particular, of maximum drawdown.

The very best way to prepare for this *psychologically* is to quantify drawdown in every way possible. It is equally important that the trader also be *financially* prepared to deal with the loss of trading income and the depletion of trading capital that will result from these events.

If the trader is not psychologically and financially prepared to endure both the typical and maximum drawdown, it may prove difficult, if not impossible, to stick by the trading strategy during the inevitable losing periods that will occur in real-time trading.

Maximum Run-up and the Trader

The *maximum run-up* in equity should also be evaluated in the same manner as maximum drawdown. The maximum run-up (MRU) is the largest improvement in trading equity between an equity low and a subsequent equity high. It is the far more pleasant opposite of maximum drawdown.

These periods of run-up define the optimal trading conditions for the trading strategy. In other words, the type of market conditions that prevailed during the biggest winning run-up are the conditions that are optimal for the trading strategy.

As previously noted, a good trading system typically excels in periods of strong trends, high volatility, and clean price swings. If the maximum winning run occurred during such a market condition, it is consistent with theoretical expectations. If, however, MRU occurs in conditions that are markedly different, this should be noted and an explanation sought.

MRU can be compared to the average run-up run as a measure of robustness and consistency. This is not quite the same as the MDD comparison, however. The best trading strategy will have a steadily rising equity curve, and as a consequence, the MRU can and should be very long.

A thorough understanding and knowledge of MRU and average run-up, however, is helpful in a psychological way. As noted earlier, a trader must be financially and psychologically prepared for the financial and emotional devastation that can be caused by an extended period of drawdown.

Whereas a big equity run-up is obviously a very positive event and the result that is sought by all traders, it too, however, can lead to a potentially damaging euphoria and a false sense of confidence that can also be antithetical to trading discipline. It is important for a trader to know the difference between a windfall and good trading. A thorough knowledge of run-up is one of the best ways to make this distinction.

Trading Capital and Risk

Undercapitalization is one of the most common causes of trading failure. The undercapitalized trading account, by definition, has insufficient reserves to withstand trading risk at its worst. This will often, though not always, lead to a catastrophic trading loss and an inability to continue trading.

Required capital (RC) is the amount of money required to trade a strategy successfully and for the long term. It was previously established that maximum drawdown is the maximum measure of risk that a trading account must be able to absorb. The issue of required capital will be explained in more detail.

Before proceeding, it should be noted that the method employed to calculate the amount of trading capital needed to trade a strategy or set of strategies, on one or a portfolio of markets will be a very large consideration in real-time trading performance. Because this is such an important issue, many ways have been developed to perform these calculations. They range from the relatively simple, but sound, method described in this section up to very sophisticated methods that employ advanced mathematics. That being said, the element common to all of these approaches is a measure of trading or portfolio risk.

Recall the earlier comments about the various inaccuracies inherent in the measurement of maximum drawdown. Risk is one of the major costs of trading. From this follows the obvious and inevitable conclusion that the more accurately risk can be measured, the more effectively, as in higher rates of return, and accurately a trading account can be capitalized.

It is beyond the scope of this book to delve into such sophisticated mathematical procedures. The strategist seeking maximum returns, however, should explore the potential of these more sophisticated ways of measuring risk.

Let us continue with our formula for the calculation of required capital. It must accommodate the two major costs of trading futures: margin and risk.

To establish a futures position, a trader must have sufficient funds on deposit to meet initial margin. Margin rates, or performance bonds, as they are more formally called, are set by the exchanges and enforced by the clearing firm. Margins change from time to time, based on the volatility of the market. The first demand made of required capital is sufficient capital to meet initial margin when a position is taken.

The second component of required capital is to have enough capital to withstand maximum trading risk. Maximum drawdown is our measure of maximum trading risk. To trade successfully, a trading account must be able to sustain a maximum, or perhaps greater, drawdown and still be in a position to continue trading.

At minimum, therefore, a trading account would require an initial margin plus the dollar value equal to maximum drawdown. Assume an initial margin of $10,000 and a maximum equity drawdown of $15,000.

$$\text{Required Capital} = \text{Margin} + \text{Risk}$$
$$RC = \$10,000 + \$15,000$$
$$RC = \$25,000$$

This minimum capital of $25,000 can sustain a $15,000 drawdown and still afford to make at least one more trade of the same size. That trade must be profitable, though. If it is a loss, the account will no longer have enough capital for initial margin and, as a result, can no longer trade. The prudent trader hopes for the best but prepares for the worst. The worst can be a drawdown larger than the maximum drawdown that has occurred in historical simulation or in real-time trading.

The prudent trader, therefore, will invest sufficient trading capital to accommodate maximum equity drawdown and have enough left over to continue trading and with some margin for error.

Consider a different formulation of required capital with a maximum drawdown of $15,000 and an allowance made for a somewhat larger future drawdown of $30,000.

$$\text{MDD} \times 2 = \$15,000 \times 2$$
$$RC = \$10,000 + \$30,000$$
$$RC = \$40,000$$

This RC of $40,000 can sustain a $15,000 drawdown and still afford at $25,000 to make a number of trades without requiring the next trade to be a winner.

Some traders extend this logic further, erring toward the conservative, and protect themselves from a maximum drawdown equal to three times the current MDD. According to this formulation, required capital will be:

$$\text{MDD} \times 3 = \$15,000 \times 3$$
$$RC = \$10,000 + \$45,000$$
$$RC = \$55,000$$

This RC of $55,000 can sustain a $15,000 drawdown and still afford at $40,000 to make a number of trades without needing the next trade to be a winner, either.

To a certain extent, the degree to which maximum drawdown is expanded as a cautionary measure for the calculation of required capital is a function of two things: personal preference and risk tolerance on the one hand and confidence in the accuracy of its original measurement on the other.

Undercapitalization has been observed to be one of the primary causes of trading failure. Erring on the side of caution, not overconfidence, is therefore highly recommended, and to use a conservative method to calculate required capital.

RISK ADJUSTED RETURN

Profit can not be correctly assessed without reference to its cost. The primary cost of profit in trading is its risk. The best measure of trading performance, consequently, is a *risk-adjusted rate of return* (RAR). Annualizing RAR further standardizes it.

Not only is RAR the most meaningful measure of performance, its annualized form consequently makes it straightforward to make an in-kind comparison for RARs for different markets as well as for returns produced over time intervals of differing lengths.

One of the interesting advantages of RAR is that it can be increased in two ways. RAR increases if the rate of profit *increases* but the risk remains the same. RAR can also increase however, if the rate of profit remains the same and if risk is *decreased*.

At the risk of repetition, profitability must be evaluated in light of the perspective of its cost. Consider the following example. A trading strategy that produces an annualized profit of $10,000 sounds great. If it requires the assumption of a risk of $200,000, however, its maximum drawdown to earn this profit represents a RAR of 5 percent per year on dollars invested and at risk of loss. This doesn't sound quite as wonderful.

Alternatively, consider a trading strategy that produces an annual profit of $5,000. Upon a first look, this appears to be only half as attractive as the first strategy. It starts to look a lot more interesting, however, when it is learned that this strategy has a risk of $2,500. This is a RAR of 200 percent.

Of course, these examples are rather extreme, but this was done to make the point more obvious. Maximum risk is typically the largest cost of any trading strategy. The only meaningful measure of the returns of a trading strategy are those adjusted for risk.

The examples cited here demonstrate that profit must be judged as a return on investment. From the formulation of the calculation of required capital presented in the previous section, it was seen how maximum trading risk is a major component of trading cost. Using that formula, let us consider a more realistic example of annualized risk-adjusted return for a trading strategy.

$$\text{Annualized Profit} = \$25,000$$
$$\text{Margin} = \$10,000$$
$$\text{Risk} = \text{MDD} \times 2$$
$$\text{Risk} = \$20,000 \times 2$$
$$\text{Annualized RAR} = \text{AP}/(\text{Margin} + \text{Risk})$$
$$\text{Annualized RAR} = \$25,000/\$50,000$$
$$\text{Annualized RAR} = 50 \text{ percent}$$

REWARD TO RISK RATIO

Given the importance that risk plays in the assessment of returns, the *reward to risk ratio* (RRR) is a statistic that provides an easy comparison of reward to risk. It its most basic form, it is:

$$\text{RRR} = \text{Net Profit}/\text{Maximum Drawdown}$$

When annualized, it is a more basic version of RAR.

For example, consider an annualized profit of $25,000 divided by a maximum drawdown of $5,000:

$$\text{Annualized RRR} = \text{Annualized Profit}/\text{MDD}$$
$$\text{Annualized RRR} = \$25,000/\$5,000$$
$$\text{Annualized RRR} = 5.0$$

The bigger the RRR the better. A bigger RRR implies that reward per trading dollar is increasing relative to the risk. In general, a RRR should be three or better. It must be noted that the validity of this number, of course, is in direct proportion to the accuracy of its components.

MODEL EFFICIENCY

This is a very unique and powerful way in which the profit of a trading strategy may be assessed. I introduced the concept of Perfect Profit (PP) in the first edition of this book. It has always been a surprise to me that this concept has not been more widely used by the trading community.

When the profit of a trading strategy is measured as a function of Perfect Profit, it is an assessment of how efficient the strategy is by its conversion of market opportunity into profit.

Markets obviously offer greater or lesser profit potential at different times. When a market is trending with high volatility, profit potential in the form of PP will be very high. Conversely, when a market is not trending and has low volatility, profit potential will be considerably lower.

The measurement of the potential profit that a market offers is an idea that is not widely understood. It is not that difficult to understand, however.

Perfect Profit is the sum total of all of the potential profit that could be realized by buying every bottom and selling every top. More precisely, it is the sum of the absolute value of every price swing formed between a price peak and a subsequent price valley. Perfect Profit is obviously an unachievable ideal measure. A review of some sample Perfect Profit values, though, shows the vast potential that exists in one market and in one time frame (see Table 12.1).[2]

Perfect Profit, even in its unachievable Ivory Tower perfection, provides an excellent measure of strategy performance. Model Efficiency is a measure of how efficiently a trading strategy converts or "transforms" the perfect potential profit offered by a market into realized trading profits.

This calculation of ME is straightforward as long as Perfect Profit is available.

$$\text{Model Efficiency} = \text{Net Profit}/\text{Perfect Profit}$$

For example, assume a net profit of $25,000 and a Perfect Profit of $300,000 for the historical period traded. Using the Model Efficiency formula,

$$\text{Model Efficiency} = (\$25,000/\$300,000) \times 100$$
$$\text{Model Efficiency} = 8.33 \text{ percent}$$

An ME of 8.33 percent is actually quite good. Trading strategies with MEs of 5 percent and better are considered very good. The elegance of ME, however, is that it is the perfect measure of performance. It is a direct measure of how much a trading strategy is capable of profiting from exactly what a market offers for a particular time frame and time period.

Like annualized risk adjusted return, model efficiency is also a statistic that makes it easy to make direct and meaningful market-to-market performance comparisons. PP and ME also provide an excellent measure of performance as markets change. A market starts to move and PP rises. The market stalls and stagnates and PP falls.

When the performance of a trading strategy is viewed solely in light of profit variation from year to year, it is sometimes difficult to interpret meaningfully. If the ME of the trading strategy remains rather stable year after year, however, it is an indication of a good, robust model. The strategy

TABLE 12.1 Perfect Profit for Five Markets and Five Time Degrees for Five Years (01/2002–12/2006)

Market	Time Degree					
	5 Min	30 Min	Daily	Weekly	Monthly	Total by Market
Crude Oil	$5,718,190	$2,385,750	$887,440	$434,310	$187,850	$9,613,540
Eurodollar	$417,100	$180,363	$56,888	$34,738	$20,250	$709,338
Japanese Yen	$3,465,650	$1,691,375	$601,000	$287,188	$114,175	$6,159,388
Soybeans	$2,810,825	$1,386,925	$783,450	$325,825	$166,888	$5,473,913
S&P Index Futures	$18,498,100	$7,842,925	$2,368,000	$988,175	$432,400	$30,129,600
Total by Time Degree	$30,909,865	$13,487,338	$4,696,778	$2,070,235	$921,563	

continues to extract a similar percentage of perfect profit even as it waxes and wanes.

CONSISTENCY

Consistency in the performance of a trading strategy is one of the most fundamental characteristics of a robust trading model. Although this may sound complicated, it really is not. The principle is very straightforward: the more consistent the trading model is in every statistical measure, the better and more robust the trading strategy is likely to be.

Perhaps it is easier to understand the importance of consistency by considering its opposite. A trading strategy that does not feature consistent performance will be a trading strategy with concentrated clusters of wins and losses, and with wins and losses of extremely variable size. When one adds extremely inconsistent performance within one market and extreme inconsistency from year to year and from market to market, the picture becomes even clearer. The bottom line is that the more inconsistent a trading strategy is, the less likely it is to be robust, and consequently the more suspect the trading strategy is.

The most robust and confidence-building model, consequently, is one that features as even as possible a distribution of:

1. Profit and loss
2. Wins and losses
3. Long and short trades
4. Winning and losing runs

Given the nature of markets and of the performance of trading strategies, however, consistency, in general, is difficult to fully achieve. Perhaps one of the easiest ways to look at this is to judge consistency by the absence of concentrations of anything.

One form of the desired trading consistency is the least possible variance in these various statistical categories. To evaluate this, it is best to calculate the average, standard deviation, maximum, and minimum for each of these categories. The smaller the span between maximum and minimum and the smaller the standard deviation, the smaller therefore is the variance and hence the more consistent the performance of the trading strategy.

Another quick way to evaluate consistency is to remove the maximum value from each category and then recalculate the average without it. If this adjusted average is considerably smaller—1 to 2 standard deviations—than the unadjusted average, this suggests excessive influence by the maximum.

The third way to evaluate consistency is to determine how well spread out each of these performance measures are throughout the historical time period under review.

The bottom line is that the most robust and attractive trading strategy is that strategy that has a relatively even distribution throughout the historical sample of:

1. Profit and loss
2. Winning and losing trades
3. Winning and losing runs
4. Long and short trades

Of course, all of these statistics can and will be affected by different market trends and conditions.

This is consequently acceptable if periods of concentration appear but can be linked to changing market conditions.

PATTERNS OF PROFIT AND LOSS

As was previously observed, one of the most important and meaningful measures of trading performance consistency is that of the evenness, or lack thereof, of the distribution of profit and loss throughout the historical sample. The distribution of profit and loss is a more important consideration than that of profit alone. A good distribution is evidence of a robust and consistent model. A poor distribution calls into question the validity of the model. Also, patterns or trends within the distribution of profit and loss have significance.

Let us examine four distinct examples of patterns or vectors of profit and loss.

Assume that a trading model has a walk-forward profit of $50,000, with a maximum drawdown of $10,000 over the five years 2001 through 2005. This profit and risk look excellent.

Four different cases of the distribution of profit and loss will illustrate the significance of these patterns.

In the first case, assume the following distribution of profit and loss displayed in Table 12.2.

A glance at the distribution of profit and loss on a year-by-year basis gives pause. Why? The biggest profit was made in the most distant year. The biggest loss was made in the most recent year. In addition, the direction of year-by-year profit and loss is on a clear, downward slope from the most distant past to the most recent past. This is a bad sign. To make matters

TABLE 12.2 Case 1—Suspect Distribution of Performance

Year	Profit	Drawdown
2001	$50,000	$5,000
2002	$30,000	$6,000
2003	$10,000	$7,000
2004	($15,000)	$9,000
2005	($25,000)	$10,000
Total	$50,000	

worse, the fact that year-by-year drawdowns are in a clear uptrend from the most distant to the most recent past raises another red flag. Furthermore, the variance of the profits and losses is quite great.

This trading strategy did very well in 2001. The profit earned in this year was large enough to mask poor performance in 2004 and 2005. This model enjoyed great prosperity in 2001 and declining prosperity in 2002 and 2003. It ran into bad times in 2004 and 2005. It is possible that this was caused by a flaw in the strategy. It is possible that these last two years were just very bad for the model. It seems that the market has been changing in a manner that is incompatible with the model. But the real question is, "How will it do in 2006?" This, of course, can only be answered by guessing whether 2006 will be more like 2001 or 2005.

Consider a second case with the following distribution displayed in Table 12.3.

Even a most cursory inspection should lead to outright rejection of this trading model. Its net profit of $50,000 is based on $110,000 of profit in 2002—the only profitable year. Every other year has a very consistent loss of $15,000. Obviously, the large net profit in 2002 exceeds and conceals poor performance in all the other years. The validity of this model is extremely questionable. Certainly, it requires a reevaluation and is likely to

TABLE 12.3 Case 2—Failed Distribution of Performance

Year	Profit	Drawdown
2001	($15,000)	$5,000
2002	$110,000	$10,000
2003	($15,000)	$7,000
2004	($15,000)	$6,000
2005	($15,000)	$4,000
Total	$50,000	

TABLE 12.4 Case 3—Excellent Distribution of Performance

Year	Profit	Drawdown
2001	$8,000	$10,000
2002	$7,000	$3,000
2003	$10,000	$4,000
2004	$11,000	$5,000
2005	$14,000	$4,000
Total	$50,000	

not be tradable in its current form. The trading strategy should most likely be rejected. At minimum, it should be seriously reexamined.

Consider the third case with the following distribution displayed in Table 12.4.

This very even distribution of both profit and drawdown reinforces confidence in the overall profit of $50,000 and drawdown of $10,000. In addition to its even distribution, performance shows a favorable upward direction in profit from the more distant to recent data. It is also shows a favorable downward tendency in drawdown from past to present. The variance of the profits is small as is the variance of drawdowns, with the exception of that in 2001. Furthermore, this model had its worst drawdown in the most distant past. All of this adds up to a very satisfying and acceptable model that is thriving in the most recent test period.

Consider the last case with the following distribution displayed in Table 12.5.

This case is the opposite of the first. It has the same questionable uneven distribution of profit and loss. It has two very desirable features, however. It has a positive upward sloping direction of profit from 2001 to 2005. It also has a favorable decline in drawdowns from 2001 forward. Furthermore, it is positively thriving in 2005 with its best performance in every category.

TABLE 12.5 Case 4—Accelerating Distribution of Performance

Year	Profit	Drawdown
2001	($25,000)	$10,000
2002	($15,000)	$9,000
2003	$10,000	$7,000
2004	$30,000	$6,000
2005	$50,000	$5,000
Total	$50,000	

The question that must be answered is, "Why?" If this model is to be traded, a sound explanation of these trends in year-to-year profit and loss should be available. Is the trading strategy better able to operate under conditions that have become increasingly more favorable? For example, a reasonable explanation of this performance would be congested and trend-less activity in 2001 and 2002 contrasted with a strong clean trend and rising volatility starting in 2003 and moving forward into 2005.

The evaluation of the distribution of profits, losses, and drawdowns is very straightforward: the more even the distribution, the better, and the more distant the maximum drawdown, the better.

Profit should not be disproportionately concentrated in one or two periods. If there is a direction or trend to profit, it should be up. Conversely, if there is a trajectory or trend to drawdown, it should be down. If there is a clear-cut trend of profit or risk, it must be noted. Just as trends change in markets, so can trends in trading model profit and risk.

CHAPTER 13

The Many Faces of Overfitting

O ver the years, a number of different expressions have been used somewhat interchangeably to describe problems that arise in the process of evaluating and optimizing a trading strategy. These terms include *overoptimization, overfitting, curve-fitting,* and *data mining.*

These words are also typically used in a pejorative and dismissive manner. There are still those who derisively, and with great ignorance, dismiss all optimization as curve-fitting, which means for those in that camp that an optimized strategy is, almost by definition, a fantasy or a delusion.

To entirely discard as garbage the very idea of optimization because an improperly optimized strategy has failed in real-time trading is itself, however, a product of ignorance and poor logic. It is the same type of logic that would cause someone who has seen only blond women to overgeneralize and conclude that all women are blondes.

It is not a coincidence, of course, that those who conclude that optimization is useless are those who have probably never seen a correctly optimized trading strategy.

It is incorrect to use these four terms interchangeably. *Overoptimization* and *overfitting* are identical in meaning. This equivalence will be seen clearly once the term "overfitting" is precisely defined.

Curve-fitting and *data mining* are often taken to have a similar sense and this too is understandable. They are two different processes, though, with little, in fact, relationship to one another. In addition, and this is important, the problem that these terms are meant to identify is really the result of poor research procedures and an abuse of hindsight. This is explained in the upcoming sections.

This problem is not simply one of semantics, however. This confusion in terminology masks a more serious confusion about the different classes of problems that can arise during optimization.

These different expressions will first be properly defined and delineated. Then, some of the other problems that can arise in the course of the development of a trading strategy will be described. Methods will also be presented for the avoidance of these other types of problems. Finally, the symptoms, causes, and solutions for overfitting will be presented.

There is some overlap in the material presented in this chapter with that presented in earlier chapters, particularly 10 through 13. There is much that is new, however, and what has been repeated has been done so from a somewhat different perspective, and so all of this important material is available together in one easy-to-study chapter.

WHAT IS OVERFITTING?

A formal definition of *fit* will help so as to correctly understand *overfitting* in an intuitive sense. The word *fit* must first be defined and understood before the term *overfit* can be understood.

One definition of *fit* in the *New Oxford American Dictionary* is, "Make suitable to fulfill a particular role."

In the context of trading strategy development and optimization, to *fit* the parameters of a trading strategy to historical data then, would be to make it suitable or capable of producing real-time trading profits.

Consider the *New Oxford American Dictionary* definition of the prefix *over:* "Excessively; to an unwanted degree."

Combining these definitions, *overfit* is defined as: "Fit to an unwanted or excessive degree."

An overfit trading strategy therefore is one that is *excessively fit* or *fit to an unwanted degree.* It is not much of a stretch then to deduce that a trading strategy fit to an excessive or unwanted degree will be one that is *not suitable or appropriate* for the purpose of producing real-time trading profits.

It is key to the understanding of overfitting to note that fitting is a process that can be correctly performed if done to the proper extent. What can be done correctly—to the proper extent—can also be done excessively or to an improper extent. As the causes of overfitting are examined, the utility of this definition will become increasingly clear.

It is helpful in this context to note that overfitting in the field of statistics means to fit a statistical model with too many parameters for the data being modeled. This should sound very familiar to a developer of trading strategies.

Overfitting occurs, then, when the various aspects of the optimization process are done to excess. There is a granularity to the optimization process. Overfitting consequently occurs to different degrees. A mildly overfit trading strategy can still produce real-time profit. A massively overfit trading strategy, however, is unlikely to do so. There are also degrees of overfitting.

Overfitting, then, is optimization performed incorrectly. More specifically, the *overfitting* or *overoptimizing* of a trading strategy is the identification of parameters that produce good trading performance on in-sample price history but produce poor trading performance on out-of-sample price history. It matters not if the out-of-sample data are an unseen historical sample or real-time data—the result will be the same.

The overall cause of overfitting is easily stated. It occurs when the rules of proper development and optimization are not followed. The different causes of this and their respective solutions are discussed in upcoming sections.

Overfitting is also readily detected by its effects. An overfit, as well as any other type of erroneously developed trading strategy will perform differently in walk-forward or real-time trading than it did in optimization. An overfit or flawed trading strategy will typically produce losses in real-time trading.

One very big difference between an overfit strategy and a strategy that is the result of flawed research is that an overfit strategy may actually be a *sound* strategy that is actually performing poorly *because of* overfitting.

A more intuitive way to explain it then is that to fit, or optimize, the parameters of a trading strategy to a market and a time period means to correctly identify those parameters that have produced profitable performance in historical simulation and will be most likely to produce comparably profitable performance in real-time or walk-forward trading.

A properly fit or correctly optimized trading strategy will perform essentially the same way in real-time trading as it did in the optimization or fitting process.

To emphasize the point, *overfitting* occurs when the fine line between proper and improper optimization is crossed. This line is easy to miss, and that is why it is essential to rigorously follow correct testing and optimization procedures.

In conclusion, the term *overfitting* refers to an improperly executed optimization, which results in the identification of parameters that are *incapable* of producing real-time trading profits. In contrast then, the term *optimization* refers to a properly executed optimization that identifies parameters that are the most capable of producing real-time trading profits. Before we explore overfitting in more detail, it is first necessary to explore what is perhaps the other main cause of strategy development failure.

THE ABUSE OF HINDSIGHT

In fact, the abuse of hindsight is really one of the most common causes of an unsuccessful strategy. This abuse falls more in the category of improper research procedures and less in the camp of statistical error. It is also an area that is not all that well understood. This lack of understanding, of course, just further promotes its abuse.

The *New Oxford American Dictionary* defines *hindsight* as: "Understanding of a situation or event only after it has happened or developed."

It brings to mind the old adage, "Hindsight is twenty-twenty."

There are some, of course, who develop trading strategies who take this issue to a counterproductive and even a prohibitive degree. It is clearly the case, however, that when the improper use of hindsight slips into the design of a trading strategy, the first person who is fooled is the trading strategist.

Consider the following somewhat simplified illustration, which uses hindsight in a manner that leads to a poor strategy. Looking back over five years of price history, the strategist observes that the market experienced an extended bull move. He consequently imparts a bias toward buying and discourages taking short positions in the strategy under design. The strategist optimizes the bullish biased trading strategy on a price history with a bullish bias and—guess what—the results are exceptional. Furthermore, the optimization set shows great statistical robustness.

The strategist, with no further testing, begins to trade the strategy in real-time. The bull move soon ends, though, and the market turns very bearish and is accented with a lot of choppy and congested periods. What do you suppose happened to the performance of his bullish biased trading strategy that was tested only on a bull market? It should be no surprise that it produces a losing streak that far exceeds the maximum drawdown produced during its development phase.

In this example, of course, hindsight colluded with an inadequate historical sample and inadequate testing to ensure failure. The outcome is predictable to all but the strategist who was duped by his own shoddy testing procedures.

Consider another somewhat simple but illustrative example of the appropriate incursion of hindsight. A longer-term trend-following strategy has been developed. It performs rather well on a historical sample with a lot of persistent trends. The strategist notes, however, that there was a very big loss on a particular trade. The strategist reasons that a $3,000 risk stop might be a good idea. Not so small as to generate a lot of whipsaw trades, not so large that it will have a derrogatory impact on overall trading performance. The risk stop is applied to the strategy, and, what do you know, profit went up 50 percent. The strategist is very excited and does not notice that it went up because the risk stop eliminated that one very large loss.

The strategist does no more research and starts real-time trading with the strategy. The market, unfortunately, has different ideas. The trend stops and market conditions change to very volatile, choppy, and trendless. Guess what happens? The strategy generates a huge string of losses triggered by the choppy, volatile conditions and maximum drawdown is exceeded once again.

Again, hindsight—fueled by a desire to eliminate that single big loss—causes the strategist to, in effect, add a trading rule that does eliminate this loss. Again, shoddy procedure and inadequate testing join to wipe out the strategist's trading account.

Consider a third example of the abuse of hindsight. The strategist develops a shorter-term strategy to trade stock index futures. The performance is marginal so far. As the strategist looks back over the performance of the strategy, however, he notices a handful of occasions when a favorable move in T-bond futures occurred at the start of a couple of some very big moves in the S&P. The strategist adds a new rule to his strategy: When an S&P signal is accompanied by a sympathetic move in T-bond futures, triple the number of contracts traded. He tests this new rule on his historical sample and finds that it more than doubles profit while keeping risk at the same level. Very excited, the strategist takes this strategy into the real-time trading arena.

What happens? The strategist finds, to his great dissatisfaction, that the "linkage" between his S&P strategy and T-bonds has become "unlinked." The resulting over leverage caused by his inadequately researched new rule, leads to catastrophic real-time trading losses.

Of course, as noted, these are relatively simplistic examples. They do illustrate the point, however. Does this mean that the strategist cannot avail himself of a review of performance on the simulation? Absolutely not. A review of the performance of a trading strategy on historical data is an important source of insight and provides an opportunity for potential improvements.

How then, in more general terms, is knowledge of past market and strategy performance abused? The first way the abuse of hindsight occurs then, is to implement a change and not test it thoroughly.

The easiest way to avoid falling into this form of error is to thoroughly test any anticipated strategy improvement over a full range of time periods and markets. If the improvement enhances performance on a limited selection of historical periods and markets, it is not really such an improvement. Conversely, if this change produces a significant enhancement over the full range of historical periods and markets, the modification in fact is a real improvement.

The second way hindsight is abused arises from the use of shoddy inductive reasoning. This is more subtle and therefore more difficult to catch. In general, the easiest way to understand this problem area is to see that it is caused by the incorrect generalization and elevation of a limited number of observations to that of the level of a principle. The effect of this error in reasoning can be seen in each of the three aforementioned examples.

The best trading strategies are those that are based on sound, and hopefully universal, principles of market behavior. As in all forms of science, the trading strategist must always defend against overgeneralization and shoddy inductive reasoning. One of the best ways for the strategist to achieve this is to find ways to empirically demonstrate the validity of his inductive conclusions.

What is the cure for hindsight? The cure is simple to state: Don't let it creep into your design process. If a new rule suggests itself based upon a more detailed review of trading performance, be sure that it is exhaustively tested before assuming it is an improvement that will hold up in real time.

THE CASE OF THE OVERFIT FORECASTING MODEL

Consider the case of a statistician who builds a forecasting model of the stock market. One of the most common and effective ways to do this would be to build a model using linear regression analysis. In this method, the statistician fits a line of regression to the stock market data. With this done, the calculation of the next point forward on the line of regression produces a forecast. Such a model will give a straight line projection. Although such a projection might not be very accurate or useful from a trading viewpoint, it is a sound forecasting model based on standard statistical practices.

Upon further evaluation of the forecasts of this model, the statistician feels that its accuracy might be improved. The statistician notes by observation that the stock market had a few large rallies and declines. Looking further for other more advanced statistical modeling methods, the statistician is able to fit a curve to these data, which better follow the contours of the rally and decline more closely. Additional review of this model shows that it fits the stock market data a bit better than the first version of the model.

Coming from a school of thought that if a little is good, then more is better, the statistician decides to apply an equation that is capable of incorporating a curve for every peak and valley in the price data. This is commonly called a higher order equation, since it requires the use of a larger number of variables. The statistician finds upon review that this newest version of the forecasting model now fits the historical price data even more closely than the two previous models. Seeing this, the statistician is already picking out the 20,000-square-foot McMansion he plans to move into and the color of his new Bentley in which he will commute between it and his world-renowned trading firm.

His dream of his fine new home and car crashes and burns, however, once the hasty statistician starts to trade with his forecasting model. The forecasts, which it makes in real time, have a much larger error than those calculated during testing.The result, of course, is a string of catastrophic trading losses. To say the least, to his great surprise it proves to be much less accurate than his first simple but statistically sound forecasting model.

What went wrong? That is simple. The effort to use established statistical modeling techniques to build a sound forecasting model turned into an exercise in overfitting. How? The statistician abandoned sound statistical theory in the construction of his forecasting model. He was seduced instead by the powerful illusion of an elegant mathematical curve with its extraordinary and seductive fit to *past* data.

This exercise in statistical modeling turned into a classic case of *overfitting* to the letter of the definition. The statistician continued to add variable after variable to his model to produce a closer and closer—but statistically unsound—fit to past data with no effort to validate its robustness.

The forecasting model was judged solely on the closeness of its fit to past price data. As a consequence, the statistician consumed too many degrees of freedom and added too many constraints. The result was a classic overfit model. To make matters even worse, the statistician did not perform a walk-forward test or analysis of the forecasting model to determine its robustness and forecasting abilities on unseen data before using it to trade with real money.

The first forecasting model had a rough, but statistically sound fit to the price data. The forecasts from the first model had broad confidence bands that proved to be untradable. The model did have statistical validity, however. It was developed with an appropriate number of variables for the data sample. This version of the forecasting model also could have been verified on out-of-sample or walk-forward data.

The last forecasting model had a much closer and attractive fit to the price data. However, this model had no statistical validity. It was developed with insufficient degrees of freedom and too many variables. Perhaps, most gravely, the forecasting model was never verified with even one walk-forward. The forecasts from this model proved to be predictably hopelessly and completely inaccurate.

Too much attention was paid only to how elegantly the model fit the past price data. This stemmed from the erroneous belief that the closeness of fit of the forecasting model to past data is a reasonable or sufficient measure of the predictive value of the model. Proper statistical modeling procedures must always be followed when building a forecasting model that is intended to produce robust predictions, just as proper optimization procedures must be followed when building a trading model that is expected to produce real-time trading profits.

Anyone who is knowledgeable about fitting equations to data knows that "With *enough* variables, a curve can be fit *perfectly* to *any* time series." Will this perfectly fit curve, though have any predictive value? Probably not—too many constraints, too few data, and not enough testing make for a bad model.

However, this is not to say that a model that fits the underlying data well is necessarily a bad model. To the contrary. The closeness of the fit and the accuracy of the forecasts come down to two important factors: the sophistication of the modeling process and the degree of nonrandom movement in the data.

A forecasting model can make valid predictions only to the extent that there is nonrandom, hence predictable, behavior in the data. A model operating within its capabilities is fit properly when adapted to that portion of price movement that is nonrandom. A model is improperly or overfit when excessively adapted to the random portion of price movement.

The proportion of the random to nonrandom components of price action sets a natural limit to the predictability of a market. The forecasting limits of a model are also a function of the limits inherent to the sophistication of the modeling process.

In recent years, the sophistication of statistical modeling procedures has undergone a renaissance. Consequently, increasingly more complex and powerful modeling procedures are becoming available.

The issue of the degree of random movement in financial time-series has also become a more hotly debated topic. This is partly the result of the emergence of these more sophisticated modeling procedures and of new and highly sophisticated mathematical approaches.

It is interesting to observe that until recently, it was widely believed in the academic community that the movements of financial markets were largely random, and hence unpredictable.

Due largely to these new modeling and mathematical methods, the academic community is more in alignment with the long-standing belief of many in the trading and investment communities that, in fact, market behavior is to some exploitable extent, nonrandom.

The increasing flow of academics to the world of trading certainly has a nonrandom look about it.

THE CASE OF THE OVERFIT TRADING MODEL

The same types of procedural errors that created the overfit statistical model will also have the same overfit result for a trading strategy. With enough variables and enough scanning of different parameters and ranges, many unsound trading strategies can be made to look profitable during optimization. Of course, as it has now been well established, that simply because a trading strategy looks profitable during optimization is no guarantee that it will generate real-time trading profits.

Consider an analogous example of a strategist optimizing a single moving average trading system. The moving average is scanned over a range of values from 3 to 15 days in steps of 1 on two years of price data. As a result of this optimization, the trader finds that one set of parameters for this model has made $10,000 in two years with a $5,000 drawdown. It is forward tested for a six-month period. It made $2,000 in this period. These are good results. It worked in forward trading at a pace roughly comparable to its annual rate of $5,000 per year during optimization. So far, so good.

However, the now overeager trader unwittingly abandons caution. A second moving average is added as a measure of a longer trend and is scanned from 10 to 100 days in steps of 2 days. The first moving average is scanned from 1 to 31 days in steps of 1. The strategist now identifies a parameter set where the in-sample profit has jumped to $25,000 for the two-year period with a drawdown of still only $5,000. The trader becomes even more frenzied in light of this dramatic increase in performance. In his excitement, he skips the out-of-sample test of this optimization.

Reasoning that the addition of a second variable boosted performance by over 150 percent, the trader adds two more variables to the model. He now scans the moving averages in the same way as he did in the second test. The first new variable, a buy volatility band, is scanned from 0 to 5 percent in steps of .25 percent, and a second new variable, a sell volatility band, is scanned over the same range. At the end of this optimization, profit has soared to $65,000 for the two-year period, with a drawdown of only $7,500.

At this point, the trader is simply beside himself. He can't wait until Monday (fortunately for him, it is still Saturday) to start making money. Frustrated, he settles for an out-of-sample test. Much to his surprise, but to the benefit of his trading account, the trading system loses $15,000 in a six-month out-of-sample historical test.

But the last optimization was over 600 percent better than the first. What went wrong? The same thing went wrong as with the forecaster. The trader paid no heed to sound research procedures and, as a result, compromised degrees of freedom, overscanned the parameters, overparameterized, used too small a data sample, and neglected to walk-forward the test. Fortunately, something (that being that markets observe the weekend!) made him do a walk-forward test and the truth was discovered. And fortunately, this occurred before the system was traded in real time when the losses would have been more than a blow to only his ego.

As clearly presented in Chapters 10 and 11, a trading strategy that has been developed according to sound research principles and evaluated and optimized by a walk-forward analysis is a trading strategy that can be reasonably expected to perform in real time in a way that is similar to the way it worked during development.

If the trading strategy developer strictly and religiously follows these principles to the fullest degree, she has done all that she can. The rest is up to the markets.

THE SYMPTOMS OF AN OVERFIT TRADING MODEL

Nothing could be simpler than describing the real-time symptoms of an overfit trading model: devastating real-time trading losses. Sound trading strategies obviously have losses; but they also have wins that make these losses endurable. The symptoms of a severely overfit or poorly developed trading strategy are typically in evidence from the very start of real-time trading. Such a strategy will show no predictive accuracy and will produce a series of real-time losses. Its real-time trading performance will be completely different—often the opposite—from that which it produced during its *mis*-development.

In cases where the degree of overfitting is not as extreme, real-time trading performance might differ from the testing profile to varying extents. It may not produce devastating losses, but it will certainly underperform its development results.

For example, the average loss string of the test profile might be 3 losses in a row with a dollar value of $4,000. The average win string might be 2 in a row with a dollar value of $6,500. In real time, the average loss string might prove to be $7,000 and four in a row and the average win string might be $4,000 and two in a row. Put more simply, if the annualized RAR in-sample was 30 percent, out of sample, it may be 15 percent. This is obviously not a disaster. Yet, it may be a warning that not all is perfectly well. It could also be the result of diminished market opportunity.

It is also quite possible that a severely overfit trading strategy can, by chance, deliver a profit or three after which it falls into the pit of unending losses. Such a turn of events can be confusing to the trader. The random profits can delude the trader into thinking that maybe there is just something a little bit wrong with this strategy. And that well may be true. But always be prepared for the worst.

As was discussed in Chapter 11 in the section on WFE, there is another subtle symptom of overfitting that is not so easy to detect. As has been previously noted, there are degrees of overfitting. It can range from the mild and insignificant to the severe and catastrophic.

The effects of a mild case of overfitting can be accurately likened to the slowdown in speed of a swift runner when weighted down by a great burden. In contrast, the effects of a severe case of overfitting is comparable to what happens to a swift race car when it accelerates at full speed off the finish line while the driver is unaware that a malicious prankster has securely anchored his rear axle to a sturdy structure and consequently leaves it behind when he has driven past the length of the chain at high speed.

The obvious way this will show up is through real-time performance that is significantly less than that of in-sample performance. Of course, real-time performance for a sound trading strategy can, in fact, be less than in-sample performance because of worse market conditions or having less market opportunity.

So, this variance in real-time versus in-sample performance can be difficult to detect if it is in fact not catastrophic. It can be most effectively detected by a comparison of the walk-forward efficiency of the trading model to its real-time performance. All things being equal, real-time trading efficiency should be relatively close to the walk-forward efficiency established from the strategy's Walk-Forward Analysis.

If the real-time WFE is radically different over a reasonable period of time and it is not traceable to a difference in market conditions, then it is likely to be a symptom of overfitting. This is usually a correctable circumstance. If the strategy passed a Walk-Forward Analysis, it is in all likelihood a sound model. Its underperformance in real-time trading then, is probably due to some degree of overoptimization. The development process should be reviewed for errors, and if detected, they should be corrected and the strategy should be reevaluated on this new basis.

THE CAUSES OF OVERFITTING

Overfitting is a direct result of the violation of some or all of the rules of evaluation and optimization. These violations generally fall into five categories:

1. Insufficient degrees of freedom
2. Inadequate data and trade sample

3. Incorrect optimization methods
4. A big win in a small trade sample
5. Absence of a Walk-Forward Analysis

Degrees of Freedom

It is a cardinal rule of statistical analysis that too many constraints—or too few degrees of freedom—on a data sample will lead to untrustworthy results. In other words, if the calculation of the formulae of a trading strategy consumes too large a proportion of the data sample, the results of the optimization will lack sufficient statistical validity and hence become unreliable. Degrees of freedom and sample size are inextricably intertwined. Insufficient degrees of freedom are still a major cause of overfitting.

To a large extent, degrees of freedom are simply a way to determine whether there are enough data remaining to produce a valid trade sample after all deductions have been made for the price data that are used to calculate the trading rules, indicators, and so forth.

Measuring Degrees of Freedom

It is simple to measure degrees of freedom. To begin, it can be thought that each data point in the sample represents "one degree of freedom." If the sample size is one thousand data points, then it begins with one thousand degrees of freedom, that is, all of the data are unconstrained.

A degree of freedom then is said to be *consumed* or *used* by each trading rule and by every data point necessary to calculate indicators.

To illustrate, consider two examples. Both use the same data sample, which is a four data-point, two year, price history composed of opens, highs, lows, and closes, or a total of 2,080 data points.

Example one is a trading strategy that uses a 10-day average of highs and a 50-day average of lows. Average one uses 11 degrees of freedom: 10 highs plus 1 more as a rule. Average two uses 51 degrees of freedom: 50 lows plus 1 as a rule. The total is 62 degrees of freedom used. To convert that to a percentage, divide degrees of freedom used by total available degrees of freedom. The result is 3 percent. This is perfectly acceptable.

Example two is a trading strategy that uses a 50-day average of closes and a 150-day average of closes. Average one uses 51 degrees of freedom: 50 closes plus 1 as a rule. Average two uses only 102 degrees of freedom: 100 additional closes plus 1 as a rule. The total degrees of freedom used are 152. Converting to a percentage, we get 7.3 percent.

While this is still acceptable, from these examples, it is easy to see how adding more indicators and rules or decreasing sample size can easily lead to decreased confidence in the results. This will be made clear in the examples in the next section.

Degrees of Freedom, Sample Size and Startup Overhead

Now consider the following two examples using the same system but with different size data samples. The trading system uses a 10-day and a 50-day close moving average and has 5 trading rules. It uses 57 degrees of freedom calculated as follows. The long moving average uses 51 degrees of freedom: 50 closes to calculate it and 1 as a rule. The short moving average only uses 1 degree of freedom because it is counted as a rule even though it uses the same data as the long average. The other 5 trading rules each use 1 degree of freedom. This brings the total count up to 57 degrees of freedom used by this trading model.

The sufficiency of the degrees of freedom is judged in relation to the size of the data sample to which they are applied. The first data sample, then, is 100 days of four field data totaling 400 data points. The indicators and rules of the trading system use 57 degrees of freedom. This is 14.3 percent of the total, leaving 85.7 percent. Generally, less than 90 percent remaining degrees of freedom is considered too few. This is reason to reject this test as it stands, or to modify it so as to free up additional degrees of freedom.

Consider a second data sample consisting of 1,000 days of open, highs, lows, and closes. Deduct 57 degrees of freedom for the trading strategy formulae. This leaves 98.6 percent degrees of freedom. This is fine. With the addition of the start-up data, the trading model can also get a proper trading test from start to finish of the target trading sample.

Furthermore, there is a start-up cost or overhead that has a direct impact on sample size independent of issues of degrees of freedom. Returning to the example strategy, it can be seen that trading cannot begin until 50 days into the sample. Why? Because a trading signal cannot occur until there are enough data points to have valid moving averages. Whereas the moving average only needs 50 closes, the nature of the trading strategy simulation process actually prevents the use of first 50 opens, highs, and lows. The overhead required to produce a valid trading simulation, in fact, consumes 200 degrees of freedom.

When this overhead cost is applied to the already small sample size of the first example, it alone consumes 50 percent of the available 400 data points. Overhead alone places an unacceptable burden on the degrees of freedom of this sample.

This start-up overhead has another equally subtle impact on the optimization process. It can impart a bias to the optimization results in favor of the shorter parameters versus the longer parameters if not enough data are available.

This has much less impact when the data sample is large, degrees of freedom consumed by the strategy are small, and the pace of trading is rapid. This is because all of these elements combine to produce fairly similar trade size samples for all of the parameter sets in the optimization set.

When the data sample is small, however, and the trading pace is slow, the degrees of freedom consumed by the formulae are quite variable and heavy on the long end of the scan range. This can have a telling impact.

Why? Two examples make it simple to see. A 3-day by 8-day moving average system on 300 data points consumes 13 degrees of freedom, and start-up overhead consumes only 8 data points. A 25-day by 100-day moving average strategy, however, consumes 102 degrees of freedom and heavily burdens the data sample by removing 100 days of data from the sample of 300 data points. The 3-by-8 MA is also going to trade a lot more actively than the 25-by-100 MA, thereby creating a decided discrepancy in trade sample size.

Start-up overhead poses a problem for Walk-Forward Analysis, which must be resolved by proper WFA software design.

At least 90 percent degrees of freedom must remain after all rules, indicators, and start-up overhead are deducted to ensure statistical validity.

Degrees of freedom can be over burdened by:

1. A data sample that is too small
2. Excessive start-up overhead
3. Too many rules
4. Too many parameters
5. Parameters that are too long

Most trading development applications do not calculate degrees of freedom. Since they can and will affect the validity and quality of the historical simulation, optimization, and Walk-Forward Analysis processes, the strategist must make some rough calculations to ensure the greatest possible statistical validity.

Common sense and careful craftsmanship in the strategy evaluation process, fortunately, can easily remedy this omission:

1. Use a large enough test sample
2. Allow for start-up overhead
3. Do not overparameterize the strategy

4. Be sure the range of parameter scans is strategy and sample appropriate

5. Test with degrees of freedom of at least 90 percent remaining whenever possible

Trade Sample Size

The importance of the size of the historical sample has been established in previous discussions in this book. It is important to fully realize, however, that the size of the historical sample is a large factor in the determination of the generation of a statistically significant sample of trades.

To state the obvious, a sample of one trade is certainly insignificant. Conversely, a sample of 1,000 trades is outstanding. Most trading strategies, however, produce trade samples in between these two extremes. In general, it should come as no surprise to hear that the bigger the trade sample size, the better. How much is enough? Thirty to 50 trades is an adequate minimum. Constraints imposed by a trading strategy, however, or restrictions made by limited data availability may occasionally force the strategist to make a judgment call on a trade sample that is less than 30. If this is the case, the strategist must be even more cautious in every other category regarding statistical validity.

Some insight into the pejorative impact of too small a trade sample size can be gleaned from three examples using a generalized formula for standard error. We can arrive at a general notion of how contracting trade sample size will expand the standard error of its population.

Examples of standard error for three different sample sizes, a sample of 10, 100, and 1,000, are presented in Tables 13.1, 13.2, and 13.3.

$$\text{Standard Error \%} = 1/\text{SqRt}\,(\text{Sample Size})$$

From these three examples, it is easy to see how standard error drops in inverse proportion to sample size.

TABLE 13.1 Standard Error

Sample Size of 10 Trades

Standard Error	$= 1/\text{SqRt}\,(10)$
Standard Error	$= 1/3.162$
Standard Error%	$= 31.6\%$

TABLE 13.2 Standard Error

Sample Size of 100 Trades

Standard Error	= 1/SqRt (100)
Standard Error	= 1/10
Standard Error%	= 10.0%

TABLE 13.3 Standard Error

Sample Size of 1,000 Trades

Standard Error	= 1/SqRt (1,000)
Standard Error	= 1/31.62
Standard Error%	= 3%

The pace of trading is highly variable from strategy to strategy. For example, a long-term trading strategy that trades, for example, 4 times a year, will require 12 years of data to produce 50 trades. Furthermore, such a strategy is likely to use indicators that consume many degrees of freedom and require a larger start-up overhead. Conversely, a short-term system that trades twice a week will only need a half of year of data to produce 50 trades. It will also typically consume far fewer degrees of freedom as well as a much lighter start-up overhead burden.

Optimization Error 1—Overparameterization

This topic has been touched upon in various places throughout this book. It is both easy to describe but not always so easy to remedy. This is the first and perhaps most damaging of these types of errors.

Overparameterization is the use of too many optimizable variables in a trading strategy. It directly relates to the discussion of overfitting at the beginning of this chapter. The use of too many parameters in a trading strategy can cause overfitting in exactly the same way that the use of too many variables can lead to the overfitting of a statistical forecasting model.

The solution, of course, is to optimize only those parameters that are necessary. It should go without saying, of course, that the more optimizable parameters a trading strategy has, the larger the historical sample and trade sample need to be. As skill and experience are acquired in the strategy development process, the selection of the proper set of optimizable parameters becomes increasingly easy.

Optimization Error 2—Overscanning

Another improper application of optimization that is another big cause of overfitting is *overscanning*. Overscanning occurs when a parameter scan uses a step size that is too small or steps over a range that is too large. A change between parameters unavoidably represents a percentage change as well. Why does this matter? Consider the following examples.

In the first example, consider a parameter scan of a short-term moving average tracking short-term price trends. The parameter will be scanned from 2 to 10 days at a step of 1. In this instance, parameter values of 3 and of 4 are separated by the minimum amount that they can be, 1 unit. As a percentage, however, this looks a little different. A 4-day moving average uses 33 percent more data than a 3-day moving average. There is little else that can be done to optimize a moving average over a short range, however, and at these lengths, there is little harm.

The second moving average, however, is intended to track changes in a longer-term trend. Such trends might range from 30 to 100 days. Because of the length of these periods, however, a set size of 1 is too small. Why? The difference on a percentage basis between a 91- and a 90-period moving average is quite insignificant at 1.1 percent. Contrast this to the 33 percent difference that 1 step produces in the short moving average. Practical experience also tells us that there will be little difference in the information provided by a 90- and a 91-day moving average.

A step size of 1 period is fine, consequently, for the short-term moving average. A scan of 30 to 100 days at a step size of 1, however, would be considered too fine.

That being said, what harm can this do, aside from wasted processing time? Recall that an important measure of the robustness of a trading strategy and of its optimization is the percentage of profitable simulations in the full optimization set. A higher average simulation and a lower variation thereof are also measures of robustness as well.

Performing an optimization scan that is too fine, as is the one in our example discussed here, then will *stack* the optimization set with a significant number of essentially *irrelevant* historical simulations. The effect of this is to artificially raise the count of profitable simulations, raise the overall average of the simulations, and lower the standard deviation. In other words, it will provide the appearance of greater robustness statistically, but it will not really be more robust because of improper procedure. The use of the overly fine optimization scan produced an optimization set with a misrepresentative population skewed by a high proportion of simulations that are really not statistically or practically different.

This two-variable optimization space will consist of 639 tests. An optimization set is considered robust if at least 40 percent, or 256, of these simulations produce statistically significant profits. It is not hard to see how this measurement could be unduly biased by the results of the over-scanned range.

Looking again at the theory behind the trading system, it is clear that a change from a 90- to a 95-day average represents a rate of percentage change consistent with the rate of parameter change for the shorter moving average. Optimizing this average from 30 to 100 days in steps of 5, therefore, is more appropriate.

This two-variable optimization space will consist of 135 tests. For this optimization space to be considered robust, 54 simulations should produce significant profit. The big difference, however, is the population of this optimization set will consist of more significantly and practically different simulations. The conclusion about robustness can be taken with far more confidence than in the first overscanned case.

The Big Fish in a Small Pond Syndrome

This phenomenon does not fall strictly in the overfitting domain, although more there than anywhere else; nor does it fall strictly in the domain of poor research procedure. Furthermore, it is really only a problem with rather long-term trading strategies that trade infrequently.

This problem can also be addressed by resorting to some other considerations such as securing a sufficiently large trade sample and avoiding strategies that have excessive concentration of profit.

The symptom must be recognized because it will crop up even with valid trading strategies. The condition is a trading strategy that offers the appearance of robust performance but has a small trade sample size—the small pond in our metaphor—and the bulk of its profit in one or two long-lasting and large wins—the big fish. This is also produced over a relatively long span of history. Is it clear why this is a symptom related to longer-term and slower strategies?

Unless this strategy, and with similar parameter sets, passes a comprehensive Walk-Forward Analysis and over the majority of a significantly diversified basket of markets, it should be rejected as overfit or statistically unsound. It is also extremely important that the optimization set feature as high a degree of robustness, given this somewhat unusual circumstance.

Also keep in mind that this symptom can arise in any trading strategy, which is highly selective, that is, infrequently traded.

The Walk-Forward Test

Now that the overfitting, hindsight abuse, and the various statistical causes of overfitting have been detailed, it is time to state that the easiest way to detect, and thereby avoid trading with, an overfit or otherwise unsound trading strategy is to perform a broad range of Walk-Forward Analyses upon it. This case was presented in detail in Chapter 11: Walk-Forward Analysis.

This runs the risk of sounding as if the solution of a complex problem has been overly simplified. It is not oversimplification however. It is a statement that is the result of extensive research and use of this technique to develop robust and profitable real-time trading strategies.

All of the methods of research and analysis presented in this book are sound. Experience has shown, however, that even when the soundest research methods and analysis are used, statistical error and overfitting can still sneak into the strategy and evaluation process.

Consequently, as stated earlier in this book, Walk-Forward Analysis was developed as an idiot-proof method of strategy evaluation, but even with its use, all the necessary cautions must still be observed. That being said, Walk-Forward Analysis is still the most essential and final stage of the evaluation of a trading strategy.

No matter how well a trading strategy performs in testing and optimization, if it does not "walk forward," that is, perform as well on out-of-sample, postoptimization trading, the trading strategy is not robust and will not in all likelihood produce real-time trading profits.

It is worth repeating that a bad strategy can be made to look great with the benefit of overfitting—that is a textbook definition of it. Conversely, a good strategy can be made to look poor in a Walk-Forward Analysis because of poor procedure and its resultant overfitting. This type of overfitting is revealed by Walk-Forward Efficiency, and this is one of the great advantages of the Walk-Forward Analysis.

How does the Walk-Forward Analysis uncover optimization excesses and statistical failure? The most important way is to determine whether it made a profit in the walk-forward. This is its major contribution to the art of trading strategy development. The second important measure is at what relative pace or degree of efficiency did it make a walk-forward profit. This is the role of Walk-Forward Efficiency.

CHAPTER 14

Trading
the Strategy

T he path that the trader must follow from idea through real-time trading is a long one. As documented in this book, this path begins as an idea, proceeds through specification and refinement, then on to evaluation and Walk-Forward Analysis and finally to end with its implementation as a profitable real-time trading strategy. The path is long and arduous at times, but it is well worth it when the well-conceived and thoroughly tested trading strategy starts and continues to produce real-time trading profits.

Before the time of the all-pervasive personal computer, it was all too common to begin trading a good idea after what would now be viewed as cursory and inadequate testing. In fact, even in this highly computerized era of ours, some traders still do it this way. The outcome was often significant trading loss. The reason for that outcome should be clear to all readers who have come to this final chapter.

The computer can save money in many ways. The main way the computer saves the trader money is by detecting bad trading ideas before those ideas erase the trader's account. Personal computer time, no matter how much is used, is usually a lot cheaper than the consequences of an untested trading strategy and its all too avoidable trading losses.

Only after a trading strategy has passed through exhaustive evaluation with robust profit should a trader even think about trading with it in real-time. Even after the most rigorous development and evaluation, the trading strategy must still be continuously reevaluated in light of its ongoing real-time trading performance.

302 THE EVALUATION AND OPTIMIZATION OF TRADING STRATEGIES

There are three main ways in which real-time performance should be monitored:

1. Return on investment
2. Maximum Risk
3. Real-time compared to test performance

This chapter will address these issues and more. But before discussing these topics, there is one other topic, somewhat unrelated but highly important nonetheless, that deserves at least a mention.

THE MENTAL ASPECTS OF TRADING

Larry Williams's quote and its topic have been mentioned in various chapters in this book. It is so important that it will be mentioned one last time: "Trading strategies work, traders don't."

The very best trading strategy will fail if it is not put into practice and followed religiously by the trader. Aside from the determination of its robustness and positive expectancy, the evaluation of a trading strategy performs another very important function. The exhaustive evaluation of a trading strategy is intended to also produce confidence in the strategy for the trader.

The unevaluated trading strategy is a lot like a new shoe: The trader or owner will never be really comfortable with either until it is broken in. How does the strategist break in a new trading strategy? The strategist tames it by fully understanding all of its nuances.

A trading strategy is a tool, albeit a relatively complicated one. If its behavior is not well understood, it can and will cause anxiety for a trader when it starts hitting performance extremes.

The well-tested trading strategy should be well understood by the strategist. The strategist should be fully conversant with the details of maximum drawdown and maximum run-up. When the best and the worst that a trading strategy can throw at the trader are known in advance, there should be little room for surprise when they raise their heads.

Some of the most corrosive character traits that will negatively affect the trader are greed, fear, and impatience. The biggest reason why so many who attempt to trade fail in the endeavor is that they do not master their own emotional and mental horizons.

Assuming that the strategist has tended to his emotional well-being and honed his discipline, he should have no problem with these corrosive influences.

And more important, an exhaustive knowledge of the trading strategy is the best cure for these influences when the trading strategy hits a period of maximum run-up, taunting greed, a period of maximum drawdown, fanning fear, or flat performance, producing boredom and the itchy desire to find something better.

Keep this brief but extremely important proviso in mind: Real-time trading success cannot be achieved if it is not followed.

RETURN ON INVESTMENT

The performance of a trading strategy in real-time trading must be compared to that of competing strategies and investments. While this may seem obvious and more like a business decision than a trading decision, it is an important measure of strategy performance. Also, the real-time performance of the trading strategy has to be compared to that of its evaluation performance.

If the return on investment of the trading strategy pales in comparison to its return produced during evaluation, the trader, as a prudent business person, also must make a decision. This is explored in detail in the section "Real-time and Evaluation Performance."

In either case, the trader must make a determination as to the cause of this decline in trading performance. It must be decided if there are any valid reasons why the strategy has underperformed.

Real-time trading performance can decline for any of three main reasons:

1. Because it is a poor trading strategy
2. Because market opportunity has contracted
3. Because unseen market conditions have emerged

Poor Strategy

If a trading strategy is performing at a subpar level, below expectations for any reason, it is always possible that it is just a poor strategy and this somehow eluded detection during evaluation. Although this is unlikely and uncommon if the strategy evaluation is done well, it is always possible. This is really the last explanation if all others fail. If poor performance continues, a business decision must be made.

Market Contraction

A market contraction occurs when favorable market conditions are replaced by unfavorable conditions. For example, a trend may pause, end, or reverse, or a trading range market that had long and very tradable swings gives way to congestion.

In any case, this is actually a fairly common cause of diminished performance. A contraction in market activity is a time when a market offers diminished profit opportunity. It is also a fairly common occurrence and not cause for alarm. Market contractions are just part of the game of trading and they must be endured from time to time.

A thorough knowledge of the historical characteristics of the market is a tremendous aid in making a sound decision in this regard. For example, consider a market that is prone to one- to two-week periods of low volatility and directionless price action intermixed with trending conditions. With this knowledge of its behavior, if the market has been in such a condition for the last four months, this may be a good justification to abandon the trading strategy even though it is performing according to expectation, in favor of superior opportunities in more active markets.

The profit opportunity offered by any market will vary from week to week, month to month, year to year, and so on. This is normal and a fact of trading life. The evaluation of the relative merit of opportunity from market to market is in itself an art and a valuable skill for the trader to master.

There are no real hard and fast guidelines to provide other than to note that the best that any trader can do is to do her homework thoroughly and thereby achieve the greatest possible assurance that she is trading the best strategy in those markets featuring the greatest known opportunities.

Unseen Market Conditions

Of course, if a trading strategy has been exhaustively tested and evaluated, it is supposed to have seen every possible market condition; this is one of the cardinal rules of strategy development. It is the nature of markets to change, available historical data may have been less than complete, the best historical sample available could have been a biased one, the strategist could have made a mistake (no, that is impossible!) and so on.

Given all of these possibilities one has to also consider the very real possibility that a market can manifest a structural shift that makes it untradable. The T-bill futures market in the early 1980s presents a case in point. From February 1980 to June 1980 this market posted a thousand basis point rally worth $25,000 a contract with very tradable daily ranges of 20 to 30 basis points. After it hit its high price, however, this market flatlined and became absolutely untradable, no matter what the style of the trading strategy.

So, whereas this is rare, it is possible that a structural change in a market can occur and be so severe as to render it untradable. Also, there are other valid reasons, as we have described, why a trading strategy that has been tested to the highest standards may still encounter as-yet-unseen market conditions.

Superior Alternatives

If the trader discovers a superior investment or trading strategy, then as a prudent businessman as well, he must objectively evaluate both alternatives on a feature-by-feature basis and follow the best course of action.

MAXIMUM RISK

The second major consideration in the evaluation of real-time performance is the risk of a catastrophic loss to trading capital and an inability to sustain trading. Before the inception of trading for a strategy, a loss threshold or *strategy stop-loss* (SSL) must be established that dictates when to abandon a trading strategy.

The factors that play a role in the calculation of the strategy stop-loss are:

1. The minimum trading capital necessary to continue financing the margin required to trade at the same level of commitment
2. A decision to limit losses to a predetermined percentage of trading capital
3. A drawdown exceeding maximum drawdown or a predetermined multiple thereof

The calculation of a strategy stop-loss follows logic similar to that of the calculation of required capital as presented in Chapter 12: The Evaluation of Performance. A calculation of required trading capital that factors in maximum risk as done in that chapter already incorporates the absorption of some multiple of maximum drawdown.

As such, an account capitalized in this manner has less of a need for a strategy stop-loss. Even the best formulated plan, however, can fail. Consequently, the incorporation of a strategy stop-loss, whereas it may be more of a formality, is still recommended as a part of a sound risk management plan.

Of course, it would be possible to set a stop loss using each of these criteria in isolation. Use of the first would be rather arbitrary. Application of the second alone, without consideration for risk would be rather arbitrary as well. Using the third criterion by itself, would be the best. All three used together as they are in the calculation of required capital, however, is the best procedure.

In practice, the loss threshold, set by the strategy stop-loss, is not always interpreted as rigidly as that of a stop order. More often, if a strategy is approaching the level of the SSL, the trader must become increasingly sensitive to the evaluation of its performance based upon current trading conditions.

A subjective—or objective, for the more quantitative-minded—evaluation is made as to whether the strategy is in free fall or whether its equity curve is finding support and may be in the process of making a bottom and then a recovery. By the way, it is worthy of mention that the equity curves of a trading strategy, especially one that trades on many markets, show the same type of technical behaviors that financial prices do.

If the strategist makes the call that the performance of the strategy is in free fall, it may prove to be prudent to stop trading the strategy even before it hits the level of the strategy stop-loss.

Conversely, if the strategist makes the determination that the performance of the trading strategy is starting to return to the expected behavior, the strategy may be allowed a bit more latitude even to a degree somewhat in excess of the strategy stop-loss.

It should be noted, however, that some traders actually do use the strategy stop loss as rigidly as a stop order. In the case of the SSL as a strict stop, trading of the strategy ceases if it generates losses that exceed the strategy stop-loss. For example, if the strategy stop-loss is determined to be $10,000 on an investment of $30,000, trading is stopped if and when losses exceed this amount, even if only by a dollar.

The strategy stop-loss is based on the risk profile of the strategy established during evaluation.

The calculation of a strategy stop-loss is as follows:

Maximum Drawdown (MDD):	$5,000
Drawdown Safety Factor (DSF):	2
System stop-loss:	MDD × DSF
System stop-loss:	$5,000 × 2
System stop-loss:	**$10,000**

The trading strategy stop-loss is analogous to the stop-loss order placed on an open position when used in the strictest manner possible. Just as a stop-loss order limits the amount of capital that will be risked per trade, the strategy stop-loss limits how much trading capital will be risked on the trading strategy as a whole. It can consequently be viewed in the same light and applied with the same relative consistency.

The need to establish a credible strategy loss level is one of the main reasons why it is necessary to accurately measure the risk of a trading system.

A sound trading system will generate losing runs. Trading can obviously continue only as long as there is sufficient trading capital. A properly calculated strategy stop-loss must factor in the amount of trading capital necessary to continue trading after a drawdown has occurred.

The evaluation profile will include the size of the strategy's maximum drawdown. Drawdown, however, can reasonably be expected to be larger in real time because of increased volatility. Also, there will be some degree of error in its measurement because of a statistical margin of error. It is consequently best if the actual strategy stop-loss uses some multiple of maximum drawdown.

The *drawdown safety factor*, that is, a predetermined value by which the maximum drawdown is multiplied, is based on the realistic assumption that the maximum drawdown derived from evaluation could possibly be exceeded, yet the strategy can still be functioning normally.

In fact, evaluation's maximum drawdown can also be exceeded in real time if, for example, a period of congestion occurs that is substantially longer than any encountered during testing. This can also be caused by the advent of other types of market conditions hostile to the trading strategy's premise.

Of course, if market conditions are seen to have fundamentally changed, this is a different type of situation. It is less one of the strategy stop-loss being approached, but rather, more a warning that there has been a structural shift in market conditions that is toxic to the strategy, as illustrated in the previous section. In this case, the trader must once again make a decision based upon this circumstance.

The bottom line is that it is necessary for the strategist to be aware of the maximum allowable level of risk for the strategy. The calculation of the strategy stop-loss is the best and ultimate limit that can be imposed on strategy risk. At minimum, if a strategy in drawdown begins to approach this strategy stop-loss level, it should be an alert that things may be going awry. For a trader using the strategy stop-loss purely systematically, the trader should stop all trading of the strategy if this level is hit or exceeded.

It was stated earlier that the best way to calculate a strategy stop-loss is one that incorporates all three contributing factors: required capital, a preset account percentage loss level, and maximum drawdown.

This formulation proceeds as follows. First, calculate required capital. It consists of required margin plus maximum drawdown and some safety factor. For example:

Required Capital = Margin + (MDD × Safety Factor)
Margin = $5,000
Maximum Drawdown = $6,000
Safety Factor = 3
Required Capital = $5,000 + ($6,000 × 3)
Required Capital = $23,000

The formulation of required capital that factors in a maximum allowable percentage of trading capital loss before trading is stopped proceeds as follows:

Margin = $5,000
MDD = $6,000
Safety Factor = 3
Capital Loss % = 40%
System stop-loss = Maximum Drawdown × Safety Factor
System stop-loss = $6,000 × 3
System stop-loss = $18,000
Required Capital = Strategy stop-loss/Capital Stop Loss
Required Capital = $18,000/40%
Required Capital = $45,000

In this way, the strategy stop-loss and the capital stop-loss are one and the same, that is, a loss of $18,000, which accommodates the strategy stop-loss plus a safety margin, is also the capital stop loss.

REAL-TIME AND EVALUATION PERFORMANCE

Typically, a trading strategy is judged solely by its trading profits. Profit is, of course, what motivates the trader. There is another equally, and sometimes even more, important way of evaluating trading profit, however, which evaluates the quality of this profit. The real-time trading performance of the strategy must be judged within the context of the way it performed during evaluation. A trading strategy is said to be functioning properly or normally if its real-time trading performance is *in line with* or *equivalent to* its evaluation performance.

In the simplest of terms, for example, if a trading strategy produced an average profit of $1,000 each month in testing, then three months of $2,000 real-time losses is not in line.

The rules of chance dictate that real-time trading can begin just as easily with a win or a loss or with a winning or a losing run. It doesn't matter. What *does* matter is that real-time trading performance, over time, be consistent with the expectation created by its evaluation performance profile.

If the real-time trading of a strategy starts with a few losses, the impatient and improperly informed trader says, "The trading strategy fell apart," and stops trading with it.

Well, maybe it did, and maybe it didn't. It is clearly impossible to know, however, if the trading strategy fell apart unless before the start of real-time trading, "falling apart" is precisely defined.

Before real-time trading begins, it is essential that the trader have a realistic expectation of what trading performance should be grounded in historical evaluation. Without this, the trader has no way of actually knowing whether the real-time trading performance of the trading strategy is consistent with its evaluation profile, whether trading is profitable or not.

The trader needs a detailed statistical profile of both evaluation and real-time trading performance to make this evaluation. The *evaluation profile* consists of a set of statistical measures of trading performance found during evaluation. The *trading profile* consists of the same measures, but of real-time trading performance.

The following statistical measures must then be recorded for both historical and real-time trading performance:

1. Annualized profit
2. Number of trades per year
3. Percentage of winning trades
4. Largest win
5. Length of largest win
6. Average win
7. Length of average win
8. Largest loss
9. Length of time in largest loss
10. Average loss
11. Length of time in average loss
12. Average winning run
13. Length of time in average winning run
14. Largest winning run
15. Length of time in largest winning run
16. Average losing run

17. Length of average losing run
18. Largest losing run
19. Length of largest losing run
20. Maximum equity drawdown
21. Length of maximum drawdown
22. Start and end data maximum drawdown
23. Maximum equity run-up
24. Length of maximum run-up
25. Start and end data maximum run-up

The standard deviation of each average value should also be calculated. It may seem like a lot of numbers, but they are necessary if one is to reliably compare real-time and evaluation performance.

Equipped with an evaluation profile and a trading profile, the trader should be readily able to judge the quality of real-time trading. It is simply the compliance of real-time trading with the expectation created by evaluation performance.[1]

COMPARING THE EVALUATION AND TRADE PROFILE

How soon can a trading strategy be judged in real-time trading? In truth, not too quickly. Just as in testing, a statistically significant number of trades must be generated to make a sound judgment, and so it is in trading. Real-time performance cannot be judged on the basis of a small sample of wins or on one loss.

Also, because of the fuzziness of these performance statistics, the comparisons are not going to be capable of complete exactness. This is further compounded by the element of variation added to these statistics, based on the impact of changes in volatility and periodic fluctuations in other market behaviors.

A flawed strategy will often show itself clearly with a series of losses that reaches the strategy stop-loss immediately. If this occurs, trading stops and capital is preserved by the strategy stop-loss.

Since a valid trading strategy can also generate a losing run in the course of normal performance, how can strategy failure be distinguished from normal performance? The answer is found in the comparison of the evaluation and trade profiles.

A bad strategy will perform differently from its test profile. For example, assume a strategy with an evaluation profile has a $4,000 maximum drawdown in 3 trades during a period of average volatility. Assume that the standard deviations of this maximum drawdown are $2,000 and 2 trades. Real-time trading produces 9 losses in row for a $10,000 loss, with market conditions the same as that of the test period. What happened? This outcome would suggest a strategy failure for any of a number of the reasons that have been discussed. This actual run of trading losses exceeds the maximum drawdown in dollars of $4,000 plus its standard deviation of $2,000 and in number of trades of 3 plus the standard deviation of 2. This is different enough from expectation to warrant the suspension of trading in the absence of a very good explanation.

Now, consider the same strategy with a slightly different start: three losses totaling $8,000 with volatility at twice the level of the evaluation profile drawdown. This real-time run of losses is the same in length, but twice in dollar size that of the test profile. Note, however, that volatility is double that of the test drawdown. This is unpleasant, but not an entirely unexpected performance. Why? Because when volatility increases, the wins should also increase in proportion just as the losses did in this example.

UNDERSTANDING THE TEST PROFILE

One of the most common causes of real-time trading failure is impatience with the performance of the strategy. Another common cause is an inadequate understanding of the evaluation profile. This lack of knowledge can prove to destabilize the trader's discipline in a variety of ways.

Nothing is more exciting than a trading strategy that starts trading with a couple of big wins. This can also be emotionally destabilizing as well, however, by fanning the flames of greed and overconfidence. The trader feels that he can do no wrong. This can cause the trader to disregard atypical losses that may follow. Or, it can also lead to false confidence, which can lead to excesses, such as doubling the number of contracts that are traded without proper regard to money management.

Knowledge from the evaluation profile that wins of this size, as attractive as they are in actual trading, are fairly typical and no cause for excessive celebration, for they will probably be followed by a couple of losses fairly soon.

It is important to know the profile of wins and their associated volatility. An unusually large profit is often caused by increased volatility. An unusually big win will often be followed by an unusually large loss. The sword of volatility cuts both ways.

Conversely, nothing is typically more disturbing to the trader than starting with a few big losses. It fans the flame of fear and can cause the trader to prematurely doubt the trading strategy and can lead to counterproductive second guessing. It can also lead to an unwarranted and premature abandonment of the trading strategy—just before the next trade, which may be a typical big win. Just as the losses were unpleasant, though, they could be viewed as typical of what was seen in the evaluation profile.

Consider another relatively common scenario. The trading strategy produces a month of small losses and wins, leading to a flat month. It would not be the first time this occurrence bored a trader. This boredom, however, may lead the trader to prematurely abandon the strategy in favor of something else or to increase the size of the trades in an effort to produce more profit. Yet, an examination of the evaluation profile would show that these types of months occurred often in evaluation. The unprepared trader is unaware of this, however, because she did not do her homework. After the trader abandons the strategy, the market picks up, and the next month after abandonment, it would have produced a healthy profit.

How can the trader avoid such mistakes? Only with knowledge. The trader must acquire a thorough understanding of the historical performance of the strategy. This is accomplished in two ways. The first is through a careful study of the evaluation performance profile. The second is by careful study of the trading strategy's performance over smaller time slices: on a day-by-day, week-by-week, and month-by-month basis. The trader must be familiar with the performance of the trading strategy, beginning at the microscopic level and ending at the macroscopic level.

The statistical analysis of trading performance presented in the Evaluation Profile[2] displayed in Table 14.1 presents the trading strategy from the macroscopic perspective.

A graphical view of these trades, runs, and equity swings can be obtained through a review of a bar chart with trades and equity curve plotted. Figure 14.1 displays a segment of these trades as an example (trades and prices only).

Table 14.2 lists the trades displayed on the chart in Figure 14.1 in a tabular form. These two present the microscopic perspective of the trading strategy. To thoroughly understand the performance of the strategy, it is recommended that every trade is examined in both graphical and tabular format.

The most thorough microscopic analysis of a trading strategy is to study its performance on a bar-by-bar basis. Review all of the daily trades, stops, positions, and equity changes. This very low-level, day-by-day, signal-by-signal review of performance is the only way to develop a true and intuitive understanding and feel for the performance of the trading strategy.

A full operating knowledge of the performance of the trading strategy can only come through the acquisition of information from the

TABLE 14.1 Evaluation Profile for a Trading Strategy

Evaluation Profile
S&P
1/2/1990 to 12/31/2005
XT99AP2dumo

Net P&L	$1,643,688			
Annualized P&L	$102,731			
Number of Trades	119			
A Number of Trades	8			
Average Trade	$13,812.50			
	Price Wins	**Time**	**Price Losses**	**Time**
Analysis of Trades				
Maximum	$146,050	95	($49,950)	16
Minimum	$4,750	5	($3,225)	2
Average	$37,188	28	($9,174)	8
StDev	$15,500	12	$8,775	5
+1 StDev	*$52,688*	*40*	*($399)*	*13*
−1 StDev	*$21,688*	*16*	*($17,949)*	*3*
Analysis of Runs	**Winning Runs**		**Losing Runs**	
Maximum	$187,375	77	($50,525)	27
Minimum	$12,335	13	($1,250)	3
Average	$31,601	25	($10,975)	12
StDev	$46,604	17	$10,776	13
+1 StDev	*$78,205*	*42*	*($21,751)*	*25*
−1 StDev	*($15,003)*	*8*	*($199)*	*−1*
Analysis of Equity Swings	**Equity Run-up**		**Equity Drawdown**	
Maximum	$535,125	190	($226,250)	65
Minimum	$35,755	25	($12,250)	12
Average	$125,755	55	($27,555)	27
StDev	$45,575	27	$12,755	17
+1 StDev	*$171,330*	*82*	*($40,310)*	*44*
−1 StDev	*$80,180*	*28*	*($14,800)*	*10*

microscopic, signal-by-signal and day-by-day behavior. With this information in hand, the trader is properly equipped to trade the strategy in real time.

PERFORMANCE QUIRKS

Consider three different real-time trading outcomes. In the first case, the trading strategy produces profits far in excess of anything in its evaluation profile. In the second case, the trading strategy begins with a dramatic, but

FIGURE 14.1 Chart of Trades

not catastrophic, losing run. In the third case, the trading strategy produces a run of small wins and losses.

The Windfall Profit

Who complains about a windfall profit? No one. Profit is profit. If it is big enough, the trader might consider early retirement. It is best, however, to not let greed and ego get the upper hand in such a fortunate situation. Such a large profit is typically a windfall. If the continuation of trading is based upon expectations of similar outsized profits, the trader is likely to be disappointed. Nor should the trader be deluded into believing this windfall is the result of his brilliance as a strategy designer. It probably was not. It was more a matter of being in the right place at the right time.

Consider the following anecdote. After the Crash of 1987, there were reports of fantastic profits. A trading firm in Chicago reportedly made over one billion dollars on their S&P and T-bond positions in a matter of a few days. The principals were reported to have done two things. They paid large bonuses and gave a paid vacation of one month to all employees. The trading operation was closed for one month while the principals decided what they were going to do with their newfound wealth. Good idea or bad?

TABLE 14.2 Tabular List of Trades

Trade Number / Type	Date	Time	Price	Contracts Profit	% Profit Cum Profit	Run-up Drawdown	Entry Eff. Exit Eff.	Total Efficiency
75	10/6/2000	00:00	1496.70	1	36.45%	177,500.00	95.25%	73.18%
Sell	11/27/2002	00:00	951.20	$136,175.00	$137,537.50	(8850.00)	77.93%	
76	11/13/2000	00:00	1406.90	1	32.39%	155,050.00	90.03%	66.15%
Sell	11/27/2002	00:00	951.20	$113,725.00	$251,262.50	(17175.00)	76.12%	
77	11/22/2000	00:00	1396.20	1	31.87%	152,375.00	89.95%	65.67%
Sell	11/27/2002	00:00	951.20	$111,050.00	$362,312.50	(17,025.00)	75.72%	
78	11/30/2000	00:00	1375.20	1	30.83%	147,125.00	86.85%	62.57%
Sell	11/27/2002	00:00	951.20	$105,800.00	$468,112.50	(22,275.00)	75.72%	
79	12/20/2000	00:00	1332.60	1	28.62%	136,475.00	83.33%	58.22%
Sell	11/27/2002	00:00	951.20	$95,150.00	$563,262.50	(27,300.00)	74.89%	
80	1/2/2001	00:00	1348.60	1	29.47%	140,475.00	85.77%	60.66%
Sell	11/27/2002	00:00	951.20	$99,150.00	$662,412.50	(23,300.00)	74.89%	
81	1/5/2001	00:00	1364.40	1	30.28%	144,425.00	88.19%	63.07%
Sell	11/27/2002	00:00	951.20	$103,100.00	$765,512.50	(19,350.00)	74.89%	
82	2/16/2001	00:00	1359.20	1	30.02%	143,125.00	96.20%	68.56%
Sell	11/27/2002	00:00	951.20	$101,800.00	$867,312.50	(5,650.00)	72.36%	
83	2/21/2001	00:00	1310.10	1	27.39%	130,850.00	91.70%	62.88%
Sell	11/27/2002	00:00	951.20	$89,525.00	$956,837.50	(11,850.00)	71.18%	
84	2/23/2001	00:00	1269.30	1	25.06%	120,650.00	84.55%	55.73%
Sell	11/27/2002	00:00	951.20	$79,325.00	$1,036,162.50	(22,050.00)	71.18%	
85	3/12/2001	00:00	1239.10	1	23.23%	113,100.00	79.26%	50.44%
Sell	11/27/2002	00:00	951.20	$71,775.00	$1,107,937.50	(29,600.00)	71.18%	
86	6/14/2001	00:00	1259.90	1	24.50%	118,300.00	96.41%	62.90%
Sell	11/27/2002	00:00	951.20	$76,975.00	$1,184,912.50	(4,400.00)	66.48%	
87	7/6/2001	00:00	1223.50	1	22.26%	109,200.00	92.15%	57.45%
Sell	11/27/2002	00:00	951.20	$67,875.00	$1,252,787.50	(9,300.00)	65.30%	
88	8/8/2001	00:00	1216.00	1	21.78%	107,325.00	94.91%	58.55%
Sell	11/27/2002	00:00	951.20	$66,000.00	$1,318,787.50	(5,750.00)	63.63%	

One can reason both ways. In truth, the huge profits that were the result of these events are the very definition a windfall. It was not a result of great skill or prognostication.

A *good* trader knows the difference between *luck* and *skill*. Skill keeps a good trader trading in bad times and produces consistent profits during good times. A good trader knows when he has been the beneficiary of a windfall and does not expect to be able to consistently reproduce such levels of profit.

A winning streak at the start of real-time trading is certainly more welcome than a losing streak, but it should not be allowed to destabilize the trader. The proper attitude is simple: take the money, smile and realize that this is luck. It could have just as easily have gone the other way and it is best to be thankful that it happened the way it did.

Win or lose, the trade profile must be compared to the evaluation profile. Real-time performance must remain in its proper context. If real-time performance remains in line with that of the evaluation, that is good. If it moves out of alignment in some way, an explanation must be uncovered. Has volatility changed? Has the trend changed? It is too common a mistake of system traders to overscrutinize loses and to gleefully and uncritically accept wins. Both extremes are hazardous to trading success.

The Losing Run

In the second case, who complains when real-time trading begins with a losing streak? Just about everyone. With such a start, a trader may panic and often without justification. The onset of real-time trading can begin with a wining or a losing run. No matter which way it starts, however, if its performance is in alignment with its evaluation profile, it is all good.

All trading strategies will produce wins as well as loses. Therefore, if this losing run, right out of the gate, gives the trader pause for concern, then it must be compared to its evaluation profile. If it is within expectation, there is no reason for undue concern. Also, the strategy stop-loss is in place to prevent catastrophic loss of trading capital. The trader should continue trading—always wary that something can go wrong—but with the confidence grounded in his thorough knowledge of his well-tested trading strategy.

Flat Production

In the third case, consider a trading strategy that produces a run of uneventful wins and losses producing a small net gain or loss after the first month of trading. This type of activity can prove almost as trying to the trader as a faster run of losses. We traders are not known for our patience. To ease the trader's mind, the trade profile must be compared to the evaluation profile. If such slow periods are not uncommon in the evaluation profile, then patience is required. In the uncommon eventuality that such a period never occurred in evaluation, however, it is an alert that either market conditions may be shifting or the trading strategy may be exhibiting the start of difficulties. In any case, the evaluation profile is there as a resource to stabilize the concerns and provide objectivity for the trader.

IN CONCLUSION

There are three tools that are highly recommended to commence and continue to successfully trade a robust and properly evaluated trading strategy in real time:

1. The test profile
2. The trade profile
3. The system stop-loss

The first two elements must be available from the start of trading. The trade profile is produced on an ongoing basis from real-time trading.

A comparison of each of the statistical measures in the trade and test profiles must be made at periodic intervals. If statistics in the trade profile are less than 50 percent or more than 150 percent of the corresponding evaluation profile statistic, whether profitable or not, then a rational explanation must be found. Equity drawdowns, in particular, must be constantly monitored with respect to the system stop-loss and the evaluation profile.

The start of real-time trading is perhaps the most critical time for the trader and his new trading strategy. The shift from design to trading is as significant as it is dramatic. It is that great leap from idea to reality that all creators experience. The trader can become excessively and uncritically optimistic if the first trade is a win, especially if it is a big one. This can be destabilizing. Conversely, the trader can become overly critical and excessively anxious if the first trade is a loss, especially a big one. This can be potentially even more destabilizing to the trader.

In both of these cases, and on through the labyrinth of what hopefully will become years of profitable long-term trading, the successful trader must manage his emotions with the iron fist of strict discipline and by rational adherence to that main principle that governs the trading of a strategy—trade the strategy as long as it performs in real time according to the expectations produced by its evaluation profile, thereby producing a steadily growing equity, which remains above the strategy stop-loss.

When this is done well, it is a long, fascinating, and profitable endeavor. Enjoy the journey and its rewards, my friends...

Notes

PREFACE

1. Thanks to Karen Harris and her masterful command of the Barclay Hedge Database for this information.

2. From the Prediction Company web site, predict.com/html/company.html

CHAPTER 1 ON TRADING STRATEGIES

1. Walk-Forward Analysis add-ins for TradeStation, MetaStock, and TradersStudio perform the methods described in this book and are available from Pardo Group Limited.

CHAPTER 2 THE SYSTEMATIC TRADING EDGE

1. The corrosive effect of negative and undisciplined emotion is explored in Robert Pardo, *The Trading Game* (Hoboken, NJ: John Wiley & Sons, 2009).

CHAPTER 4 THE STRATEGY DEVELOPMENT PLATFORM

1. The Walk-Forward Analysis add-in for TradeStation and TradersStudio is available from Pardo Group Limited.

CHAPTER 6 THE HISTORICAL SIMULATION

1. Perry Kaufman, *Smarter Trading* (New York: McGraw-Hill, 1995), 22.

2. Sam Kash Kachigan, *Statistical Analysis: An Interdisciplinary Introduction to Univariate & Multivariate Methods* (New York: Radius Press, 1986), 145.

3. Conveyed to me by Art Collins in private conversation and received by Collins from Dennis during an interview.

4. William Poundstone, *Fortunes Formula* (New York: Hill and Wang, 2005) last plate, before page 149.

5. Both the rise and fall—arguably caused by an unwillingness to admit error, extraordinary arrogance, over-leverage and under-diversification—of Long-Term Capital Management are brilliantly documented in the classic and very-well titled book by Roger Lowenstein: *When Genius Failed* (New York: Random House, 2001).

CHAPTER 7 FORMULATION AND SPECIFICATION

1. The author was the developer of Advanced Trader, one of the pioneering applications in this vein. Some of the more widely used applications, in alphabetical order, are Metastock, TradersBlox, TradeStation, TradersStudio, and Wealth-Lab.

CHAPTER 9 SEARCH AND JUDGMENT

1. Walk-Forward Analyst, TradeStation, Metastock, and TradersStudio add-ins from Pardo Group Limited provides fully featured Walk-Forward Analysis.

2. Thanks to Bruce DeVault for his excellent material, which I adapted for the Simulated Annealing, Genetic Optimization, and Particle Swarm Optimization sections.

3. P.J. van Laarhoven and E.H. Aarts, *Simulated Annealing: Theory and Applications* (New York: Springer, 1987).

4. David Goldberg, *Genetic Algorithms in Search, Optimization & Machine Learning* (Reading, MA: Addison-Wesley, 1989).

5. Lawrence Davis, *Handbook of Genetic Algorithms* (New York: Van Nostrand Reinhold, 1991), is a classic starting point. For the

contemporary perspective, consider *Biologically Inspired Algorithms for Financial Modeling*, by Anthony Brabazon and Michael O'Neill (New York: Springer-Verlag, 2006).

6. James Kennedy, Russell C. Eberhart, and Yuhui Shi, *Swarm Intelligence* (San Francisco: Morgan Kaufman Publishers, 2001).

7. Thanks to my old friend and mentor Bo Thunman for the basic idea for PROM.

CHAPTER 11 WALK-FORWARD ANALYSIS

1. Done with Walk-Forward Analyst add-in for TradeStation from Pardo Group Limited.

CHAPTER 12 THE EVALUATION OF PERFORMANCE

1. A good place to start is *The (Mis)Behavior of Markets: A Fractal View of Risk, Ruin And Reward* by Benoit B. Mandelbrot and Richard L. Hudson (New York: Perseus Books Group, 2006).

2. Thanks to Valerii Salov for these numbers. His book, *Modeling Maximum Trading Profits in C++* (Hoboken, NJ: John Wiley & Sons, 2007), develops a variant of Perfect Profit as presented in this book and provides software for its calculation.

CHAPTER 14 TRADING THE STRATEGY

1. TradeProfiler TradeStation add-in from Pardo Group Limited creates and monitors the trading and evaluation profiles of a trading strategy automatically.

2. Produced with TradeProfiler, from Pardo Group Limited.

Index

Page numbers set in *italic* indicate figures and tables.

Printed and bound by CPI Group (UK) Ltd, Croydon, CR0 4YY

23/04/2025

14661005-0003